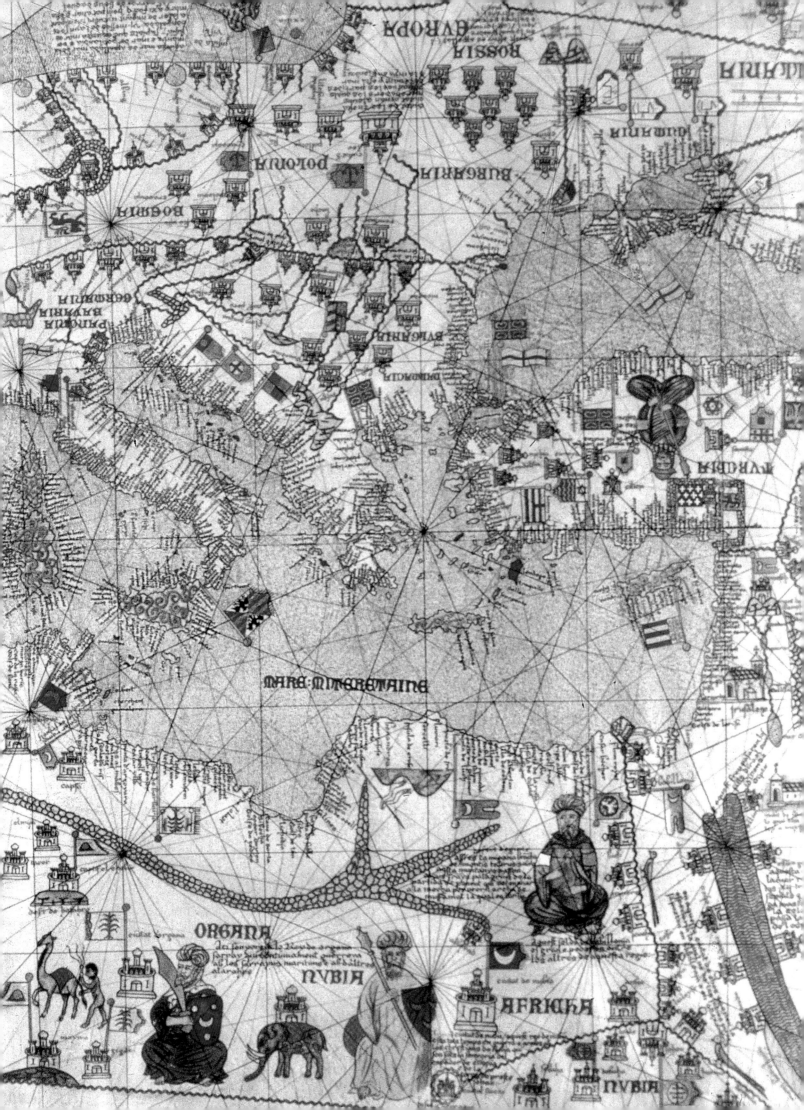

CONTENTS

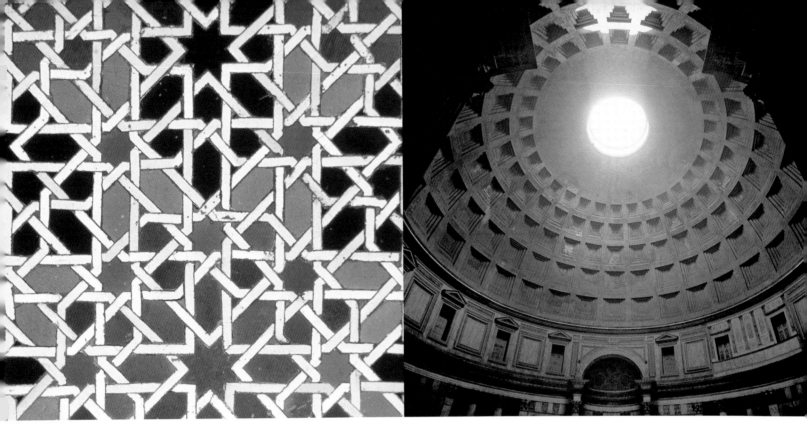

INTRODUCTION

BELOW: The defeat of the Persians in the 5th century BC was a turning point in history, and helped ensure that Greek culture dominated the story of Europe. The Greek states were able to thwart Persian invasions, first at the Battle of Marathon in 490 BC, and then at this, the decisive Battle of Salamis, in 480 BC.

The Mediterranean touches the lives of tens of millions of people, even those of us who live far from its inviting beaches and sparkling blue waters.

From Spain to Turkey, and from Italy to Tunisia, the region's many resorts hold a seemingly endless attraction for tourists. Whether it is for the virtually guaranteed sunshine, the stunning views, the enchanting light or the varied nightlife, the Mediterranean lures a constant stream of visitors to its shores and islands each year.

The sea and its lands offer other pleasures, too, both of the senses and of the mind. Much of the wine and the olive oil that we consume will have begun its life in the sunshine of the region, while Mediterranean-style cooking has an enduring popularity throughout Europe and beyond. Even gardening and interior design have been influenced by the variety of plants and the colour and vibrancy of the landscape. The architecture and art of the classical Mediterranean continue to impress and dazzle visitors and to inspire succeeding generations of artists and architects. The beguiling light of the region, too, has made it ever popular with painters.

The Mediterranean also touches us in less visible but more profound ways. The politics and history of the region, its many cultures and languages, the intellectual creativity, artistic insight and ingenuity of its peoples, and its many traditions of faith – all have played their part in shaping the face of modern Europe. There is, perhaps, a case for stating that the history of the Mediterranean, at least until the Middle Ages, is in effect the history of the modern western world. The great 19th-century British philosopher and champion of liberty John Stuart Mill once remarked that the victory of the Greeks over the Persian Empire in the 5th century BC was a more important event – even in the context of British history – than the Battle of Hastings and the Norman invasion of England in 1066. His point was that, without the legacy of 5th-century BC Athenian thought and democracy the world would have been a very different place.

Of course, other great civilizations have shaped history and continue to have an impact on the world. The sophisticated ancient cultures of China, India and Mesopotamia generated advances in technology, governance, science, religion and agriculture. Yet none has had the enduring and direct impact on modern European life that the Mediterranean world has provided.

At the same time, one of the great strengths of the region and its many diverse cultures has been the ability to absorb new influences from outside and to transform and improve them. For example, early Greek philosophy can trace some of its early themes back to eastern thought and religion. In math-ematics, too, the Greeks who set the standard of insight and excellence for 2,000 years drew upon the work of Babylonian scholars. The Islamic world, which came into the Mediterranean with the Arab invasions of the 7th century AD, brought knowledge and technology from the Far East and South Asia: paper from China, for example, and sugar to sweeten the diet of Europeans. Indeed, much of the food that we now regard as typically Mediterranean originated in areas such as India and the Americas. The aubergine is but one example of this trend.

A glance at any map of the Mediterranean shows why it has been so open to outside influences. Though the sea is almost literally enclosed – only its small opening on the Atlantic attaches it to the rest of the world's great waters – the lands that surround it constitute gateways to several very different and important cultures. To the west lie the Atlantic and the great seafaring nations of Spain and Portugal. To the south are North Africa and the vast expanse of the Sahara; though the desert has acted as a barrier, it is by no means impassable and has allowed influences from sub-Saharan Africa to reach the Sea. Flowing in from the north are some of the great rivers of Europe, such as the Rhône and the Po, which have served as channels of communication with other, more northerly parts of Europe. To the east is the Black Sea, a body of water that has long

been important in the development of the Mediterranean, offering a route into the expanses of central Europe, the wide–open steppes of Eurasia and, ultimately, the Far East. At the sea's south–eastern extremity lie Egypt and the Levant, from which communications have long existed with Arabia, the Red Sea, the Persian Gulf and the Indian Ocean.

Through all these gateways have poured – in both directions – new and exotic produce, learning and philosophies, faiths, technologies and, of course, armies. Just as the waters of the Nile and the Rhône still run into the sea, so new ideas and influences have constantly flowed into the Mediterranean. In turn, the region has passed on its legacy to the modern European world.

ABOVE: This early map shows the complexity of the Mediterranean coastline and illustrates some of the gateways into the region; from the south through Africa, from the north through central Europe and from the north-east via the Black Sea.

The Mediterranean: Cradle of European Culture charts these various trends and describes just how the region has shaped our present society. As well as tracing the the vast, unseen social forces involved, the book also turns a spotlight on many of the brilliant, colourful and sometimes wayward personalities who have helped shape the region's destiny.

For convenience, the book is divided into five chapters, each covering a major theme of the Mediterranean world.

The first chapter reviews the natural life of the region – the geology of the sea, the story of its often surprisingly varied climate, the plants and animals that dominate the area, and the natural disasters that have brought about change and, sometimes, devastation. Among the latter, the destructive force of Mount Vesuvius, the massive super-eruption of the island of Thera, and the Greeks' own, little-known version of Pompeii are treated in particular detail.

The second chapter considers the political and military history of the region. From Julius Caesar to Suleiman the Magnificent, and from Alexander the Great to the last of the Byzantine emperors, it describes the bewildering rise and fall of great empires, recounts stories of military conquest, and traces the origins of democracy and the gradual formation of the nation–states that now dominate the area.

In the third chapter the book turns to the huge achievements of Mediterranean artists and intellectuals, and their impact on modern western thought. It looks at the great philosophers of Greece, such as Thales, Socrates and Plato, and the innovative Greek dramatists; the genius of the Roman poet Virgil; and the impact of the classical world on Renaissance artists such as Raphael and Titian, and on architecture and writing more

BELOW: The volcanic Mount Vesuvius has brought death and destruction over many centuries and is still a real threat to nearby settlements. The Mediterranean has often suffered from natural disasters caused by geological weaknesses in the region.

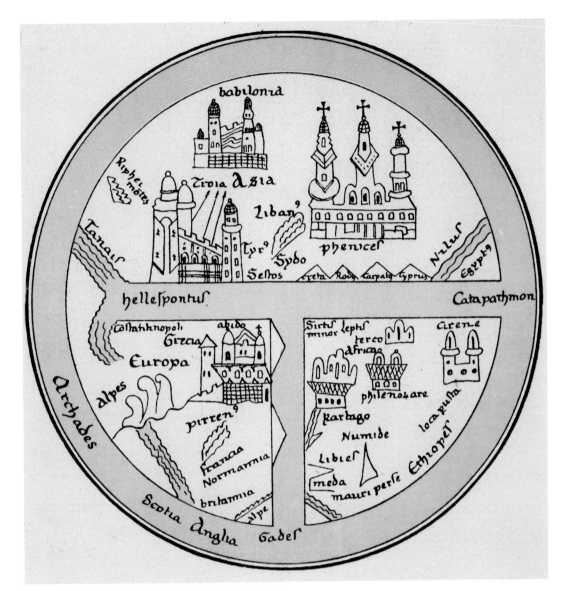

broadly. It also looks at the plight of women and, particularly, slaves in the ancient world, and the lasting importance of laws from the classical past.

The fourth chapter describes the extraordinary thirst for adventure and inventiveness of the Mediterranean peoples: the great sea explorations of the Phoenicians, Arabs, Spanish and Genoese; the ingenuity of the Arabs and Greeks; and the apparently boundless capacity for technological innovation of the Romans. From the use of concrete to public drinking water, this chapter describes the simply enormous number of ways in which the Romans transformed the physical world around them. It also reflects on how much of classical Greek science was saved from obscurity by the Islamic world and eventually passed on to Christian Europe at the start of the Middle Ages.

Finally, the fifth chapter looks at the belief systems that have dominated the region for millennia. It considers the worship of the many gods and cults of the ancient world, and looks at their controversial links with the birth of Christianity. Above all, this section charts the rise of the three great 'faiths of the book' – Judaism, Christianity and Islam – each of which has played a fundamental role in establishing the landscape of the modern European world.

Together, these lavishly illustrated chapters piece together the astonishing story of the Mediterranean and show just how extensive, and how profound, the influence of this beautiful region has been on the world of the 21st century. Above all, they demonstrate why the Mediterranean truly is the cradle of European culture.

CHAPTER 1
THE NATURE OF THE MEDITERRANEAN

The usual modern image of the Mediterranean is of blue skies, a sparkling sea, long sandy beaches, and a rich and exciting diet of food and wine. Yet, behind this commonplace view lies a far more complex picture. The climate may appear benign, but in the past it has posed dangers to many species of plants and animals – as well as to humans. There is also the constant threat from the region's numerous earthquakes and volcanoes, and fears that deadly giant waves – tsunamis – could batter the Mediterranean's coasts as they have in the past. Despite these dangers there is a diversity in the nature of the Mediterranean that has sustained an abundance of life and has helped give rise to the development of European civilization along its beautiful and varied shores.

RIGHT: When people think of the Mediterranean the usual image they have is of blue skies, sandy beaches and inviting waters, though the area boasts many other stunning geographical features and has a fascinating diversity of plants and wildlife to delight visitors.

The Mediterranean is a sea of many moods, many sounds and many colours. Indeed, the Mediterranean is not simply one sea at all, but a collection of many different, smaller seas that combine to make one large and magnificent body of water. From the Ligurian and Tyrrhenian seas to the west and the Adriatic, Ionian and Aegean seas to the east, the Mediterranean is a complex system stretching some 3,860 kilometres (2,400 miles) from Gibraltar to Beirut – about the distance from New York to Los Angeles. Its vast shoreline of 46,000 kilometres (28,580 miles) connects three continents: Europe, Africa and Asia. It is this central position at the junction of three crucial regions that gives the Mediterranean Sea its key role in the story of human civilization.

A magnificent diversity

One has only to consider the range of more than 20 countries that border the sea to grasp the huge diversity in the region. To the south are Islamic North African countries, such as Algeria and Libya, to the west lie the familiar European nations of Spain and France, and to the north the nations that once boasted powerful empires that dominated the sea: Italy, which gave birth to the Roman Empire, and Turkey, which produced the Ottoman – as well as Greece, home of the glories of the classical world. In the east lie countries with complex histories going back to the earliest civilizations: Syria, Lebanon, Israel and Egypt. All these very different countries, each with their own languages, customs and religious traditions, face out on to the same blue waters of the Mediterranean.

Yet the countries that fringe the sea are not the only players in its story. The Mediterranean is punctuated throughout its extent by islands, large and small, often

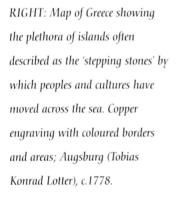

RIGHT: Map of Greece showing the plethora of islands often described as the 'stepping stones' by which peoples and cultures have moved across the sea. Copper engraving with coloured borders and areas; Augsburg (Tobias Konrad Lotter), c.1778.

NAMING THE SEA

The Mediterranean Sea has been given a variety of different names by different peoples throughout the centuries. The name Mediterranean Sea (mare mediterraneum) comes from the Latin *mediterraneus*, meaning 'inland' sea; this expression, however, did not come into usage until after about AD 300. The Romans tended to use a name that expressed their own power: *mare nostrum*, meaning 'Our Sea'. Though referring to it in such a way may seem a little arrogant to modern ears, the description accurately reflected the fact that their empire controlled both eastern and western 'halves' of the sea. It was the first and last power to do so. The Romans also referred to it as the 'Great Sea', as do biblical writers. In ancient times, when Jews came across the sea they gave a blessing to God 'who has created the Great Sea'. Another old name used in the Bible is the 'Western Sea', while the Turkish name *Akdeniz* means 'White Sea'. In modern English usage the sea's name has been contracted and it is often referred to simply as 'the Med'.

ABOVE: Few islands have as long and varied a history as Malta. The island occupies an important strategic position between the European and African coasts, as well as being on the narrow stretch between the east and west sections of the Mediterranean. The capital Valletta was ruled successively by the Phoenicians, Greeks, Carthaginians, Romans, Byzantines, Arabs and the Order of the Knights of St John. Valletta's 320 monuments, all within an area of 55 ha, make it one of the most concentrated historic areas in the world.

RELIEF MAP OF THE MEDITERRANEAN

Atlantic Ocean

Rhine

Seine

Loire

Bay of
Biscay

MASSIF
CENTRAL

Garonne

Rhône

A L P S

Po

CANTABRIAN MTNS

PYRENEES

Ebro

A P E N N I N E S

IBERIAN

Tagus

PENINSULA

Corsica

Balearic Islands

Sardinia

Tyrrhenian
Sea

Guadalquivir

Mediterranean Sea

Strait of
Gibraltar

Sicily

A T L A S   M O U N T A I N S

S   A   H   A   R   A

0 — 500 miles

0 — 500 km

CARPATHIANS

GREAT
HUNGARIAN
PLAIN

Dnieper

Don

Black Sea

DINARIC ALPS

Adriatic Sea

Danube

BALKAN MTNS

RHODOPE

Bosphorus

PINDUS MTNS

Sea of
Marmara

Kizil Irmak

Dardanelles

ASIA MINOR

Aegean
Sea

Ionian
Sea

Crete

Cyprus

Malta

Mediterranean Sea

Libyan Desert

Gulf
of
Suez

Gulf of
Aqaba

Nile

Red Sea

described as the 'stepping stones' by which peoples and cultures have moved across the sea. Among the larger islands that have figured prominently in the history of the region are Crete, Sicily and Cyprus, while among the many smaller ones tiny Malta, which has a total surface area of just 316 square kilometres (122 square miles), has time and again taken a key role.

The chief reason why Malta and Sicily have been so important is that they occupy one of the defining areas of the Mediterranean: the gateway between the eastern and western parts of the sea. This gateway is the relatively shallow stretch of water that lies between the southern tip of Italy in Europe and the coast of modern-day Tunisia in Africa. The location of Sicily in between the two narrows the gap yet further, leaving only a slender section of sea – known as the Straits of Messina – between the island and Italy, and a larger expanse of water to the south and west between the Sicilian port of Marsala and the fertile lands of Cap Bon in Tunisia. Historically, whoever has controlled either or both of these two routes between the eastern and western Mediterranean has been in a position of power.

The division between the eastern and western seas is more than simply a geographical one. During the long human history of the region, the east has been influenced more by the cultures of the ancient Greeks, the Ottoman Empire, the Egyptians and the peoples of the Levant, while to the west the distinct cultures of the Romans, Berber and Moorish (Islamic) Spain, and, later, the Franks have tended to dominate. At times the two parts of the sea have been in close partnership with each other, exchanging peoples, cultures and, above all, trading goods, while at other periods they have operated almost as separate regions.

The cultural differences between east and west Mediterranean are underlined by the very different physical influences at either end of the sea. Beyond the mere 13 kilometres (8 miles) that separate Europe from Africa at the narrow Straits of Gibraltar – the 'Pillars of Hercules' to the ancient Greeks – lie the open expanses of the strongly tidal Atlantic Ocean. In the east, on the other side of the Sea of Marmara – traditionally regarded as part of the Mediterranean – and the Bosphorus at Istanbul, is the enclosed and virtually tideless Black Sea. The contrast between the raging, free-flowing waters of

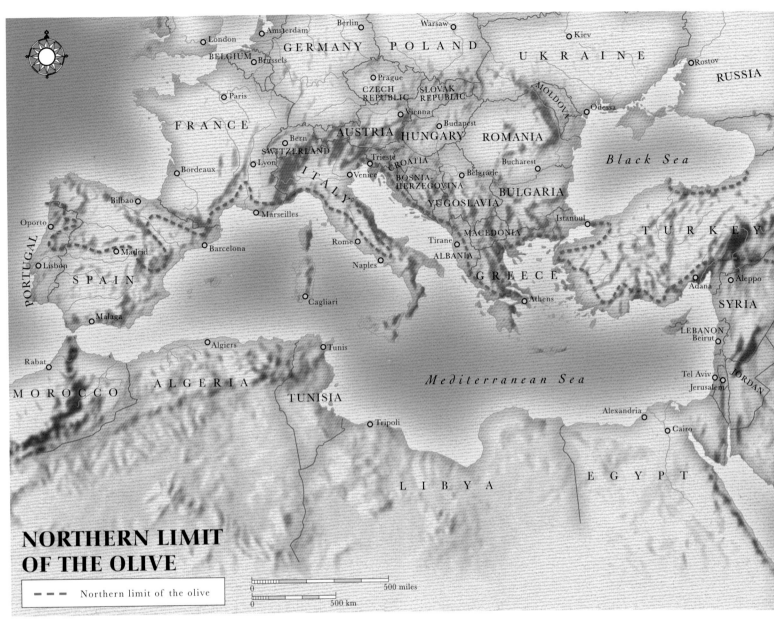

NORTHERN LIMIT OF THE OLIVE

- - - Northern limit of the olive

0   500 miles

0   500 km

the Atlantic and the often calm surface of the now heavily polluted Black Sea could not be more marked.

To these two traditional maritime entrance points a third must be added. Since 1869, the Suez Canal has linked the Mediterranean to the Red Sea and thence to the open waters of the Indian Ocean. This outlet has had a significant impact not only – as intended – on world trade, but on the marine life of the Mediterranean too.

The sheer spread and diversity of the sea can make it hard to define just what we mean by the Mediterranean region. If we define it by climate and culture, then there is a good argument for including Portugal among the Mediterranean nations, for in climate, agricul–ture, trade, Islamic occupation and Christian reconquest it has shared in much of the same story as its Spanish neighbour to the east. Yet Portugal's entire coastline juts out into the Atlantic Ocean. It is also hard to discuss the region without moving into adjoining areas whose influence on the geography, history, culture and beliefs of the Mediterranean have been immense. From the well–known 'fertile crescent' of ancient Mesopotamia (modern–day Iraq) to the fecund lands bordering the Black Sea and the dry deserts of Arabia, many outside areas have played their part in the story of the sea and its adjoining countries.

Yet another way to define the area is to consider the northern extreme of the 'olive line', the area in which that quintessentially Mediterranean tree can grow – and an area

ABOVE: One way of defining the Mediterranean region is to include within it all those lands where the sun-loving and drought tolerant olive tree can grow. It is true that all the region's ancient cities developed south of this line; however such a definition would also include countries that have no physical connection with the sea, such as Portugal.

that, incidentally, includes Portugal (see map, p. 19). It is true that all the region's ancient cities developed south of this line; however, such a narrow botanical measure is needlessly restrictive. Instead, this book will regard the Mediterranean in the way most people would understand it, and include those countries that border on the sea, its many islands and, of course, its entire surface area of some three million square kilometres (1,145,000 square miles).

From sea to desert, and back

Though it may seem stable and familiar to us, the Mediterranean has not always looked the way it does now. There was once a great sea between the continental masses of Africa and Europe called Tethys (in Greek mythology Tethys is the wife of the god Oceanus), which was obliterated as the land masses slowly collided over millions of years. Around 14 to 18 million years ago, the eastern channel from this sea to the Indian Ocean was closed, and much of the old Tethys was squeezed up to become part of the Alps. The Mediterranean was formed from remnants of the oceanic crust of the southern part of Tethys. Like Tethys, the Mediterranean Sea, too, is being squeezed between the continents and will one day vanish from Earth – though not for another 10 to 15 million years.

For millions of years the Mediterranean Sea was connected, as it is now, to the Atlantic Ocean. However, the almost unimaginable pressures caused by the continuing collision of the land masses gradually raised the level of the 'sill' that marks the small gap between the Atlantic and the Mediterranean at the Straits of Gibraltar. This, coupled with a fall in world sea levels – probably caused by an Ice Age – meant that around six million years ago the

two bodies of water became separated by a narrow spit of land. The result was startling. Within a relatively short period of time in geological terms – some 100,000–200,000 years – the sea dried to a puddle and then soon became a desert. Indeed, it is thought that the sea bed then must have been rather like the Sahara Desert is now. It has been suggested that some species of fish may have survived in a few small remaining lakes, but the over-whelming majority of its warm–water marine life would have perished at this time.

The reason for this transformation is simple. In a warm and relatively dry area such as the Mediterranean, the huge loss of water through evaporation in the constant hot sunshine is not matched by the influx of water from rainfall or rivers. Though some sizeable rivers do flow into it – for example, the Nile and the Rhône – a body of water this large would require far more and larger rivers – waterways on the scale of the Amazon – to keep its waters restocked. Lacking these, the Mediterranean relies on the reviving waters of the Atlantic to replenish it, and without these it is doomed to become desert. Such was the case some six million years ago when its link with the ocean was cut.

One can only imagine the scene some hundreds of thousands of years later when, at the end of the Ice Age, world sea levels rose again and the waters of the Atlantic began to flood back into the dry Mediterranean basin and the sea filled up once more. This time, though, there was a crucial difference. Before the link with the Atlantic was cut the sea had been stocked primarily with tropical, warm–water species, inherited at least in part from its ancient links with the Indian Ocean. The influx from the Atlantic now brought with it cold–water marine species, species that have existed in the sea to this day.

Some experts have suggested that this arrival of marine species more suited to cold waters may explain the relative poverty of marine life in the Mediterranean. Another

ABOVE: Though we now take the presence of the sparkling waters of the Mediterranean for granted, there was a time around six million years ago when it became cut off from the Atlantic and the sea dried up. Then its bed must have resembled a desert, perhaps rather like the Sahara is today.

reason is the low level of nutrients in the Mediterranean. For while tuna and oysters, for example, are fished and harvested in the sea, and while we may have fond memories of the seemingly abundant supplies of frutti di mare we have eaten on summer holidays, the truth is that marine stocks are relatively low in comparison with, for example, the nutrient-rich waters of the Atlantic or the North Sea.

Among the reasons for the low nutrient value of the sea is the lack of rich material being pumped into it by rivers. This shortage was exacerbated by the building of the Aswan High Dam on the Nile in the 1960s. While of undoubted value in many ways, this project sharply reduced the flow of water and nutrients from that great river into the Mediterranean. For example, the haul of sardines caught by fishermen off the Egyptian coast in the late 1960s fell to a quarter of pre-Aswan levels, and although the catches have since improved, that fall has been directly attributed to the reduction in food for the fish.

A century earlier, the opening of the Suez Canal also set off a change in the fishing stocks of the eastern Mediterranean. It seems that, after a gap of five million years or so, warm-water tropical fish have been taking advantage of the man-made waterway to swim in from the Indian Ocean and Red Sea and find a new habitat in the Mediterranean. For a variety of complex reasons – again including the building of the Aswan High Dam – this process has been accelerating in the past few decades, and the presence of Indian Ocean and Red Sea fish and crustaceans in the Mediterranean is becoming more and more pronounced. This movement is called Lessepsian migration, in honour of the man credited with the plan for the canal, Ferdinand de Lesseps (1805–1894) – a curious and doubtless unforeseen legacy for the French diplomat and engineer.

Every year, between five and ten new species of marine life are discovered in the eastern Mediterranean, and local fishermen have been taking advantage of the new species to increase and diversify their catches. Not all the incomers are necessarily welcome, however: among them is the highly venomous striped eel catfish. It is thought that today around 10 per cent of the fish in the so-called Levant Basin between Cyprus and Egypt are visitors from the Indian Ocean and especially the Red Sea. Only time will tell what the impact of such marine migration will be, though some have speculated that it could in fact stabilize the marine population by introducing species better adapted to the conditions of the sea.

RIGHT: The building of the Aswan High Dam in the 1960s has been of enormous economic benefit to Egypt, but it has also had an impact on the sea by reducing the flow of nutrients, which in turn initially reduced the number of fish in the Mediterranean near the Nile Delta.

The many Mediterranean climates

If the Mediterranean waters hold some surprises, then so do the surrounding lands. The widely held assumption that the Mediterranean climate and landscape form a continuous and uniform whole right around its shores does not bear close examination. In fact, there is marked variation from area to area. For example, the driest place in Europe can be found on the Mediterranean in the area near Almería in south–east Spain, where the Tabernas Desert receives barely an inch of rain a year. This barren but fascinating rocky landscape has been the setting for numerous Hollywood Westerns and other movies, including such classics as *A Fistful of Dollars*, *The Good, the Bad and the Ugly* and *The Magnificent Seven*. Parts of Crete are also desert-like in their dryness. Perhaps more surprising is the fact that the Mediterranean region also contains the wettest location in Europe: Crkvice in Montenegro, which has an annual rainfall of around 493 centimetres (194 inches).

The contrasts become even more pronounced when one considers that the southern coastline of the Mediterranean is dominated by that great sea of sand the Sahara Desert, stretching for hundreds and hundreds of miles, while to the north snow is commonplace within a short distance from the sea in many parts of the Balkans, southern France, Italy and north–eastern Spain – and anyone who has spent time in Venice in January or February will know just how cold that city of the Adriatic/Mediterranean can be in winter. Even a single island, Sicily or Crete, for example, can contain within its confined area a mixture of soaring, forbidding peaks, belts of fertile land and more arid, barren zones.

One of the reasons for these numerous and significant variations is the presence of so many mountains. For example, within the space of a few miles one can find the contrast between the generally calm sunny weather of Nice in the south of France and the often

ABOVE: A key aspect of the geography of the region is the presence of so many mountains, such as the Alps. The effect of their dominance has been to restrict the amount of flat cultivable land.

unpredictable weather of the Alps immediately to the north. A glance at a physical map of the area (see map on pages 16–17) shows immediately that towering peaks dominate the landscape. All across the region, from the Alps in France and Italy and the Pyrenees in France and Spain to the Atlas mountains of North Africa, the Greek and Balkan high peaks, the rugged interior of Turkey and even the high lands of the Levant, the waters of the sea meet high ground. The flat plains of what are now Libya and parts of Egypt constitute one of the few long, unbroken stretches of low ground around the sea, though even here the desert to the south forms a kind of barrier of its own.

Thus the land around the Mediterranean often feels hemmed in, relatively narrow strips of coastline sandwiched between mountains or desert on one side and sea on the other. It is hard to be certain what impact the proximity of mountains and hills to the coastline had on the development of early civilization in the area; one obvious point, though, is that nearly all the great settlements and later cities of the ancient world were built on or very near to the sea shore.

Some experts have suggested that the mountains acted as cultural barriers, closing off small societies from each other and leading to the emergence of a multiplicity of small and relatively distinct communities. Certainly the mountains have proved a formidable obstacle to invading military forces, even if in the case of the great Carthaginian general Hannibal – who took elephants across the Alps to invade the Italian peninsula in the 3rd century BC – they were not always insurmountable.

Others have claimed, on the contrary, that the existence of different landscapes and micro-climates, separated by high land, effectively forced people to trade and exchange

BELOW: Because of the different climatic challenges of the area humans have had to learn to be adaptable to make areas habitable, as seen here through the use of irrigation canals to harness the powerful waters of the Nile.

THE FLOOD MYTH
AND THE MEDITERRANEAN

The ancient stories in many cultures and religions of a devastating flood that wrought havoc in the world may be linked to events involving the Mediterranean around 7,500 years ago. The Black Sea, now joined to the Mediterranean by the Sea of Marmara and the Bosphorus, was once a low-lying freshwater lake. The theory is that, as ocean levels rose after the end of the last Ice Age, the waters from the Atlantic and Mediterranean eventually burst through the Bosphorus and flooded the area with vast quantities of salt water. The sound of the flooding waters would have been awesome – compared by some to 200 times the noise made by the Niagara Falls. Human settlements on the edge of the lake would have been swamped; killing many people and displacing even more. The enormity of such an event would certainly have stayed in the consciousness of anyone affected by it, and may have given rise to tales such as the Babylonian flood myth in the Epic of Gilgamesh and the later story of Noah and the Ark in the Old Testament.

goods with other communities in order to survive. Some of this communication would have taken place, where possible, over the mountains, or at least through mountain passes; but, increasingly, the preferred method was by boat over the coastal waters, with commerce gradually expanding from the first very short local trips through longer and longer voyages. Thus the very geography of the Mediterranean lands may have encouraged the peoples of the region to turn inwards upon one of the most valuable resources they possessed: the sea.

Seasonal Patterns

The many local variations of geography and micro-climate serve as a reminder of the risks of generalizing about so large an area as this. However, the region has given its name to a form of climate – 'Mediterranean' climates exist in locations as far apart as regions of Chile, California, South Africa and south-west Australia – and there are some generally accepted features of weather in the Mediterranean area. The summers are typically hot and dry, with very little of the annual rainfall occurring in these months. The winters are usually mild or cool and wet, with frost and snow relatively rare – a mildness caused in part by the proximity of the warm Mediterranean waters.

Although this is a form of temperate climate, the heat and, especially, the dryness of summer can make conditions difficult for agriculture, even if they are ideal for tourists seeking virtually guaranteed sunshine. In some parts of the area the summer is effectively a 'dead' time for plants, which take advantage of the more moderate temperatures and higher rainfall of winter and spring to do their growing. Yet the availability of so much sunshine – 300 days or more in many places – means that if irrigation is available intensive growing techniques can be very fruitful.

The switch between the summer and winter weather of the Mediterranean is triggered by the planet's vast weather systems. During the summer, the weather is dominated by subtropical high-pressure zones over the Azores, which provide stable, hot and dry weather. Very occasionally, moister air from the north-west or the

ABOVE: The lack of rainfall in much of the parched lands during summer means that the region is often at risk from damaging forest fires, though fortunately most of the plant life is quick to re-grow afterwards. In this photograph, fires continue to burn out of control on Samos in the Aegean Sea.

south-east will move in and cause heavy deluges of rain or even hail. During the autumn, as the high-pressure zone retreats, weather systems from the west – that is, the Atlantic – become more important, bringing with them cooler temperatures and, above all, rain. However, though the Mediterranean usually gets a number of Atlantic storms in winter, most of the rain and low-pressure zones in the region are generated locally.

Areas noted for significant rain and storms include the waters west of Crete and the gulfs of Lion and Genoa. Sometimes this rain can be very heavy indeed, and flash floods are not uncommon. Indeed, much of the Mediterranean's rainfall comes during torrential downpours and storms rather than in the steady, soaking rain associated with areas such as the west coast of Britain. On the last day of October 1963, the meteorological station on Mont Aigoual, north of Montpellier in the south of France, recorded some 607 millimetres (24 inches) of rain in just 24 hours.

Violent storms are another problem. In January 2004, both the Dardanelles and the Bosphorus (the narrow stretches of water that link the Mediterranean to the Black Sea), as well as the Suez Canal, had to be closed because of storms and high winds that also brought severe sandstorms to Egypt and snowstorms to Greece and Bulgaria. In the western part of the sea, too, deadly storms can blow up quickly, causing havoc both to boats at anchor in harbour and to those caught out in the open sea.

The Wicked Winds

Among the key features of the Mediterranean climate, affecting shipping, agriculture and today tourism, are the sea's many and famous winds. Traditionally, of course, mariners in particular have always paid close attention to the patterns of winds, recording carefully from which direction they blew, how often they blew and how long they lasted, so that they could venture onto the sea in safety and reach their intended destination. Any sudden and unexpected changes in the wind patterns could spell disaster. Four of the best-known of the Mediterranean's winds are the Mistral, the Bora, the Etesian (or Meltemi) and the Khamsin.

The notorious Mistral blows down the valley of the river Rhône in France and out on to the Golfe du Lion, where it heads east along the coast past Marseille towards Toulon. The Mistral often occurs when a cold front moves across France, with the cold air from the high lands of the Alps or Massif Central tumbling down with ever-greater vigour into the valley of the Rhône and seawards. It is a dry wind that heralds clear weather in the area, but it can also be bitterly cold and is usually associated with the winter or spring – though it can blow in the summer, too. Residents in the areas that suffer this often unpleasant and fierce wind, which may blow for as many as 100 days a year, often complain of feeling in low spirits just before it starts to blow, and of headaches and migraines when it does engulf them. One local name for the Mistral is the 'idiot wind', as people say that its incessant cold force can drive people to the edge of insanity. The name 'Mistral' comes from a local dialect word for 'master', a testament to the wind's influence on both humans and the environment. In fact it is said that the Golfe du Lion is so named because the sound of the Mistral ripping through the waves and rigging of ships resembles the roaring of a lion.

Apart from threatening shipping and ruining sports matches, the Mistral can fan dangerous forest fires in the tinder-dry lands of Provence. Yet there is one group of people who welcome it – windsurfers, groups of whom can often be found lounging around on shore waiting for the Mistral to whip up the waves that make the usually calm Mediterranean surface ideal for their sport.

The Bora blows from the north-east, funnelling down from the mountains into the top of the Adriatic, through cities including Trieste and Venice. This is another cold wind and can be dangerous for shipping in the northern Adriatic, causing sizeable waves to form very quickly. It is triggered in a similar way to the Mistral, with cold air coming down from the mountains to the north, the Dinaric Alps that run from Slovenia down to northern Albania. The Bora takes its name from the Greek god of the north wind, Boreas, and a similar wind blows into the north of the Aegean. Though the Bora is seen as cold, capricious and dangerous, the people of Slovenia have also traditionally made use of it by hanging legs of pork in its path to cure the meat for their local delicacy *prsut* (prosciutto).

ABOVE: The saying that 'It's an ill wind…' could hardly be more appropriate for this Slovenian ham delicacy known as prsut, *which is air-dried by being hung in the often biting cold wind called the Bora, one of many well-known winds in the Mediterranean.*

The Etesian wind comes from the north as well, but unlike the previous two is essentially a summer wind. It blows from the mainland of Europe and Eurasia through the Balkans and Turkey, where it is known as the Meltemi. Though it too can be a violent wind – the Roman poet Horace wrote of its dangers to the unwary sailor – its coolness can also bring welcome relief from the high temperatures of July and August. In Athens, for example, it is credited with removing much of that city's pollution for at least part of the summer.

Last of these four is the Khamsin, which blows northwards from the Sahara through Libya and Egypt in the eastern Mediterranean. It is triggered by low-pressure areas moving along the North African coast from February to early summer and is an exceptionally hot and dry wind. It often picks up sand and dust from the desert (as does another wind from the Sahara, the Scirocco), lending the sun an eerie, almost orange glow shining through the thickness of the storms. The Khamsin, feared for its potential to destroy crops, takes its name from an Arabic word for 'fifty', as this is the number of days the wind is commonly thought to last.

A Pattern of Constant Change

These descriptions of seasonal weather trends and wind patterns give an impression of predictability in the conditions of the Mediterranean. In fact, there are signs that the climate of the region has been changing constantly since the glaciers of the last Ice Age retreated from most of Europe around 10,000 years ago.

Indeed, scientists believe that about 8,000 years ago a catastrophe hit the sea, with

devastating effects on its marine life. Geological records suggest that a time of exceptionally heavy rainfall caused the rivers around the Mediterranean to swell in size and pump countless gallons of fresh water into the salty sea. The Nile, in particular, may have reached the size of the present-day Amazon. According to this theory the very rapid influx of rainwater caused, within just a few decades, a curious phenomenom in which the fresh water helped form a kind of 'cap' over the sea that effectively deprived the deeper waters below of oxygen. As a result, much of the marine life in these lower depths of the eastern sea would have died from oxygen starvation. In other words, the entire deep ecosystem of the eastern Mediterranean would have been wiped out.

Curiously, early humans living on the shores of the sea may not have noticed any immediate change in the water, or in the fish that they were able to catch; for only those species living in or visiting deeper parts of the sea would have been affected. Yet over time the knock-on effects to all marine life of this catastrophe would have been significant. Some were exterminated altogether, with others reduced in number, though other species benefited from the new conditions. In all it took more than 3,000 years for the deep sea to re-oxygenate after the flood waters had ended. It may even be that some species have still not recovered to this day.

It is believed, moreover, that this was not a one-off event, but that such episodes of torrential rain, followed by the death of deep-water marine life in the Mediterranean, are regular occurrences that may happen as 'often' as every 20,000 years or so. If that is so, then we are at roughly the halfway point between the last deep-sea catastrophe and the next one.

There are also signs that the climate in the region has been changing, albeit less dramatically, in the years following the last deep-sea disaster. Around 7,000 years ago – roughly 4,800 BC – the weather seems to have started to become drier and more seasonal, and to resemble more closely the area's current climate. There is evidence of unstable and unusually wet weather again in the first half of the 2nd millennium BC, and again of another similar period around AD 700. Much more recently, the period commonly known as the Little Ice Age – from the 14th century to the 19th, when temperatures in Europe were significantly lower than today – also saw wetter weather in the Mediterranean.

In hindsight, then, it seems that stable, dry weather in the Mediterranean, of the kind we are currently experiencing and consider normal, is more the exception than the rule. Though one must be careful about making direct correlations between climate and the development of civilization – humans, after all, have a habit of getting on and coping with whatever is thrown at them – it should also be mentioned in passing that the main expansion of the Roman Empire (roughly 200 BC to AD 400) took place during what seems to have been another period of relative climatic stability.

Terrain and plants

During the current phase of relatively settled climate, the terrain of the Mediterranean has taken on a number of distinctive appearances, associated with the plants it supports. One typical form of vegetation associated with much of the area is usually called *maquis*. This is a landscape of mostly evergreen shrubs and low–growing trees that would form woods and forests if not restricted by, for example, the grazing of animals, fire and wood–cutting. This form of densely covered shrubland lent its name to a group of French resistance fighters against the German occupation during the Second World War, the men and women who took to the bushes or *maquis* to carry out their campaigns of intelligence and sabotage. A common tree among the maquis landscape is the evergreen prickly oak (*Quercus coccifera*); others often found in this environment include the Greek or Grecian strawberry tree (*Arbutus andrachne*), Holm oak (*Quercus ilex*) and Atlas cedar (*Cedrus atlantica*).

Another common type of landscape found along the shores and islands of the sea, characterized by smaller shrubs in slightly more open terrain, is known as *garrigue* or *phrygana*. Plants typically found here include members of the broom family, heathers, colourful small shrubs such as species of *Cistus* (popular in northern Europe in rock gardens), and many herbs, including mint, rosemary, thyme and, of course, lavender. It is these areas that give so many parts of the Mediterranean its distinctive colours and aromas, especially on warm evenings in late spring and early summer. Corsica, one of the most beautiful of all Mediterranean islands, is known as 'the scented isle' because of the wonderful perfumes of the *garrigue* and *maquis*, said to be smelt by sailors as they approach its shores.

The plants of the region have had to adapt to a number of difficult conditions, including long, dry, hot summers, constant grazing by sheep and goats, frequent forest and bush fires, and, of course, human activities. One plant that has adapted well to the rigours of the heat is Spanish broom (*Spartium junceum*), a familiar plant in the *garrigue*. It loses its leaves during the extreme heat of the summer, unlike most deciduous plants, which shed their leaves in the winter. The reason *S. junceum* and other plants such as the woody spurge (*Euphorbia dendroides*) perform this trick is that leaves are one of the main parts through which a plant can lose moisture; so doing without them for the heat of the summer enables them to cope better with aridity.

Evergreens also need to shed their leaves, although, unlike their deciduous cousins, they lose them gradually over the course of a year so that the plant always retains its greenness. Many evergreens lose their leaves gradually during the winter and experience their main growing season in the spring and summer – even if there may not be much moisture around to help in this growth. It is possible that this habit is a throwback to the

ABOVE: *Rosemary grows wild in the Mediterranean region where it can grow from from 2 to 6+ feet high. It bears shiny, dark-green leaves that are grayish-white beneath and small, white, blue or violet flowers. In masses, blossoming rosemary looks like blue-gray mist blown inland from the sea. Its name translates from Latin as sea dew from the words 'ros' for dew and 'marinus' for the sea, probably in reference to its inhabiting sea-cliffs.*

times when the regional climate was less dry than it is now, suggesting that perhaps not all plants have adapted to the changing conditions of the region. The main mechanism by which evergreen plants protect themselves against loss of moisture is to grow small, thin leaves with a minimal surface area or thick, waxy leaves to shield the vulnerable interior of the plant from the heat.

One by-product of the huge numbers of visitors to the area over recent decades has been an increase in Mediterranean-style gardening and interest in the plants of the region. This enthusiasm has seen many beautifully coloured and fragrant species native to the warm shores of the sea transplanted into gardens across northern Europe. So far, the results have been mixed. Many plants from this warmer, drier region have shown themselves surprisingly able to adapt to the air frosts of northern climes; however, they are far less able to cope with being immersed in the wet, cold earth that is typical of north European gardens in winter. The Mediterranean climate has not moved to Cardiff, Cologne or Copenhagen just yet.

The Missing Forests

A less common habitat in the region is forest. There are many trees in the Mediterranean, but compared with much of northern and central Europe it is lightly wooded. Tree growth in recent times has been limited by various factors, including the growing aridity of the climate, but the paucity of woodland is in large part the result of human activity over many centuries. Wood has been used to build homes and, especially, ships, and new growth is restricted by the grazing of domesticated animals – as noted above, large areas of *maquis* are capable of growing into full-scale woodlands if left ungrazed. Populations of cork oaks have been particularly badly hit by human exploitation in North Africa, where there were once vast forests of trees, including this species alongside others such as the Berber thuya (*Tetraclinis articulata*) and wild olive. It is estimated that the extent of cork-oak forest today in North Africa is barely a third of what it has been in the past, while areas of wild olives in Algeria amount to just a tenth of what they once were. It is also estimated that some one million cork oaks were lost in the land around Cadiz in Spain in just 20 years early in the 20th century, when they were felled for the extraction of tannin.

The mountains of the region, however, provide an exception to this general picture, for here great expanses of forest remain. Moreover, large-scale planting of trees has begun throughout the Mediterranean in an attempt to improve the environment and reduce erosion.

The relative lack of available timber in certain areas around the sea has had an impact on human development in the past. In Egypt, where natural woodlands have long been rare, the pharaohs traditionally looked to the wood-rich lands of Lebanon and the Amanus mountains of what is today Syria to provide timber – much of it cedar, but also some oak – for ships and everyday materials. The result was an established trading pattern between the Nile delta and the Levant coast, a good example of how environmental diversity can encourage the transfer and exchange of goods between communities.

The animal world

The animal life of the sea itself is rich and varied. Whale-watching and dolphin-spotting are now regular tourist pastimes. Whale species seen include the mighty sperm whale and the pilot whale, while the occasional killer whale swims in through the Straits of Gibraltar from the Atlantic. Among the dolphin species are the striped, Risso's and bottlenose. The sea also contains numerous species of shark, among them the giant but harmless basking shark; even the much-feared great white shark has been frequently (if irregularly) sighted in the sea, especially in the strip of water between Sicily and Tunisia, but also on occasions as far north and east as the Bosphorus.

The presence of seals comes as more of a surprise, for these animals are more usually associated with cooler waters. The Mediterranean monk seal is, however, only just surviving, with a very few – possibly only 500 – still living off the shores of Greece and Turkey and in their other habitat, off the north–west coast of Africa in the Atlantic.

Ancient Animals

On land, the changing climate and the competition with humans have obliterated many of the larger animals that were once native to the region. Lions were once relatively common and existed around ancient Greece long enough to be recorded – and killed – by humans. The Barbary lions of North Africa survived rather longer, though by the 19th century they were an exotic rarity. In the early 1920s, the last one was shot in the Atlas Mountains in Morocco, and the breed is now officially declared extinct in the wild, though strains of the lion may have survived in captivity. In the days of the Roman Empire, this large and powerful beast – the male could weigh more than 500 pounds and sported a distinctive dark brown mane – was commonly trapped and taken back to Rome to perform in the 'games' and attack and devour Christians and other doomed prisoners.

Another large mammal, the brown bear, was once found in many parts of Europe and all around the northern shores of the Mediterranean. It still clings on to its Mediterranean habitat, with a few tiny colonies existing in Greece, Spain, Italy, Turkey and parts of the Balkans. A less well-known survivor from the past is the golden jackal, which lives on in Greece in three main locations: the Fokida, the Peloponnese, and the island of Samos. Its continued existence is perhaps especially surprising when one considers that until the last decade of the 20th century it was still legal quarry for

BELOW: Among the many wonderful sights of the sea are bottlenose dolphins, just one of several species of sea mammals found in the Mediterranean; others include whales and even seals. This Minoan, 13th-century BC wall painting is from Thera (Santorini). Athens, National Archaeological Museum.

ABOVE: Roman, mid 3rd-century mosaic showing four animal wrestlers fighting with four leopards. Found at Amira (Smirat-Moknine, south-east of Sousse, Tunisia). Sousse (Tunisia), Archaeological Museum. Lions were also once relatively common and existed around ancient Greece long enough to be recorded – and killed – by humans.

hunters. However, the jackal is known to be dwindling in numbers and there may be no more than a few hundred left.

When conditions were wetter, the hippopotamus was widespread in areas bordering the Mediterranean. In fact, this large, water-loving mammal managed to survive in parts of the Nile delta until the first years of the 19th century – the last one apparently being shot in 1816 – long after it had vanished from elsewhere in the Mediterranean. Elephants, too, once flourished in the region.

The lion, bear, jackal and hippo may seem exotic to the Mediterranean, but in the distant past the region boasted even more unusual animals. Remains found on Crete and other islands show the pre-historic existence of curious dwarf elephants and hippopotamuses the size of large dogs. On Crete there was also a strange deer-like creature that was unable to run – unlike its fleet-footed modern counterpart – apparently because there were no large predators. On Malta, meanwhile, the remains of an enormous prehistoric swan-like bird have been found.

On a grimmer note, one animal that came to the Mediterranean from India as long ago as Roman times and was destined to have a hand in human history was the black rat. This creature has been widely blamed for helping to spread the bubonic plague, which caused such misery in the region in the 6th century AD and then again from 1347, when it was known as the Black Death.

Migrating Birds and Native Reptiles

Vast numbers of birds fly south from their summer breeding grounds in the north of Europe in order to winter in Africa or around the Mediterranean before returning north the following spring. The fate of many is a tragic one. It was estimated in 2005 that as many as 1,000 million – a billion – birds are shot or otherwise killed each year in the

Mediterranean, many of them during their migration. This staggering figure represents around 15 per cent of the total population of wintering or migrating birds, and includes many birds of prey and colourful species, such as bee-eaters. They are shot and trapped by hunters for sport in countries all around the sea, from France, Spain and Italy to Tunisia, Egypt, Jordan and Lebanon. The islands provide scant refuge, many of the birds being killed on Cyprus and especially Malta. It is a huge and indiscriminate slaughter that is having an impact on a number of species.

As well as providing a home to migrating birds, the Mediterranean has many distinctive native species, including the Dalmatian pelican and the white pelican, the great egret, the huge Griffin's vulture, the snake–eating short–toed eagle and the hoopoe.

Thanks to the warm climate, the Mediterranean is also home to numerous snakes and other reptiles, including the gecko, chameleon, the extremely poisonous nose-horned viper and the Montpelier snake, which grows to 2 metres (6 feet 6 inches). The most famous story involving a snake is that of the last Ptolemaic ruler of Egypt, Cleopatra, who, according to tradition, committed suicide in 30 BC by allowing a venomous snake, an asp, to bite her. Experts believe that the snake in question was an Egyptian cobra (*Naja haje*) – the name 'asp' was used to describe a number of different poisonous snakes. The bite of the Egyptian cobra, which can grow to a length of 2.4 metres (8 feet), is extremely toxic and can kill a human quickly. The reptile was also a royal symbol adopted by the queen. Another snake that is still called an asp is the aspic viper (*Vipera aspis*), which can be found in northern Mediterranean countries such as France and Italy. It is unlikely that anyone would choose this snake to take their own life. Its bite can be treated nowadays and is unlikely to be fatal, but the venom can cause excruciating pain.

ABOVE: *Each year, a massive number of birds cross the region to spend the winter in Africa and then return to mainland Europe to breed. Sadly, many of them – as many as a billion – are shot and trapped on the way, including the beautiful bee-eater.*

The Effects of Domestication

Aside from the wild animals of the Mediterranean, those domesticated by humans have also made a substantial impact on its landscape and history. One animal domesticated relatively recently is the camel, the 'ass of the south', first tamed and used by humans in Arabia. An earlier example is the horse, an import from the vast open steppes of Eurasia. The horse was known in ancient Greece from the 2nd millennium BC and played an important role in military history throughout the succeeding centuries. In particular, the rapid and devastating Islamic conquest of large areas of land around the Mediterranean in the 7th and early 8th centuries AD owed much to the speed, stamina and strength of their Arabian horses and the skill with which the Muslims deployed them as cavalry.

Other animals domesticated early in the human history of the region include dogs, cats, sheep, goats, pigs and cattle. Cattle were once as popular as sheep in the region, but they require large amounts of water and as the climate has become drier their numbers have declined significantly. The widespread grazing of sheep and goats, however, continues to shape the landscape of the Mediterranean.

Among the great innovators when it came to taming animals were the Egyptians. They successfully managed to domesticate chickens, pigeons, Nile geese and, of course, cats. Cattle were very popular in ancient Egypt as a source not only of milk but also of meat

RIGHT: One of the most
important animals in
Mediterranean history and
elsewhere in the world is the horse,
shown here in this wood engraving
from 1845, featuring a battle
between a saracen and a
crusader; they were also used for
transport.

and leather, and owning large herds of them was considered a sign of prestige. However, it seems the Egyptians also tried – with uncertain results – to bring under their control a range of other animals from Africa, including herons, pelicans, antelopes, gazelles, and even hyenas and leopards. We know that the Egyptians were successful in keeping cheetahs as pets.

Agriculture

As important as the domestication of animals was the cultivation of crops. The development of agriculture is often regarded as one of the two clear signs of the beginning of modern civilization, the other being writing. Key food crops such as barley and wheat first began to be farmed roughly 10,000–11,000 years ago in what is known as the 'fertile crescent' stretching south and east from the Levantine coast of the Mediterranean, including the ancient settlement of Jericho, and gradually spread throughout the Mediterranean lands. In later centuries, parts of what is now Tunisia and, in particular, Sicily would flourish as providers of grain and would become known as the 'bread baskets' of the Mediterranean and especially the Roman Empire. Indeed, the Romans' deadly rivals at Carthage – near the site of modern Tunis – were renowned for their expertise in agriculture and in making the most of the fertile land near the North African shores of the sea. Even the Romans – who obliterated Carthage in 146 BC, though they were later to rebuild a city there – seem to have valued the Carthaginians' farming acumen.

Pliny the Elder informs us that after the destruction of Carthage the Romans cared little about the many books kept by their enemy, except for one. This was a 28-volume work on agricultural techniques written by a man called Mago. The Senate decreed that

these volumes be translated into Latin, and they were also consulted later by Islamic and Byzantine scholars. This masterpiece of the ancient world – Mago was described as the 'Father of Agriculture' – included advice on how to make wine and how to select the best cattle, and underlines just how fertile this part of North Africa could be, as well as how refined farming had become by the second half of the 1st millennium BC. Sadly, none of the original volumes have survived; all we have today are a few extracts cited by later writers.

The Illustrious History of Wine

Two vital crops that are inextricably linked with the Mediterranean are wine and olive oil. Vines have been cultivated to make wine for thousands of years. Some believe the grape vine (*Vitis vinifera*) originated in the foothills of eastern Anatolia; traces of the earliest wine known to have been produced have been found in a 7,400-year-old jar unearthed at Hajji Firuz Tepe in Iran, and we know that wine was made in Egypt and Syria perhaps 5,000 years ago. For the early Egyptians, wine was an imported luxury, probably brought in from Syria and Palestine, as no vines grew in the wild in their own land; in time, however, their descendants became skilled at viticulture themselves, and many surviving images from ancient Egypt show trellises being used to train vines.

The ancient Greeks enjoyed their wine, too, as is clear from the many references to it in their literature. They were probably the first to introduce the vine to Provence in the south of France. On the Italian peninsula, the Etruscans were also keen wine-makers. However, it was the Romans who, over the course of several centuries, spread both the drinking and the making of wine to other parts of Europe. As early as 160 BC, Cato had written a treatise on wine production around Rome and its territories, and in the 1st century AD, Pliny the Elder spent considerable time pondering the problem of preventing wine from turning into vinegar. One technique was to put tree resin into the wine during production. This age-old practice is still used to make the Greek wine retsina, and is doubtless the reason why many describe its unique and acquired taste as 'sappy'.

Initially, the Romans controlled the making of wine, and for a while tried to restrict

ABOVE: A 3rd-century BC Roman mosaic of an olive oil press. Found at St.Romain-en-Gal. St-Germain-en-Laye, Musée des Antiquites.

its production in such places as Gaul (France), preferring to sell wine to the inhabitants in exchange for slaves. It was said that the people of Gaul were a good market for this commodity, though the Romans noted disapprovingly that they usually drank it neat, without first diluting it with water as was the usual custom. It seems the French love affair with wine started a long time ago.

Viticulture eventually spread to many parts of Europe, including Spain and France, and the Romans even established vineyards in Britain, an unlikely location that is nevertheless enjoying a modest boom in winemaking at the start of the 21st century.

Mediterranean Cuisine

Olive trees need relatively little water once established, seem to thrive on neglect and even relish the regular harvesting of their fruit. These are important qualities in a region that – despite its reputation for abundance – suffers from aridity and a shortage of large areas of good cultivable soil. Outside the narrow coastal strips the soil can be poor, thin or rocky, and the land very steep – hence the existence of so much terracing in the Mediterranean. In a few areas, though, notably the Nile valley, the problem can be too much water; over centuries the Egyptians had to learn how to cope with the annual flooding of the waters and turn it to their advantage.

Despite these problems, and thanks in part to modern irrigation techniques, the Mediterranean is nowadays a significant provider of high-value food products. Indeed, the first years of the 21st century have seen a strong vogue for 'Mediterranean-style' cooking and produce, based on the culinary practices and lifestyle of the region's inhabitants.

Curiously, many of the 'traditional' ingredients of this cuisine do not originate in the Mediterranean but are introductions from other parts of the world. For example, aubergines, now a staple of Mediterranean food, are originally from Asia, in particular India, and made their way into the Middle East before being introduced to Spain by the Moors after their invasion in AD 711; rice, too was brought to Spain by the same route and cultivated especially in the land around Valencia, which became a major rice-producing area. Yet another Mediterranean favourite, the tomato, is an introduction from the New World and is thought to have been grown and eaten in Europe for the first time in Italy in the 16th century. Even the courgette, an essential part of the Provençal dish of ratatouille, is thought to have originated in the Americas, while the ever-popular pepper or sweet pepper (*Capsicum annuum*) is yet another import from the American tropics, brought back by the Spanish and Portuguese. The potato, whose thirst for water makes it poorly adapted for the region, also came to the Mediterranean from across the Atlantic. Thus, Mediterranean cuisine reflects a general feature of the region's cultures: the ability, even eagerness, to accept outside influences and to forge something new and distinctive from them.

A more basic but nonetheless essential food commodity is salt, which has long been used, traded, taxed and fought over in the Mediterranean. The Phoenicians and, later, the Carthaginians were early exploiters of salt deposits in the region and traded widely in this valuable commodity, while the Greeks used to pay for slaves in salt. The Romans doled out rations of the mineral to their soldiers: hence the expression to be 'worth one's salt'. The Latin for salt is *sal*, giving rise to the English word for a monthly payment – salary. The Romans also put the 'sal' into salad. The word comes from *herba salata* or salted herb/vegetable, after the Romans' habit of adding salt to their vegetable dressings. The Egyptians used salt for preserving bodies as well as for preserving and adding taste to vegetables. Much later, the medieval city-states and trading rivals Genoa and Venice traded and fought over the business of salt, the latter helped by the fact that it could obtain raw salt on its doorstep – from its own lagoon.

LIQUID GOLD

The olive tree is a true native of the Mediterranean region, and wild olives have flourished there for many thousands of years. The olive is famously tough, and some trees in parts of the Middle East such as Israel are thought to be up to 1,000 years old. Its cultivation is believed to have begun in the eastern Mediterranean lands and spread throughout the region – there is evidence of very early olive cultivation on Crete, possibly from as far back as 3000 or even 3600 BC. Ever since then, this remarkable tree and its unpromising-looking fruit have retained their value and popularity. The oil has also been used for medicinal and cosmetic as well as culinary purposes. The Greek athletes of antiquity used to rub their bodies with olive oil, while the Old Testament tells us that in King David's time, doubtless because of the value of the product, it was considered necessary to have separate overseers put in charge of olive trees and of olive oil supplies. The great classical writers such as Homer and later Virgil wrote glowingly about olive oil, while since biblical times an olive branch has been a symbol of peace.

As with wine, the Romans did much to help the spread of olive-tree cultivation from its eastern Mediterranean stronghold, and later the Moors in Spain played an important role. Today, Italy and Spain are the most important sources of olive oil in Europe. In the first decade of the 21st century, the olive oil industry worldwide was estimated to be worth some US$125 billion – a sign of the continued importance of this ancient Mediterranean staple.

Geological riches

Salt was one of the most important natural minerals found and used by early Mediterranean cultures, but it was not the only one. Vast deposits of limestone cover the area, and it was these that were used to build the pyramids in Egypt. Much of the distinctive white limestone used for this monumental enterprise was mined at quarries such as those in the Muqattam hills on the west bank of the river Nile.

But stone was used to make Mediterranean buildings even before the pyramids. The most stunning examples of these early constructions that remain are on the islands of Malta and its neighbour Gozo, where seven megalithic temples still stand. The oldest may date back as far as 3600 BC and thus predate the first pyramids of Egypt by hundreds of years. At one time it was thought that other ancient stone structures, such as those at Stonehenge in southern England, were based on these Mediterranean megaliths. Though this is no longer believed to be the case, the question remains – in respect of both the megaliths of Malta and those of Stonehenge – who built them? The structures on Malta and Gozo suggest a fertility cult linked to the worship of a goddess representing Mother Earth, but no one can be sure. Indeed, it is unlikely that we will ever understand who these early peoples were, how they lived and where they came from. However, they must have been relatively highly organized communities to build these impressive structures.

Other important minerals and metals have played their part in the shaping of European and world history. At some point near the start of the 3rd millennium BC, humans discovered that by mixing a certain quantity of tin with the already well-known metal copper, they could make a much stronger metallic alloy, which came to be called

ABOVE: *As well as its food and vegetation, the Mediterranean has deposits of important minerals such as limestone, used, for example, to make the famous and beautiful pyramids of Egypt.*

bronze – a material that gave its name to an entire period of human history. The Bronze Age in the Mediterranean is usually dated from *c.* 3000 BC to *c.* 1200 BC. There is evidence that tin was mined in the far east of the region, at Kestel in the Taurus mountains of Anatolia. The Egyptians are known to have traded in Sinai for copper, while much later the Phoenicians traded for tin from Spain and may even have voyaged as far as Cornwall in the south-west of England – way beyond the shores of the Mediterranean – in search of this valuable and relatively rare commodity.

Natural disasters

We have already seen how extreme forms of weather can produce hazardous conditions for mariners and land-dwellers alike in the Mediterranean. But more deadly still are the threats posed by the weaknesses of the earth's crust, lying just beneath the sea and surrounding lands. As a result of these and the pressures beneath them, human societies in the region, from the earliest settlements to the present day, have periodically had to cope with the extreme dangers posed by earthquakes, volcanoes and tsunamis.

The principal causes of this instability are the awesome forces created as the land mass of Africa continues its slow but relentless progress into the landmass of Eurasia. The

Mediterranean lies at the point where the tectonic plate – a section of the rigid outer shell of the earth – of Africa is colliding with the Eurasian plate (see map on page 42). The position is further complicated by the movement of two smaller plates, known as platelets, the Arabian platelet and the Anatolian platelet, the former forcing the latter westwards towards Greece. It is these remorseless movements that generate the numerous volcanic eruptions and especially earthquakes experienced in the area.

Earthquakes are a regular occurrence in the eastern Mediterranean and, as recent history has shown, Turkey and Greece are especially at risk. In 1999, two devastating quakes hit Turkey, both of them measuring more than 7 on the Richter scale. The first and larger measured 7.4 and hit the Izmit area in the north-west of the country on 17 August, leaving at least 17,000 people dead and many more injured and/or homeless. The economic cost of this disaster was estimated by the United Nations to be around US$16 billion. Just three months later, on 12 November, another quake, this time measuring 7.2, struck just 100 kilometres (60 miles) to the east, leaving nearly 1,000 people dead. In between these two appalling events, an earthquake of a more modest size (5.9) hit Greece near the capital, Athens, killing 143 people and causing widespread damage.

Both countries have had a long experience of such events. In 1509, for example, Istanbul, which at that point had been in the hands of the Ottoman Empire for

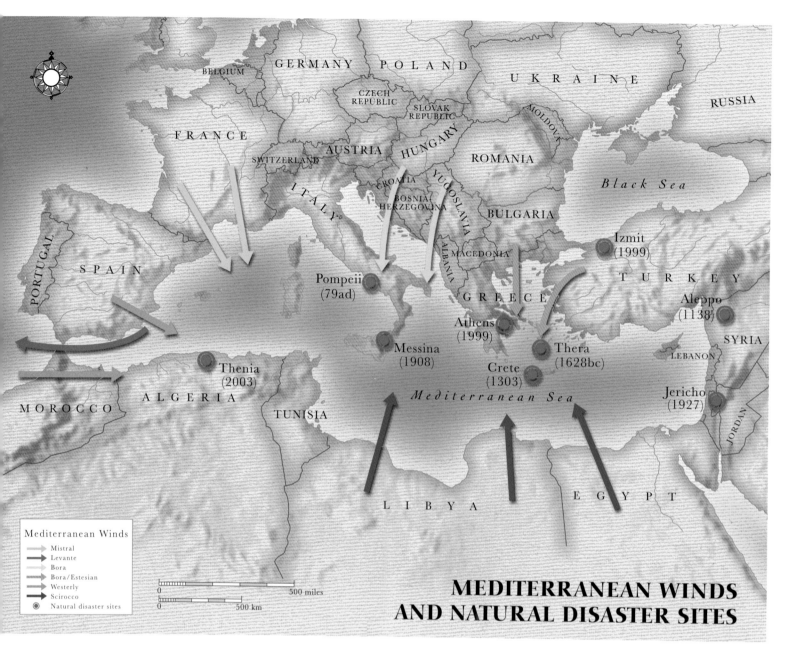

Mediterranean Winds

→	Mistral
→	Levante
→	Bora
→	Bora/Estesian
→	Westerly
→	Scirocco
◉	Natural disaster sites

0 — 500 miles
0 — 500 km

MEDITERRANEAN WINDS AND NATURAL DISASTER SITES

ABOVE: Life in the Mediterranean has long been influenced by powerful forces of nature both above and below the earth's surface. The many and various winds that blow across the region have had a major impact on human navigation of the sea and also the climate; while the course of history has often been punctuated by destructive earthquakes and volcanic eruptions.

only just over half a century, was partly destroyed by an earthquake. Thousands of years earlier, a serious quake that hit the ancient Greek city-state of Sparta in around 469–464 BC caused widespread damage and may have killed as many as 20,000 people. The resulting discord both inside and outside Sparta led to a conflict with its neighbours that has been described as the 'earthquake war'. Four decades later, in 426 BC, another earthquake, this time north of Athens, is also said to have caused damage and loss of life, in part from a series of tsunamis or giant waves caused by the shocks.

Further east, the area that is now Lebanon has also suffered from its share of earthquakes, including one that hit the ancient trading port of Byblos in 1365 BC and another that devastated Beirut in AD 551; and in neighbouring Syria a huge earthquake that today would measure more than 7 points on the Richter scale is thought to have claimed thousands of lives in AD 1202. Nor is the risk confined to the east of the region: the quake, rated 6.7, that hit Algeria in May 2003 was just one of many destructive tremors that has affected that country in recent decades.

The fact that so many earthquakes have occurred in the Holy Land has led to speculation that these natural phenomena may lie behind some of the intriguing stories in the Old Testament. For example, in the Bible the fall of Jericho, an ancient settlement east of Jerusalem, is attributed to Joshua's soldiers marching around its walls and his priests blowing their trumpets until the walls collapsed. Though to modern minds this seems unlikely, it is quite possible that Jericho's walls did come tumbling down at around this time as the result of an earthquake. In 1927, for example, the area around Jericho was hit by a quake measuring 6.3 which killed some 200 people. Similar tremors are known to have hit the same area in the more distant past.

More controversially, some experts explain the biblical description of the destruction of Sodom and Gomorrah with reference to the destructive power of an earthquake. The book of Genesis describes how God was so angry at the behaviour of the towns' inhabitants that he decided to destroy them – with the sole exception of Sodom's one good man, Lot, who was allowed to escape with his family (though his wife ignored God's instruction not to look back at the town as she left and was turned into a pillar of salt). It has been suggested that the two towns were hit by a huge earthquake and landslide that caused them to vanish into the waters of the Dead Sea. However, this is conjecture; some scholars still doubt whether Sodom and Gomorrah ever existed.

The Eruption of Thera

One natural disaster that certainly did occur was the eruption of Thera in the Cyclades, the group of islands that lies between Crete and the main waters of the Aegean sea, east of mainland Greece. This cataclysm happened roughly 3,500 years ago, though exactly when remains a matter of controversy. The date has usually been put at around 1450 or 1500 BC, but recent scientific findings in the Mediterranean and also from ice cores in Greenland suggest that a huge eruption took place somewhere in the globe nearer to 1650 BC. Whether this was Thera or another volcano is unclear.

There is less doubt about the sheer scale of the Thera eruption. Some geologists now believe it had a ranking of 7 on the Volcanic Explosivity Index (VEI). To put this into context, the huge eruption at Krakatau in Indonesia in August 1883 has been given a VEI value of 6 – and that explosion could be heard around 4,800 kilometres (3,000 miles) away and darkened the sky in the area for three days. A value of 7 is described as 'colossal' by volcanologists; the only equivalent eruption of the past 10,000 years is thought to have been the one at Tambora in Indonesia in 1815, after which clouds of volcanic material entered the atmosphere causing the infamous 'year without summer' of 1816, with unseasonal cold, crop failures and even famine occurring in many parts of the globe.

The scale of the eruption at Thera is particularly important because it may have been responsible for a crucial event in the history of the Mediterranean – the end of Minoan civilization. This is the name given to the flourishing society based on the island of Crete from as early as the 3rd millennium BC. Soon after 2000 BC, the Minoans were building impressive palaces and had developed an early form of writing and a beautiful style of pottery. For many centuries thereafter they dominated trade in the eastern Mediterranean. Yet, by about 1450 BC, this great early civilization had fallen steeply and apparently swiftly into decline. Indeed, at about this time their island and way of life were effectively taken over by the Mycenae, people of the mainland to the north and

ABOVE: When a volcano erupts the lava, ash and gas it spews out can cause total devastation to nearby areas. This picture shows the black smoke column from the crater of Mount Etna, on July 24, 2001. Mount Etna is the highest and the most active volcano in Europe, and was billowing huge clouds of smoke and black ash, and spitting rivers of lava, which lead the government to declare a local state of emergency.

MACEDONIA

ALBANIA

Eurasian
Plate

GREECE

Limnos

TURKEY

*Aegean
Sea*

Lesbos

Likades

Evvoia

Chios

Anatolian
Platelet

Mediterranean Sea

African
Plate

Andros

*Aegina
Methanal*

Naxos

Nyseros

Milos

Thera

Rhodes

Crete

0   100 miles

0   100 km

– – – Hellenic Arc

Major faults

◎ Volcanic complexes

**FAULT LINES AND TECTONIC PLATES
IN THE EASTERN MEDITERRANEAN**

*ABOVE: The cause of so much
geological instability in the eastern
Mediterranean is the slow but
unimaginably powerful, ongoing
collision between the tectonic
plates of Africa and Eurasia. The
results of this movement are areas
of fault lines, volcanoes and
recurring earthquakes.*

forerunners of the later classical Greek civilization. The intriguing question is whether it was the eruption at Thera some 110 kilometres (68 miles) to the north that brought Minoan society to its abrupt end.

The eruption effectively blew the island apart and poured out perhaps 30 cubic kilometres (7 cubic miles) of volcanic material, including vast quantities of ash and rock. The collapse of the volcano during the eruption led to the formation of the enormous 'caldera' or cauldron-shaped depression whose flooded centre dominates the island to this day. The ash and dust in the atmosphere could have changed the weather in the region for years afterwards, lowering light levels and temperatures, and causing crops to fail completely. This would have had a catastrophic impact on both the Minoans and their vital trading partners around the sea. More immediately, the explosive collapse of the volcano would almost certainly have triggered a series of large tsunamis or giant waves, which would have smashed into the island of Crete and wrought havoc on its ports and shipping.

It has been estimated that the tsunamis triggered by the Thera eruption could have been as high as 9 or even 15 metres (30 or 50 feet). The awful potential of tsunamis to lay waste coastal regions was graphically underlined in the first decade of the 21st century by the earthquake–induced tsunamis that struck the Indian Ocean on 26 December 2004.

The Thera eruption is also thought likely to have sent a great plume of debris into the sky, perhaps as high as 35 kilometres (22 miles), which in turn spewed ash and dust across a vast area of the eastern Mediterranean. Examinations at a lake in south–west Turkey, some 320 kilometres (200 miles) away from the island, have revealed a layer of ash from the volcanic blast that may once have been as deep as 25 centimetres (10 inches). Geological evidence also shows that ash reached the island of Rhodes, the Nile delta and, of course, Crete itself. The effect of the ash on the agriculture of the Minoans could have been devastating. Crops would have been ruined and later rainfall would have brought down more ash into low-lying farmland, acidifying the soil. Life on Crete and other smaller islands nearby would have been, at the least, uncomfortable and unpleasant for many years.

The volcano may also have caused widespread fires in Crete. There are signs that many Minoan palaces were destroyed by fire, and scientific evidence suggests that these blazes and the falling of the volcanic ash occurred at about the same time. No one can be sure how they are linked. The volcano was too far away to have caused fires directly, as the hot ash would have cooled by the time it fell upon the Minoan dwellings. It is also unlikely that the fires were set off by the earthquakes that certainly accompanied the eruption, as these were more likely to have occurred before Thera exploded. One possible explanation is that the force of the explosion on Thera caused shock waves in the atmosphere that overturned oil lamps, which in turn set the palaces ablaze, though this is simply a theory based on observations of the effect of the Krakatau eruption of 1883.

The Thera catastrophe occurred at a time when writing was still in its infancy, and so it is not surprising that no direct account of it exists. However, some scholars have sought

PLINY THE ELDER

Gaius Plinius Secundus, or Pliny the Elder as we know him, was born in AD 23 in northern Italy and has become one of the best known of Roman writers. Pliny was many things – an historian, biographer, soldier, military theorist and lawyer – and he also travelled widely. One of the literary achievements for which he is most renowned is the immense *Naturalis Historia*, or 'Natural History', which ranges widely over subjects including science, art, the natural world and agriculture. It is an epic work, which Pliny said drew on the existing literature of the time as well as his own observations, and thus offers invaluable insight into the thinking of the classical world. It was sadly ironic that Pliny's scientific curiosity led to his death. In AD 79, in charge of a Roman fleet at Misenum, he set sail across the Bay of Naples to examine the eruption of Vesuvius, a journey that turned into a rescue mission for friends. While ashore he died, probably overcome by toxic gases released by the eruption, and it was left to his nephew, Pliny the Younger, to record his observations of the cataclysm.

to link it to events outlined in the biblical book of Exodus. This describes waters turning red, darkness falling, and storms of thunder and hail. Certainly, the description of pillars of cloud by day and of fire by night (Exodus 13, verses 20–22) are suggestive of a volcanic eruption. The events related in Exodus are thought to have taken place around the 15th century BC, so the posited link between Thera and Exodus would support the later possible date for the eruption of *c*. 1450 BC.

Attempts have also been made to link the eruption with various elements of Greek myths, and even with the legend of the lost city of Atlantis. However, as we shall see shortly, there are more plausible explanations for that particular story.

The Tragedy of Pompeii
If the story of Thera is only slowly becoming better known, then the same cannot be said of the infamous events that took place in AD 79 in the forbidding shadow of Mount Vesuvius, the volcanic peak that has dominated the landscape around the Bay of Naples for many thousands of years. The mountain, 1,280 metres (4,200 feet) high, is situated on a volcanic arc and is part of what is called the Romana volcanic belt. Vesuvius itself lies where two major fractures in the earth's crust meet roughly at right angles – one a fault following the line of the Appenines in mainland Italy and the other a fault coming in from under the Tyrrhenian sea through the Bay of Naples.

Vesuvius has many times brought death and destruction to those living near it. However, the eruption of the 1st century AD is the best known, partly because it was the first properly described volcanic eruption in history. The prolific Pliny the Elder, a dedicated chronicler of the natural world, saw the event at first hand and would have been an ideal reporter of its enormous destructive power. Tragically, however, Pliny died in the disaster (see box on page 43) and it was left to his nephew, known to us as Pliny the Younger, to describe what he saw of the eruption in letters to the Roman historian Tacitus. As a result of his descriptions, large and explosive eruptions, such as that of Vesuvius in AD 79, are described as 'Plinian'.

Though the eruption of AD 79 clearly caught the inhabitants of Pompeii and its often

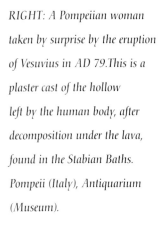

RIGHT: A Pompeiian woman taken by surprise by the eruption of Vesuvius in AD 79. This is a plaster cast of the hollow left by the human body, after decomposition under the lava, found in the Stabian Baths. Pompeii (Italy), Antiquarium (Museum).

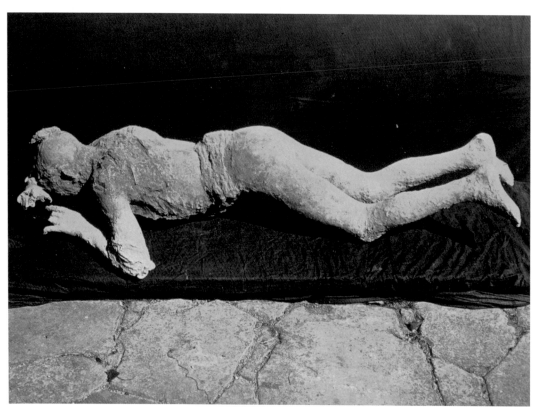

forgotten sister settlement of Herculaneum by surprise, there is intriguing evidence that the volcano had been active some 300 years before and had even been briefly documented at that time. Ancient writers, such as Plutarch and Silius Italicus, referred to the sky being 'on fire' and to the mountain 'hurling flames worthy of Etna' (a reference to the volcano on Sicily) in around 217 BC. These accounts are supported by geological evidence of an active volcano in the area at this time. Going still further back, recently discovered evidence shows that Bronze Age settlements in the northern part of the bay were destroyed by an eruption around 1800 BC.

Yet if there were age–old warning signs that Vesuvius might erupt again with deadly fury, then they were lost or ignored. It is true that the ancients were well aware of the power of earthquakes and volcanoes, both in Italy and in the even more susceptible lands of Greece and Turkey. But their occurrence was usually ascribed to religious causes – the anger of the gods – rather than to any underlying geological fault in an area. Certainly, no connection was made between the phenomena of earthquakes and volcanoes.

Of course, volcanic slopes and the nearby areas, which are usually rich in minerals, often make excellent agricultural land, and there is no doubting that the wealthy towns of Herculaneum and Pompeii were wonderfully situated on the Bay of Naples below the gaze of the mountain – two compelling reasons for people to settle there. Also, the inhabitants of the two towns had only recently repaired the damage done to buildings by a severe earthquake in AD 62, a restoration that would have caused them considerable inconvenience and, presumably, expense. (Following this earthquake the philosopher Seneca noted that a flock of 600 sheep near the town had been wiped out, a loss he attributed to poisons coming from the earth – probably volcanic gases seeping through fissures they had created in the ground.)

Given all these reasons, we cannot perhaps blame the Romans for getting caught in the firing line in AD 79 and for not having considered leaving the area for safer parts –

ABOVE: Once the eruption of Vesuvius had begun, the once-elegant streets of Pompeii were soon buried under mountains of ash, followed later by deadly surges of hot gases and particles known as pyroclastic flows; no one stood a chance of surviving.

even if modern experts can recognize the tell-tale signs of impending doom with the aid of 19 centuries of hindsight. Pliny the Elder, his nephew tells us, took note of the earthquakes that occurred before the eruption but dismissed them on the grounds that such tremors were commonplace in the surrounding area of Campania. Even the sight of a column of smoke pouring out of the summit of the mountain at first did little more than arouse the curiosity of the elder Pliny. And the inhabitants, having endured that earthquake less than two decades before – Naples was also hit in AD 63, while the Emperor Nero was giving a concert – were in no mood to relinquish these beautiful and prosperous locations on the basis of a few mild tremors.

When Vesuvius finally erupted on the morning of 24 August it did so with devastating force, probably deserving a rating of 6 on the VEI, which volcanologists class as 'huge'. Vast amounts of ash and pumice exploded into the atmosphere and within perhaps 30 minutes the panicked inhabitants of Pompeii, 10 kilometres (6 miles) away, would have been watching in horror as much of this debris began to fall on their town. It would have been like a storm of dark-coloured snow falling at the bewildering rate of up to 20 centimetres (8 inches) an hour; the sun and sky would have been obliterated from view and all would have become darkness.

In his letter to Tacitus, Pliny the Younger described how the cloud looked as the eruption began.

The cloud was rising from a mountain – at such a distance we couldn't tell which, but afterwards learned that it was Vesuvius. I can best describe its shape by likening it to a pine tree. It rose into the sky on a very long 'trunk' from which spread some 'branches'. I imagine it had been raised by

BELOW: One of the many fascinating discoveries from the excavations at Pompeii were these gladiator barracks where combatants lived and trained before their contests. Many weapons and items of armour, such as helmets, were found at the site, as well as examples of gladiators' graffiti on the walls.

a sudden blast, which then weakened, leaving the cloud unsupported so that its own weight caused it to spread sideways. Some of the cloud was white, in other parts there were dark patches of dirt and ash.

By midnight, this deadly cloud, a part of which would reach as far as North Africa, had dumped pumice and ash to a depth of more than 6 feet in places. Roofs had caved in, and anyone who had not fled the initial eruption would have almost certainly been asphyxiated or crushed to death. Yet some people, especially in Herculaneum, had found shelter and had managed to withstand the awful barrage of ash and pumice.

At this point, Vesuvius produced an even more deadly horror. Just after midnight, a series of what are called pyroclastic flows started their swift and appalling descent from the summit. A pyroclastic flow is typically made up of two parts. The first is a cloud of fine particles and volcanic gases, probably at temperatures of 100 degrees Celsius, which travels exceptionally quickly – up to 300 kilometres (190 miles) an hour. The second, much denser surge is made up of large particles and rocks, moving far more slowly but, at temperatures of up to 400 degrees Celsius, burning just about everything in its path.

In Herculaneum, which, thanks to the direction of the wind, had been spared much of the initial ash, hundreds of survivors had fled to the harbour, where they huddled with a few scant belongings and valuables under some protective arches. Perhaps they had hoped to escape by boat, or perhaps they were expecting to brave out the rest of the night sheltered from the falling ash. But as soon as the first of the pyroclastic flows fell upon the town they were killed instantly, all hope of escape vanishing in a split second of searing heat. Over the next eight hours, five more pyroclastic surges bellowed out of Vesuvius, the later ones enveloping Pompeii as well as Herculaneum. No one who had remained alive in the vicinity stood a chance of surviving.

The eruption seems to have caused at least one tsunami as well. Pliny the Younger describes how along the coast he saw the sea 'sucked away', leaving marine creatures 'stranded on dry sand'. This is a description of what happens when the trough – the low point – of a tsunami hits shore just before the main wave crashes into the land.

We can never be sure just how many died in the appalling events that overtook Pompeii, Herculaneum and the surrounding countryside and settlements, though some estimates have put the death toll between 10,000 and 16,000. After the earthquakes that had damaged the two towns in AD 62, people quickly rebuilt the damaged structures and continued to live there. This time, after the wholesale destruction caused by the eruption, there was no attempt to resuscitate the settlements. Pompeii was eventually covered in a layer of volcanic debris more than 5 metres (15 feet) thick, while the depth of ash and pumice on top of Herculaneum reached more than 20 metres (60 feet) in places. The total volume of ash and pumice belched out by Vesuvius over the surrounding area during the 19 hours of the eruption was at least 4 cubic kilometres (1 cubic mile).

Even had there been the will to rebuild, there were very few survivors left of the two towns' original inhabitants to attempt the task. There is evidence that a few may have escaped the effects of the eruption and have tried later to tunnel into the area to retrieve precious possessions; certainly the sites were looted by thieves as well.

ABOVE: One of the great Roman observers of the natural world, Pliny the Elder (Gaius P. Secundus Plinius, AD 23/24-79), was a witness to the explosion at Vesuvius. However, he tragically lost his life after he sailed too close to the carnage in an attempt to get a closer look, and to rescue survivors. It was left to his nephew, Pliny the Younger, to record the events for posterity. Engraving by Bollinger, after an antique bust; colour added later.

ABOVE: The late 3rd- or early 4th-century Christian martyr St Januarius, also known as San Gennaro, is credited with the posthumous power to stop eruptions at the volatile Vesuvius, though occasionally when his powers have not stopped eruptions local crowds are said to have vented their anger on his statue, as depicted here after the eruption of 1872.

Curiously, though the smoke and ash billowing from the mountain were visible from Rome, and despite Pliny's letter to Tacitus, the memory of the cataclysm in the Bay of Naples did not appear to linger long in the public consciousness – at least, not in surviving published writings. Within a few decades, much of the northern part of this beautiful bay recovered its economic clout and its appeal to wealthy visitors, even if it was never quite the draw of pre–eruption years.

Meanwhile, the buried towns of Pompeii and Herculaneum and their inhabitants were quietly forgotten. It was not until 1,500 years later that workmen digging in the area began to unearth the remains of the tragedy, and by the 1760s some archaeological excavation work had started. Even then, as slabs of marble and statues were uncovered they were more likely to be carted off to adorn new villas than to be studied as the precious historical artefacts they were. It was not until the 19th century, thanks in particular to the efforts of an archaeologist called Giuseppe Fiorelli, that a systematic excavation of Herculaneum and especially Pompeii was embarked upon. It was Fiorelli who discovered in the 1860s that, by pouring liquid plaster into the holes or 'moulds' where bodies had been entombed in the ash, he could produce very accurate representations of the victims of the disaster – in some cases even capturing the expression on a person's face.

It was then, too, that the remarkable state of preservation of the remains began to be appreciated. Decorated walls, statues, furniture, jewellery, household utensils – and, of course, human bodies – all preserved by the layers of ash that had covered them, provided a unique snapshot of how Romans had lived their lives in the 1st century AD.

ST JANUARIUS

St Januarius (or San Gennaro, the Bishop of Beneventum) was an early Christian martyr who died during the reign of the Roman emperor Diocletian around AD 300 or 305. He was beheaded at Pozzuoli near Mount Vesuvius, and his body was later taken to the cathedral in Naples, where it was buried. Meanwhile, his skull and phials of his blood became holy relics. The saint is believed to have the power to stop volcanoes – more particularly, to stop the eruptions of Mount Vesuvius. According to one account, a crowd set fire to the gates of the cardinal archbishop's residence in Naples after the eruption of 1767 because he had refused to bring out the relics of the saint to quell the volcano. It was later claimed that when the archbishop bowed to pressure and brought the skull out into public view the mountain immediately stopped erupting. The saint is also credited with protecting Naples from a lava flow from Vesuvius in 1832. Each year the powdery remains of the saint's blood, still kept in a phial, are brought out and placed near the supposed head of the saint, at which point the blood then liquefies in what believers say is a miraculous sign.

The discoveries at Pompeii, and the techniques developed by those working there, were important steps in the development of archaeology. Meanwhile, the study of Mount Vesuvius helped lead to the science we now call volcanology. Sir William Hamilton, a British envoy in Naples at the end of the 18th century, became fascinated by the mountain and began to observe it and other volcanoes in detail. Sir William's many letters and two books on the subject were the first modern written attempts to under–stand the scientific processes of volcanoes, and the diplomat is sometimes referred to as the 'Father of Volcanology'. By the middle of the 19th century, an observatory had been built high up on the mountain, and in 1872 a physicist called Luigi Palmieri stayed at this vantage point to observe an eruption at first hand.

For Vesuvius had not been quiet since AD 79; indeed, the volcano was very active right up to the 13th century. There was then a lull of several hundred years, during which vineyards returned once more to the mountain's slopes, until it erupted again with devastating force in 1631, killing up to 3,000 people. Since then the volcano has erupted periodically, including once in 1906 when it killed 100 people and again in 1944, leaving 26 dead. Many experts believe that when – not if – the next eruption occurs it could be on the scale of that of 1631.

The 'Greek Pompeii'

For a third and final example of the natural disasters that can strike the Mediterranean, we move back in time to four centuries before the calamity at Pompeii, when the Greek cities of Helike and Bura flourished on the Gulf of Corinth about 160 kilometres (100 miles) west of Athens. Helike in particular was an important and powerful centre. Its citizens had founded settlements in Italy and Asia Minor, and it was home to a famous grove dedicated to the worship of Poseidon, the revered god of earthquakes as well as the sea.

Then, one day in 373 BC, Helike and Bura simply vanished from the face of the Earth. A huge earthquake accompanied by a tsunami destroyed the area and caused the

BELOW: A representation of the lost city of Atlantis based on excavations on Crete. After a draw‑ing by Walter Heiland. From: A. Herrmann, Katastrophen, Natur-gewalten und Menschenschicksale, Berlin (G.Schoenfeld) 1936, p.39. Coll. Archiv f.Kunst & Geschichte.

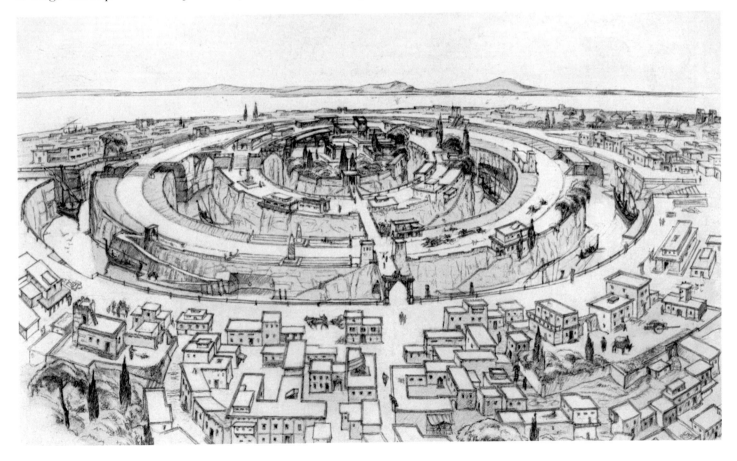

surrounding land to sink into the sea. So high was the wave that at one point only the tops of the trees of the sacred grove could be seen – according to much later accounts, at least. Thousands of people perished, and even Spartan ships that lay at anchor nearby were lost.

Visitors to the scene in later ancient times claimed to have seen evidence of the demolition of Helike and Bura. They spoke of buildings visible through the clear blue waters and even a bronze statue of Poseidon under the waves that was apparently a hazard to fishermen's nets. Eventually, though, Helike silted over and for centuries lay forgotten and ignored. No one was even sure where the city had once been. Then, in 2001, a team of scientists discovered traces of the ancient city less than a mile inland near the town of Aigio, close to the south–west shore of the Gulf of Corinth. The evidence suggests that the city had been buried by an inland lagoon that had itself silted over. The experts also found evidence that an earlier Bronze Age settlement had existed on the spot some 2,000 years before Helike and that this, too, had suffered a similar fate.

The discovery of Helike has excited much interest in the archaeological world, and the site has been dubbed the 'Greek Pompeii' because of the wealth of detail it has revealed and is expected to continue to yield in the coming decades as excavations progress.

One intriguing suggestion is that the loss of so great a city may have given rise to the stories of Atlantis, the fabled lost city alluded to earlier. The story of a once–great civilization that perished in a natural disaster comes from the great Greek philosopher Plato. His account of the civilization and its demise was probably written about 15 years after Helike's tragic fate and about a decade before his own death in 348 BC. Plato describes how the area was hit by earthquakes and floods and Atlantis was then 'similarly swallowed up by the sea and vanished'.

As with all supposed discoveries of the 'real Atlantis', there are problems in reconciling Plato's account with the site at Helike. The philosopher located the city far away, somewhere in the Atlantic Ocean, and also said it happened thousands of years before the time he was writing. But Plato was alive during the loss of Helike, and the destruction of

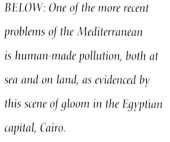

BELOW: One of the more recent problems of the Mediterranean is human-made pollution, both at sea and on land, as evidenced by this scene of gloom in the Egyptian capital, Cairo.

so powerful a society in just one winter's night of mayhem is bound to have had a lasting influence on the mind of a thoughtful and brilliant man. The truth is that we will probably never know where Atlantis was located or even whether it ever existed at all. But the tales of its destruction, with their echo of the very real events at Helike, serve as yet another reminder of the destructive power of nature in the Mediterranean.

There seems little reason to doubt that natural disasters such as those just described will continue to affect the Mediterranean in the years to come. Sadly, there will be more deeply damaging earthquakes such as those experienced in Turkey at the end of the last century. The only questions are when they will happen, and how big they will be.

A problem of more recent origin is that of pollution. Sewage, shipping and the influx of waters from the heavily polluted Black Sea have all taken their toll and have damaged the flora and fauna of the sea. Since 1975, Mediterranean countries have agreed to abide by the Barcelona Convention, committing them to controlling and reducing levels of pollution entering the sea.

More difficult to assess is the impact of climatic change on the Mediterranean region. While few doubt the reality of global warming, it is less clear what its precise impact on the weather will be. Scientific models suggest that in the northern half of the region winter rainfall may increase, but that in the southern half it may decrease, while temperatures in both parts will rise. Implicit in such models is the worrying prospect that the least economically developed parts of the region – North Africa and parts of the eastern Mediterranean – will be hardest hit by drought and that there may even be an increase in the area reduced to desert. The impact on agriculture, in particular, and water supplies could be very significant. Rising sea levels – a predicted result of global warming – could also have a disproportionate impact on a region that by its very nature depends on coastal strips for agriculture and large-scale human settlement. Yet the Mediterranean has experienced massive and sometimes rapid changes in climate in the past and coped. One must hope that the many peoples and cultures around the sea today will be able to meet the new challenges that lie ahead.

CHAPTER 2

HISTORY AND POLITICS

Humans have lived on or near the shores of the Mediterranean for tens of thousands of years. Some of the earliest evidence of human activity in the region is provided by the extraordinary cave paintings that have been found in the Mediterranean countries of Spain, France and Italy. From those distant beginnings onwards, the history of the region and its dominating sea has been bewildering. Dazzling empires have come and gone, great religions have been born and bloody battles have been fought, all ultimately helping to form the many nation-states and peoples that make up the Mediterranean today.

RIGHT Alexander the Great's troops defeating the Persians led by Darius III in the important battle of Issus in 333 BC. The conquests of Alexander enabled the influence of Greek culture to spread far beyond the Aegean Sea and changed the history of the entire region. Roman mosaic, imperial time, from the Casa del Fauno in Pompeii after a Greek painting by Philoxenos from the 4th century.

Stone Age illustrations go back to the distant recesses of human memory. Tablets of stone bearing painted images of an animal and a human figure, found in Fumane Cave near Verona in Italy, may be as much as 35,000 years old. Even more impressive are the slightly younger paintings – about 30,000 years old – found at Grotte Chauvet in the Ardèche region of southern France, which feature mammoths, owls, bears, large cats and rhinoceroses. No one can be quite sure what the significance of these and later paintings is, or why they were made, though many of them point to a possible religious significance – they show a fascination with animals, and the power of nature is often associated with the first-known forms of religious worship. Yet it is becoming clear that human society all those thousands of years ago was rather more sophisticated than we might suppose.

The earliest times: farming, settlement, worship

Another key sign of the start of modern civilization was the development of farming. Once humans learned to grow rather than merely just gather or hunt their food, they could remain in one place and start to build larger communities. There is evidence that the eastern shore of the Mediterranean was one of the earliest places at which this crucial change occurred. From the 11th millennium BC, rye was grown in what is now Syria, and by 9000 BC at the latest, wheat and barley were being cultivated in the Jordan valley. Excavations have revealed ancient settlements, the earliest known in the region, at the famous site of Jericho (occupied since at least 9000 BC) and also at the equally important if far less well-known site of Çatal Höyük in what is today southern Turkey.

Situated near the modern city of Konya, Çatal Höyük dates from roughly 7000 BC and, because of its size at the time, is sometimes described as the 'first city' – even though by current standards it was a modest-sized town or large village. Estimates of its likely population range from under 5,000 to 10,000. The people lived in mud-brick houses tightly packed together with no doors, the only way in and out being through holes in the roofs. Here archaeologists have found clay figurines, pottery and works of art; the main 'industries' of the area would have been agriculture (growing corn and raising cattle) and the making of tools from obsidian (volcanic glass). There is no sign of any hierarchical structure, nor any evidence of any grand houses or palaces where leaders might have lived, and we know little about just who these late Neolithic people were and how they organized their society. The site provides, nonetheless, a tantalizing glimpse of how, very gradually, the peoples of the Mediterranean began to coalesce into larger and more complex communities as they emerged from what we have labelled the Stone Age.

It can be hard for us, living as we do in a fast-moving world where events of even a few decades back feel 'old', to understand how slow and gradual the development of human society was so long ago. The gap between the origins of settlement in places such as Çatal Höyük and the emergence in the eastern Mediterranean of what we call the Bronze Age is a matter not of centuries but of millennia. During this lengthy period, humans gradually developed new techniques, technologies, beliefs and social structures, in processes of which we know relatively little. But, just occasionally, out of this darkness of prehistory, occasional shafts of light emerge to surprise and dazzle us.

One such glimpse, dating from just before the start of the Bronze Age, is provided by the impressive but baffling temples found on Malta and its neighbouring island of Gozo. As stated in Chapter One, we do not know a great deal about these 'megalithic temples of Malta' or where the people who built and used them may have come from, though

their ancestors seem to have arrived on the island via Sicily about 5000 BC. As far as we can tell their culture had no direct connection with any other society at the time, and experts are unsure how they fit into the 'story' of the development of Mediterranean civilization. And yet they built these magnificent temples, structures considerably older than the equally mysterious structure at Stonehenge in England, older even than the first pyramids in Egypt.

The advance of Egypt

The first major civilization to emerge in the Mediterranean was in Egypt at the dawn of what we call the Bronze Age in the 4th millennium BC. Egyptian society developed roughly in parallel with that of Mesopotamia (the area around the rivers Tigris and Euphrates), though there appears to have been only limited contact between the two.

Both cultures had this much in common: plenty of sunshine and, thanks to the Nile and the other two rivers, an abundance of water. For the Egyptians, the presence of the Nile was crucial. From roughly 3000 BC – it is impossible to be precise about such a phenomenon – the Sahara, which in the past had contained grasslands, became markedly more arid and began to assume something like its present form. Without the Nile, therefore, it is hard to imagine the development of an Egyptian civilization.

The waters made the Nile and its delta good for agriculture as long as humans could control the flooding and the marshes – which were full of dangerous wild animals such as crocodiles and hippopotami, and of disease. By some point in the 4th millennium BC, the Egyptians were learning how to channel the flow, using canals to direct the stream as the waters rose. Gradually, as society became more organized and the amount of food grown increased, more non-farming people could be supported. These people performed other valuable roles in the settlements, as craftsmen, builders, artists and, later, scribes. On top of this growing society stood a solitary ruler – the king.

Egypt was originally divided into two countries, upper and lower. The first king of Egypt, the man credited with uniting the country, is usually reckoned to be King Narmer of Upper Egypt, who lived some time around 3200–3100 BC. His victory over Lower Egypt is commemorated in the famous Narmer Palette, a decorative version of the kind of palette used for preparing make-up. (There is an element of confusion here, because later Egyptian sources claimed that the founder of Egypt was someone called Menes; it is possible Narmer and Menes are the same person.)

The triumph of Narmer heralded what we now know as the First Dynasty of Egypt, the beginning of a sequence of dynasties that would number 31 by the time they ended in the 4th century BC. After that came the so-called Hellenistic Period, heralded by the invasion of Alexander the Great and divided between the Macedonian and Ptolemaic dynasties. The latter lasted until 30 BC, when Roman dominance was established.

Over those 3,000 years between Narmer and Roman times the fortunes of Egyptian society waxed and waned, but its achievements were huge. The pyramids were built, as was the Great Sphinx; magnificent cities such as Memphis were founded; and control was exercised over lands as far north as Syria and as far south as the Sudan. Many rulers – who became known as pharaohs after the name used for the Great House in which they lived –

BELOW: The Narmer Palette, shown here, was discovered at the end of the 19th century by British archaeologist James Quibell, and depicts the bringing together of Upper and Lower Egypt into one kingdom by King Narmer in roughly 3100 BC. The votive plaque shows Narmer with a defeated enemy and the Horus falcon. Found at Nekhen (Hierakonpolis). Cairo, Egyptian Museum.

LEFT: *The reign of Amenhotep III (Egyptian King of the 18th Dynasty, 1411–1375 BC) was a period of great cultural achievement in Egypt and also a time when its empire stretched from Sudan to the Euphrates. This procession figure of Amenhotep III shows the king wearing the double crown of upper and lower Egypt. Luxor Museum.*

achieved fabulous accumulations of wealth, in particular apparently limitless amounts of gold, and presided over the development of a form of early writing, art and complex religious beliefs. For many in the ancient world, Egypt was a byword for wisdom and learning as well as great splendour and riches.

Even the invasion of the Hyksos, a Semitic people who seized control of Egypt and ruled in the Nile delta in the mid–2nd millennium BC, may ultimately have strengthened rather than weakened the kingdom, for by the time they were deposed after ruling for more than 100 years, they had overseen the introduction of new weapons and new gods. Soon after the start of the post–Hyksos New Kingdom in 1548 BC, Egypt was undoubtedly the most powerful empire in the region, rich in wealth, culture and military might. Its fame had spread far and wide among trading partners, as did its usually ample supplies of grain, and it produced powerful leaders, such as Amenhotep III (1388–1348 BC) and Rameses II (1279–1212 BC).

Yet Egypt never gained control of a huge cultural or trading Mediterranean empire, as the Greeks and Phoenicians were later to do, or a vast territorial empire of the kind carved out by the Romans and then the Arabs and Ottomans hundreds of years after-wards. For all its wealth and power, and the longevity and continuity of its culture, Egypt largely retained influence only in its own eastern corner of the Mediterranean. Though one must be wary of forming judgements at so great a distance of time; perhaps this can be explained in part by a certain insularity in the Egyptian outlook, prompted by the belief that Egyptians were a superior people and that their way of life was sufficient in itself. From this viewpoint, the purpose of military action was to protect borders and maintain trade, not to spread Egyptian religion or culture to the rest of the world.

Nevertheless, Egypt's legendary wealth and fertility made it an inevitable target of envious Mediterranean neighbours, who sought to get their hands on the kingdom's riches by trade or, quite often, by conquest. Indeed, that is the later story of Egypt, beginning with assaults first by the Persians and then, more conclusively, by Alexander the Great – constant conquest by the latest regional superpower.

Bronze Age kingdoms

The eastern Mediterranean was not the only place where early societies developed. Humans on the western, southern and northern shores were not sitting around waiting for history to happen to them; they too developed settlements, local trade and agriculture. Yet, it is true to say that there existed in the western half of the region no large empires such as those that predominated to the east. In the early days of Mediterranean civilization it was the east that led the way.

Another important Bronze Age empire was the one based on Crete, which we generally call the Minoan civilization. In fact, it is probably an exaggeration to call the Minoan culture an empire. The Cretan society was above all a trading phenomenon, with a network of commercial partners in the Aegean and right across the eastern section of the Mediterranean. As an island, Crete depended on ports and shipping for its survival, and it must undoubted-ly have had a powerful merchant fleet at its disposal. Its inhabitants settled at trading posts in the Aegean, in the Levant and in Anatolia, and its merchants voyaged to the

LEFT: This amphora artwork (540-530 BC) depicts the myth in which the Greek hero Theseus slays the half-man half-bull creature known as the Minotaur, on Crete. Theseus was able to escape from the Labyrinth where the Minotaur had dwelt thanks to a trail of thread supplied by his lover Ariadne. Paris, Musée du Louvre.

Nile delta. Yet, though undoubtedly it could be warlike when the occasion demanded, it was not a land-conquering empire seeking to impose its control on other societies.

The building of the famous palaces of Crete began around 2000 BC when Minoan culture was beginning to develop: the potter's wheel had arrived, and the use of wheeled wagons was adopted. The most famous palace was the one at Knossos, supposedly the home of the great King Minos. Thanks to a British archaeologist, this legendary character gave his name to the whole Minoan civilization.

When Sir Arthur Evans was excavating the site at Knossos at the start of the 20th century, the vastness and intricacy of the 5-acre site reminded him of the legend of King Minos and the Labyrinth, and so he coined the name 'Minoan' for the civilization whose past he was unearthing. In this tale, Minos asks the craftsman Daedalus to build a structure to hold the Minotaur, the half-man half-bull created out of the liaison between the Cretan queen Pasiphae and a magnificent white bull sent to the king by the god Poseidon. The result of Daedalus' labours was the Labyrinth, a house from whose maze of passages it was thought impossible to escape. Each year the Greeks were forced to pay tribute to Minos by sending youths to be eaten by the Minotaur, as a form of sacrifice to the gods. Eventually the Greek hero Theseus managed to kill the Minotaur and escape from the Labyrinth thanks to a thread supplied by his lover Ariadne – who was King Minos' own daughter. This Greek story seems to symbolize the way in which the Mycenae – forerunners to the Greeks of the classical period – eventually came to rule over Crete.

The legend of Minos certainly underlines the wealth and prestige that Crete once had in the world. The Cretans had writing – though the language is as yet indecipherable – produced some fine art and pottery, traded in wool, and may even have been the first to develop a flourishing olive trade and the production of wine in the region. Even the destruction of their palaces, presumably by earthquakes, in around 1700 BC did not long interrupt Crete's prosperity, for the buildings were promptly reconstructed.

Yet at some point around the middle of the 2nd millennium BC the Minoan civilization on Crete disappears from view, and by 1450 BC it had been replaced by the Mycenaean culture. No one is quite sure how or why Minoan society ended so abruptly, though, as we saw in Chapter One, some believe that the volcanic eruption of Thera may have been responsible.

Early Greeks

What became of the Minoans themselves is unclear. Undoubtedly, some, maybe many, stayed where they were to become absorbed in the new Mycenaean culture. Others probably scattered around the Aegean and other parts of the eastern Mediterranean. The Mycenaeans, meanwhile, took over not just their Cretan homeland but the Minoans' trade routes too.

The Mycenaean culture is named after the main city of the peoples who inhabited the Aegean and its islands, and who from around 1650 BC became a dominant force in the area. The ancient city of Mycenae lies between Argos and Corinth in the north-east of the Peloponnese. Though not usually classed as one of the Bronze Age empires, the Mycenaeans nevertheless played an important, if relatively short-lived, role in the development of civilization in the Mediterranean. These people were among several groups of immigrants who came from the north and north-east and who spoke what are called Indo-European languages. This particular group, who spoke an early version of Greek, are known as Achaeans – the northern part of the Peloponnesus was later known as Achaea after them – though more often referred to as Mycenaeans.

The Mycenaeans travelled widely in the Mediterranean, inheriting and extending the old Minoan trade routes. They reached Italy, Sicily and Sardinia, and began to establish permanent colonies in the western Mediterranean, trading in luxury goods and metals, and also exporting their metal-making skills. These westward journeys were important, cross-fertilizing the eastern and western halves of the sea, which up to now had been largely separate. They also set a

BELOW: One of the most powerful stories from the siege of Troy was the killing of the Trojan hero Hector by the Greek warrior Achilles, who then dragged his dead foe's body around the walls of the city. Though this particular story could well be a literary invention, scholars believe that Troy really existed and probably was besieged by Mycenaeans, or early Greeks. From the town Virunum, capital of the Roman province Noricum. Kaernten, Austria.

precedent of trade and settlement in those areas that would be remembered and developed later during the rise of classical Greece.

For the most part, however, the Mycenaeans still looked to the east, and it was here that they entered into a long-running conflict that was to spark the most famous siege in ancient history – the siege of Troy.

The mystery of Troy

The *Iliad*, the epic poem attributed to the Greek poet Homer of the 8th century BC, tells the story of how a Greek fleet headed by the most powerful of the Mycenaeans, Agamemnon, King of Mycenae, was launched to rescue Helen from her Trojan abductors. However, it is not the only source of this tale; indeed, the *Iliad* describes only a small part of the long siege, focusing on how the great Greek hero Achilles, angered by Agamemnon's assertion of kingly rights over him, briefly turns his back on his fellow Greek warriors before returning to the fray to kill the Trojan hero Hector. For the rest of the story of Troy we rely on other Greek tales, including Homer's *Odyssey*. All these narratives drew on oral Greek tradition that went back well before the 8th century and may indeed stretch back to the times of the Mycenae.

Although in western Europe this epic tale was usually regarded as 'just' a story, it was considered a factual record by the ancient Greeks for many centuries. For them, Troy was as real a place as Mycenae or Knossos. This is now the view of many modern experts, too. Though most of the details of the Trojan War can never be verified and may well be simple storytelling, there is little doubt that a place called Troy did exist and that it was destroyed, and it is highly likely that the people responsible for its downfall were the Mycenaeans.

The city is thought to be at a place known as Hisarlik, a strategically important stronghold lying on the mouth of the Dardanelles in the north-west of what is today Turkey. Around it would have been valuable farming land, while the city itself controlled the route into the Sea of Marmara and was an important and ancient staging-post on the route of the traders in tin – the vital and scarce metal that, combined with copper, makes the strong alloy bronze.

The date for the war with the Mycenaeans is generally said to be around 1250 or 1270 BC, at a time when the Mycenaean society was probably at the peak of its powers. By this point the Mycenaeans had been active in the west of Asia Minor – west Anatolia – for many years, trading and also plundering the lands. It was here, on what we would now call the coastal frontier between modern Greece and Turkey, that the powerful Mycenaeans came into conflict with another power, mightier than them – the Hittites.

The forgotten Hittites

The Hittites have not had a particularly bad press in the annals of history; their main problem is that for many hundreds of years they had no press at all. Until the 19th century, when the discovery of various documents and archaeological digs in Turkey suddenly began to excite interest, the Hittites had effectively been lost to history. The ancient Greeks never referred to them, and though the Hittites are mentioned in the Old Testament there is little to dispel the impression that they were just another tribe in the region. In the book of Chronicles, Solomon, king of the Israelites, is mentioned as sending valuable Egyptian horses to 'all the kings of the Hittites' (2 Chronicles 17). Perhaps with hindsight, we can see this as a sign that the Israelite leader had to keep on good terms with the powerful Hittites.

In the late 19th and early 20th centuries, it became clear that the Hittites once controlled a powerful empire based on the lands of Anatolia, spreading west to the

ABOVE: The Iliad *tells that the Trojan War erupted after the beautiful Helen left her husband Menelaus, the king of Sparta, and eloped with Paris, a prince of Troy. The Greeks laid siege to Troy for ten years without success. Then the siege was lifted and the Greeks apparently sailed away, but a large 'horse' fashioned from wood was left outside the gates of Troy. The 'horse' was, in fact, hollow and contained a band of armed Greeks. The Trojans opened their gates and drew the wooden horse inside. That night the concealed Greeks emerged from the Trojan Horse to open the city gates, thereby facilitating the sacking of Troy by the returning Greek army.*

Aegean and east as far as the Euphrates. The Hittites came, as the Mycenaeans had done, from the north and north-east, settling in Anatolia from about 2000 BC. By around 1650 BC, their empire was growing in size and stature.

In many ways the Hittite Empire was well placed. It was ideally positioned for trade, with excellent communications to both the Mediterranean and the Black Sea, and some of the land was fertile and productive – though drought seems to have been a problem. Yet there were disadvantages, too; its location meant that it was surrounded by potential enemies. To the east were Babylon and the Assyrians, and to the south there was always the risk of confrontation with Egypt, which saw the area of the Levant up through to Syria as part of its sphere of influence. For a while, too, there was the threat from the Mitanni empire of Mesopotamia, which the Hittites eventually defeated.

Thus the Hittites seem to have been in a near-permanent state of war with one or other of their neighbours. Yet the Hittites were far more than a war machine, and in fact the discovery of many of their court documents – their diplomatic files – reveals them to have been skilled in negotiation, often seeking ways to avoid conflict. Doubtless this diplomacy was primarily designed to avoid fighting on too many fronts at once.

Nevertheless, the sending of emissaries or diplomats between various kingdoms seems to have been quite a routine activity at this time, with the aims of extending trade and establishing colonies as well as maintaining peace. In about 1380 BC, for example, the Egyptians sent a delegation to travel around the Aegean and to visit the Mycenaean capital at Mycenae, a mission that doubtless helped to cement trade links between the two peoples. And a Hittite document from about the same time quotes the powerful king Suppiluliumas (1368–1328 BC) as saying: 'Of old, Hatti [the name the Hittites used to refer to their land] and Egypt were friendly with each other... Thus let Hatti and Egypt be friendly with each other continuously.' Politics in the Bronze Age Mediterranean was not always just about war.

It was Suppiluliumas who is credited with reinvigorating the Hittite Empire and who boosted the prestige of its capital at Hattusa in central Turkey, a remote site now called Bogazköy. The remains of this once sizeable capital were discovered fortuitously in July 1834 by a Frenchman, Charles Texier, an event that restored the Hittites to history.

Despite Suppiluliumas' successes in war and the empire's ceaseless diplomacy, the Hittites soon had another problem on their doorstep, this time to the west – the Mycenaeans. The Hittites controlled the western flanks of their empire, western Anatolia, by dominating smaller self-contained lands or mini-kingdoms, which owed their allegiance to the Hittite king even if they were not directly ruled by him. Into this mix came the Mycenaeans from across the Aegean. Not only did they trade with these vassal Hittite states and fight with them or take their peoples as slaves, they also set up a colony of their own at Miletus, on the river Meander in south-west Turkey. The Hittites seem generally to have accepted this as a Mycenaean outpost, but this did not stop them attacking it at least twice, once in the 14th century BC and again around 1250 BC. Thus there are clear signs of tension and conflict between the mighty Hittite Empire and the upstart Mycenaeans both before and roughly at the same time as the presumed date of the Trojan War.

BELOW: The exact reasons why the once-mighty Hittite Empire collapsed so swiftly at the end of the 13th century BC are still unknown, though it may have been connected to the arrival of the mysterious sea peoples in the eastern Mediterranean. This funeral stele depicts a Hittite merchant with a pair of scales, possibly from Marash (Syria). Paris, Musée du Louvre.

The story of Troy suggests that the Mycenaeans were close to the peak of their powers in the middle of the 13th century BC. Yet soon they and the Hittite Empire, and indeed many of the societies of the eastern Mediterranean, were to disappear as a new and turbulent era in history was to begin. For after the glory of the Bronze Age and its empires came the mysterious and controversial era we call the Dark Ages.

The sea peoples

The Dark Ages of the eastern Mediterranean are generally dated from the start of the 12th century BC until around 900 BC or a little later, when a new Greek civilization began to emerge. This is traditionally seen as a time of a great movement of peoples, social dislocation and the quest for new lands and identities, as one might expect in a period between the collapse of empires and the establishment of new societies.

Clearly, when talking about any period described as a 'dark age' we have to guard against assuming that somehow history 'stopped' or did not exist at such a time. People would still have traded, fought, built houses, farmed and formed settlements; the problem is simply that we know very little about what went on at this time, partly because the societies of which we have records – for example, the Mycenae and Hittites – simply ceased to exist. (Some experts now suggest there were no long 'Dark Ages' at all, and have controversially claimed that the traditional dating of this period is simply wrong by as much as 250 years, and that the Bronze Age and its societies ended around 950 BC rather than around 1200 BC.)

Exactly why the Mycenaean and Hittite societies collapsed as quickly as they did – in approximately 1230 and 1200 respectively – is uncertain. Towards the end of its existence, the Hittite Empire, divided by internal faction–fighting and threatened by the Assyrians, was hit by a shortage of food. The last Hittite king, Suppiluliumas II, wrote to the leader

ABOVE: For thousands of years the Hittites were virtually lost to history, though historians now recognize their importance. This is a 9th century BC Hittite bas-relief depicting three warriors marching. It was found at the Fortress of Zincirli. Istanbul, Archaeological Museum.

of Ugarit, an important trading city in what is now Syria, begging in desperation for a ship to transport grain, plus as many boats as possible to transport the king, his retinue and army from their base at Cilicia, on the south-east coast of Turkey. The letter stresses that the issue is a matter of 'life and death', and even now, so many centuries later, one can sense the urgency and near-panic of the plea. In the event the people of Ugarit, traditionally a vassal state of the Hittites, had no ships to spare; and soon, certainly by 1190, both Ugarit and the Hittite capital at Hattusa had been destroyed. Individual Hittite states survived for a while, but the empire itself was no more.

What had happened? Prolonged drought leading to famine, though potentially serious, would not have led to the kind of urgent alarm that such a letter conveys. There are clues to other possibilities. The Hittites and the people of Ugarit, as well as the pharaohs of Egypt, were involved in battles at this time with a group of people known collectively to us only as the 'sea peoples'. Who they were, exactly where they came from, what their purpose was and where they eventually went, we cannot be sure. Nor can we be certain to what extent they were a cause of the Bronze Age 'crisis' that led to the Dark Ages, and to what extent they were the product of that crisis.

Some experts believe that the peoples of the sea were invaders who provoked the collapse of the Mycenaean and Hittite societies. Others believe that they were a mixed group of peoples displaced – possibly by famine and drought – from the Aegean and western Anatolia and other areas, who moved southwards in search of better places to live. Here they came into conflict with existing societies. Thus the sea peoples may have included displaced Mycenaeans and Hittites as well as peoples from other cultures and areas.

Much of the evidence for the existence of the sea peoples comes from Egyptian records. Reliefs in the Medinet Habu temple of Thebes depict how, during the reign of Rameses III (1198–1166 BC), a powerful force involving many different peoples threatened Egypt. *The foreign countries made a conspiracy in their islands… No country could stand before their arms.'* This inscription is part of a tribute to Rameses III who, it relates, was able to defeat these threatening forces in battles on land and sea in about 1180 BC, so one has to allow for a certain element of propaganda on the part of the author. Yet it suggests that a disparate force of people was indeed roaming around the eastern Mediterranean at this time, and that it reached Egypt.

One group of people mentioned in the Egyptian inscription were the Peleset, who later invaded the coast

BELOW: Though the Phoenicians had an enormous impact on the region's history we still know relatively little about them. Ironically, though they gave the Greeks their alphabet, very little Phoenician writing has survived. An inscription is shown here in a memorial stone (cippus) dating from the 2nd century BC, which was found in Gozo (north west of Malta).

of the Levant, where they become known to us through the Bible as the Philistines. The Philistines often fought with the Israelites – hence their bad press in the Old Testament. It is likely that they were of Mycenaean/Greek origin, and came out of the collapse of the Mycenaean society.

Historians now believe that, far from being simply nihilistic invaders engaged in war and disrupting the region, the sea peoples helped to bring about the formation of new societies and cultures. Certainly one great civilization was about to emerge out of the apparent turmoil – that of classical Greece.

Greeks and Phoenicians

So, who were the Greeks and where did they come from? As we have seen, their forebears, the Mycenae, were an Indo-European people who had, over time, moved down to the north of the Aegean from the Caucasus in a great movement of populations of which these early Greek-speakers were just a part. After the destruction of their culture some Mycenaeans stayed in the lands that would eventually become modern Greece, while others left.

During the next few centuries, up to around 900 or 800 BC, they were joined in these sparsely populated lands by other Greek-speaking peoples. Among these were the Dorians, tough farmers and warriors who came from the north and the west, through and from Macedon. In the past they have been 'blamed' for destroying Mycenaean society, though this seems unlikely as they arrived some 100 years or so after the main flight of the Mycenaeans. The Dorians spread right through western and central Greece, into the Peloponnese and eventually across to Crete and as far east as the island of Rhodes. The other two main Greek-speaking peoples in this period were the Ionians and the Aeolians. The Ionians spread from the area around Athens – in effect, they were keepers of the flame of Mycenaean culture – to the coast of Asia Minor around Miletus. The Aeolians moved down from Thessaly in central Greece across the Aegean to Asia Minor, around Smyrna, near the modern Turkish cities of Izmir and Abydos (near Çanakkale).

These processes of migration and the resulting blending between locals and newcomers, all Greek-speaking, continued over hundreds of years. Slowly, they led to the formation of the city-states that would ultimately make up the golden age of the Greeks, with their powerful combination of physical toughness, cultural sophistication, trading acumen and, ultimately, democracy.

At the same time as Greek civilization was evolving, however, another people was beginning to develop an advanced and adventurous farming, manufacturing and, above all, trading culture. The Phoenicians occupied a strip of coastal land that is now Lebanon and part of Syria. Their principal cities included Byblos, Tyre and Sidon, the last two very familiar to us from the Bible.

The Phoenicians are an intriguing phenomenon. They gave the Greeks, and thus modern western civilization, the alphabet, yet few of their own writings have survived. So the relatively little that we know about them comes from the Greeks, the Bible, and the evidence of their trading and settlement around the Mediterranean.

Though we know them as Phoenicians, it was the Greeks who gave them that name; the lands they lived in were called Canaan, which is why they are referred to as

ABOVE: The Phoenicians were great traders who bought and sold goods all over the Mediterranean and even beyond, possibly as far as Cornwall. In their trading empire they often used silver coins, such as this Phoenician silver coin with the depiction of a Phoenician ship and a hippocamp. Beirut, National Archeological Museum.

ABOVE: *Statue of the ancient Phoenician goddess, Baalat, the mistress of the city, the 'Lady of Byblos'. Musée du Louvre.*

Canaanites in the Bible. There are various theories about the Phoenicians' origins, but the likelihood is that they were a mixture of indigenous, Semitic and northern immigrants who, from around 3000 BC, began to use a common language and worship similar gods. Some of those immigrants could have been the sea peoples referred to by the Egyptians, an idea supported by the coincidence of their advent with the usual dating of the rise of Phoenician society in about 1200 BC. However, at the start of the 21st century scientists carried out DNA testing of peoples around the Mediterranean in areas where the Phoenicians were known to have settled. The results suggest that there is no significant genetic difference between the Canaanites, Phoenicians and the modern-day Lebanese and that they were in turn very similar genetically to their neighbours in the Levant. This would indicate that the impact of the newcomers to Canaan/Phoenicia was more cultural than racial.

Phoenicia was not a centrally controlled, unified state but rather a collection of smaller, flourishing cities and communities ruled by their own kings, linked by shared beliefs and language but remaining independent from one another. In this respect the Phoenicians were symbolic of the huge changes that were occurring in Mediterranean society at the time. Some of the old centralized monarchies – the so-called palace economies of the Hittites and Minoans, for example – had gone, to be replaced by more fluid and dynamic ways of doing business. The Phoenicians were trail-blazers for a revolution in trade and settlement patterns, their merchants on the ground responding to need and opportunity rather than to the demands and dictates of remote courts.

Though we know relatively little about them, there is no doubt of the Phoenicians' importance to the history of the Mediterranean and the development of European civilization. They traded and settled far and wide via the sea, reaching Sicily, Spain, Sardinia and North Africa. They brought luxury goods from the east and took back raw materials from the west, possibly even reaching Cornwall to buy tin. This process of trade, following and expanding the old commercial routes of the Mycenae, slowly helped to re-establish communications between the east and the west of the Mediterranean, gradually beginning a permanent relationship between the two 'halves' of the sea that would wax and wane over the millennia.

We must not assume that the story at this time was simply one of the advanced peoples of the eastern Mediterranean lording it over more primitive peoples in the west and south. Though comparatively little is known of the societies existing in Spain and southern France at this time, around 1000 BC there was a flourishing trading society known as the Tartessians in southern Spain. We also know that a relatively advanced culture existed on the west Mediterranean island of Sardinia from around 1500 BC. These people made sophisticated pottery and bronze figures, were relatively wealthy and built at least 7,000 stone towers called *nuraghi*. These curious towers were often joined together by walls to form defensive areas where people could take shelter. Who these people were we do not know, though their towers may have been built to protect themselves in later years from the Phoenicians. The *nuraghi* culture remains one of the Mediterranean's enduring mysteries.

Aside from opening up lines of communication, the Phoenicians played another crucial part in history. From the 9th century BC onwards, they found themselves and their cities under growing threat from other cultures, notably the Assyrians from the east. Eventually, their centre of gravity moved west, and one of their early settlements in North Africa grew in size to become the centre of the Phoenician world. It was at this point that the Phoenicians become known as Carthaginians, the inhabitants of the great city of Carthage in what is today Tunisia. But Carthage's glory comes a little later; first we must return to the area that was beginning to develop one of the definitive cultures of Mediterranean history.

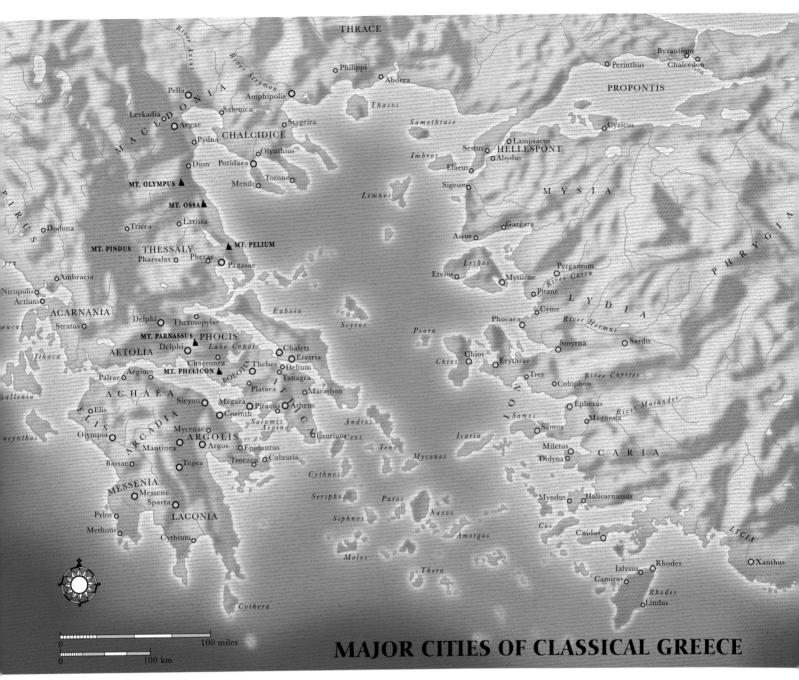

MAJOR CITIES OF CLASSICAL GREECE

Classical Greece and the Persian Empire

As in Phoenicia, a prominent feature of the rise of classical Greece was the development of relatively small city–states, which shared gods and a common tongue – albeit with different dialects – but which jealously guarded their own independence and individuality. This pride in identity was to be a source of strength in many ways, with cities seeking to outdo their neighbours in philosophy and argument, in the arts, and in athletics. The pan–Hellenic games were first held in 776 BC. Yet while this healthy competition was pursued in the knowledge that they were all Greeks, and that being Greek was something to be prized and appreciated, the constant sparring among the various Greek societies ultimately contributed to their political downfall.

Though ancient Greece is best known for its contributions to the arts, literature, history, science and philosophy, the Greeks were traders, farmers and settlers, too – and, of course, warriors. So it was that an important part of the Greek story took place along the south–west coastline of Asia Minor – Ionic and Doric Greece – and further to the

ABOVE: Though Athens and Sparta dominate our view of classical Greece, the Greek world was in fact made up of many different cities and states, which while bound by a common identity, also had many differences in culture and outlook. For example, many of the great Greek cities, such as Miletus, the home of influential philosophers, were on the mainland of what is now Turkey.

ABOVE: The Spartans were a warlike people who became great rivals of the Athenians for effective leadership of the Greek peoples. This 5th-century BC, marble head and torso of a Spartan soldier, thought to be king Leonidas was found in the sanctuary of Athena Chalkioikos in Sparta. Sparta, Museum of Classical Antiquity.

north in Aeolian Greece. Greek merchants and settlers also ventured further east, into the Black Sea, and set up important colonies along its shores. Later, these colonies would oversee the importation of vast amounts of grain from the fertile lands to the north to feed the growing populations of Greece. Further south, the Greeks traded in Egypt and North Africa and also travelled westwards, settling there to such an extent that in later centuries parts of Italy and Sicily would be called (in Latin) Magna Graecia – 'Great Greece'. The Greeks also established an important settlement near the mouth of the mighty Rhône river in France at a place called Massilia; we know it as Marseille.

In the western Mediterranean the Greeks competed and sometimes fought with the Phoenicians and Etruscans (of whom more later in this chapter), all the time spreading their influence and culture throughout the region. The extent and longevity of this trading and political empire helped the later transmission of Greece's cultural values to the rest of the world – above all via the Romans.

Central to the Greek civic system was the *polis* or city–state. This was a defined, self-governing geographical area, with a strong urban centre, which lent its citizens a sense of identity and to which they gave their allegiance. The best-known city–state of classical Greece is Athens, but that was not the first Greek entity to come to prominence. The people of the large island of Euboea were among the first to start trading and voyaging. The discovery of a previously forgotten Euboean city called Lefkandi, where gold and luxury items from the Levant were found, shows that this area was prosperous as early as the 12th century BC. As well as showing that Euboea was among the first Greek areas in the new era to trade both locally and further away, the prosperity of Lefkandi during the 'Dark Ages' is a further reminder of the continuity of life and society during that period.

Corinth, too, quickly became a major force, and by 733 BC its citizens had founded the strategically important city of Syracuse in Sicily, destined to become one of the more important regional cities in the Greek world.

By the middle of the 1st millennium BC two major powers were starting to emerge in Greece – Sparta and Athens. Between them they would epitomize much of what was good and bad about the Greek world and shape the destiny of the Greek states for centuries to come. From the start there were important differences between the two. Athens and its surrounding lands – Attica – were generally more sophisticated and cultured than Sparta, which was situated on the Peloponnesus, south-west of Athens, and which retained many of the simple traditional Doric values, including martial discipline. Athens, as we shall see, became the true home of democracy, while Sparta was a far more closed, authoritarian and, above all, militaristic society in which discipline and the need to serve the greater good of the state at the expense of individual freedom of expression were dominant themes. (Spartan military prowess and austerity were both notorious in the Greek world; there is a story that a visitor from the wealthy Greek city of Sybaris in Sicily once tasted the plain broth that was a staple food in Sparta and declared that only then did he understand why Spartans did not fear death.)

The Persian Threat

From the mid-5th century BC onwards, the rivalry between these two powerhouses of ancient Greece would prove disastrous both for them and for other Greek communities. But first they had to unite – or at least co-operate – against a common enemy, one that threatened the destruction of Greek society.

The Persian Empire at the start of the 5th century BC was immensely powerful. Its rise had begun under Cyrus the Great, its leader from 559 BC, who united the peoples of Persia. He began a series of conquests that would ultimately encompass Babylon, Egypt, other parts of North Africa, Macedon and Anatolia.

It was in Asia Minor that the Persians came into contact and eventual conflict with the Greeks who inhabited its Aegean shores. Here the cities of the Ionian, Aeolian and Dorian Greeks were effectively forced under the subjugation of the Persian dynasty, a situation most of them found repellent and against which they rebelled. Athens decided to help its fellow Greek-speakers in this struggle, though the Spartans opted to stay out of the fight. Meanwhile, the new Persian leader Darius saw that Greece could be a constant irritant and resolved to conquer the area, starting with the part that had impertinently taken up arms against his empire – Athens.

It was generally thought at this time that the huge and well-armed Persian army was just about invincible. Moreover, Greece's own crack troops, the much-vaunted Spartans, were not in this fight. Instead, it fell to the soldiers of Athens and a force from the small city of Plataea to defend the Greeks against the invading Persians in 490 BC, the empire having already crushed Ionian resistance by this time.

The Greeks fielded a mere 10,000 men at the Battle of Marathon, against a vastly larger Persian army. Yet, somehow, the Athenian forces won a dramatic victory, saving the

BELOW: The threat of the Persian Empire for a long time cast a shadow over Greek politics. However, in the Battle of Marathon (490 BC) the Athenians under Miltiades defeated the much larger Persian army under Darius and Ataphernes. Colour print, 1925, after a drawing by Karl Bauer (1868-1942).

city from Persian attack – for the time being at least. They were probably helped by the fact that their general, Miltiades, had previously fought alongside the Persians in their battles against the Scythians who lived to the north of the Black Sea. The battle also spawned the famous story of the messenger Pheidippides, who was despatched to run the 26 miles from Marathon to Athens to inform the city of their salvation. According to the story, he delivered the news and then dropped dead.

The Greek historian Herodotus informs us that the Persians lost more than 6,000 men at Marathon, while the Greek forces lost fewer than 200. These figures seem rather extreme, but do suggest a stunning victory. Nevertheless, the importance of this famous battle can be overstated, for the Greeks would have to fight the eastern empire again before the enemy was finally defeated, and Athens would be briefly overrun by the Persians. Yet it is

also true that had Darius been able to extend his empire over large parts of Greece at this time the story of Mediterranean culture and history could have been very different.

If the Athenians had had their day against the Persians, then a few years later the Spartans would have their chance to make their mark in one of the most remarkable rearguard actions in military history.

The Persian king Darius was determined to take revenge for his force's defeat, but died before he could do so, leaving it to his son Xerxes to launch a yet more concerted attack on the Greeks. It came in 480 BC. This time the Greeks had more warning of the Persians assault, and were better prepared. Though differences among them still persisted – many Greek cities remained neutral, while others for a variety of reasons actually sided with the Persians – this time the Spartans were put at the head of a pan-Hellenic force that was boosted by the presence of thousands of well-armed Spartan troops and a size-able, mostly Athenian fleet.

Yet even this force was dwarfed by the massive number of troops and ships at the disposal of Xerxes, which included perhaps 200,000 men and 1,000 ships – many of them provided by their allies, the Phoenicians. Indeed, for such a powerful empire as Persia the defeat of a relatively small number of squabbling Greeks should have been little more than a formality.

The Persian king had decided to take his huge army across the Hellespont – the stretch of water dividing Europe from Asia, now called the Dardanelles – so that he could march on Greece from the north. He faced little opposition and was soon in a position to enter the heart of Greece, though he was obliged to do so via a narrow mountain pass at Thermopylae. What followed was one of the most heroic defeats in military history. As the Greek fleet held its own against the Persian and Phoenician ships, the new Spartan king Leonidas, with just 300 fellow Spartans, some soldiers from Thespiae and some very reluctant recruits from Thebes, rushed to defend the pass. For several days Xerxes kept his men in camp, perhaps assuming that the vastly outnumbered Greek contingent would retreat or flee. When Leonidas showed no sign of doing either, the Persians finally attacked. In the narrow pass the Greeks stood firm, resisting attack after attack as many of the Persians perished on the end of the long Greek spears. The Spartan king knew, however, that his force could not last for ever – a contingent of Persians had found a mountain track by which they could encircle the defenders – and sent many of his men away to spare their lives. After two days of fighting, Leonidas, his fellow Spartans and the equally brave Thespians were slaughtered where they stood; the reluctant Thebans surrendered and their lives were spared.

Though the eventual Greek defeat was total, this brave stand showed that even a relatively small number of Spartans and other Greek soldiers could prove hard to beat. Coupled with the inability of the Persian fleet to defeat its counterpart, this was a bad omen for Xerxes. The defensive battle also briefly delayed the march into the heartland of Greece, and became a symbol of heroic Greek resistance. The historian Herodotus, who wrote detailed accounts of the Persian wars, gives us a revealing glimpse into how the Spartans viewed the selfless bravery of their men, in the fate of one of the few Spartans who had escaped death, the messenger Pantites. 'He had been sent with a message into Thessaly and on his return to Sparta found himself in such disgrace that he hanged himself,' writes the historian.

Nonetheless, Xerxes continued his advance and sacked Athens, which by the time he arrived had been abandoned. The Greek defensive line had been pulled back to defend the isthmus protecting Peloponnesian Greece, while the fleet sailed off to the island of Salamis.

Once more the whole culture of Greece was under threat; and once more the Athenians stepped forward to protect it. Though they had lost their city, they still controlled the Greek fleet, which was under the astute leadership of Themistocles. Themistocles is an intriguing character, a man possessed of self-confidence bordering on arrogance, who a few years earlier had successfully argued that his native Athens should invest in a strong fleet – even if at the time he had in mind rivalry with other Greek states rather than the Persians. Now his foresight offered him an opportunity to secure a famous victory, and he did

BELOW: The battle of Thermopylae in 480 BC is famous as one of the most heroic defeats in military history. For two days a small group of Spartans and other Greek troops held off the massive army assembled by the Persian leader Xerxes. Coll. Archiv f.Kunst & Geschichte.

not waste the chance. Luring the hapless Persian fleet into the narrow waters of the Bay of Salamis, the Greeks won a crushing and wholly unexpected victory. Many of the ships of the proud Persian fleet were destroyed and sunk, their sailors drowned.

Xerxes withdrew, and though he left an army behind under the generalship of Mardonius, this force was beaten decisively at the Battle of Plataea the next year, 479 BC, thanks largely to the determination of Spartan troops.

At last the Persian threat had been removed from the heartland of Greece. But how had the Greeks prevailed against such overwhelming odds, particularly as by no means all Greeks had fought alongside the Athenians and Spartans?

Greek Identity

Part of the reason for the Greeks' success lies in their military weaponry and tactics. The Greek infantry, the *hoplite*, were generally well armed and well disciplined. They worked in rows or phalanxes, protected by their helmets and shields, and used long spears against the enemy. This cohesive fighting form was particularly good at turning a numerically small group of men into a formidable fighting machine; the whole really was greater than the sum of the parts. In his account of the Battle of Thermopylae, Herodotus describes how the technique and arms of the Spartans told against the Persian troops, with 'the two armies fighting in a confined space, the Persians using shorter spears than the Greeks and having no advantage

ABOVE: The Persian leader Xerxes looks on in despair as his huge fleet is defeated by the Greek commanders, effectively ending his dream of going one step further than his father Darius and conquering all of Greece. Coll. Archiv f.Kunst & Geschichte.

from their numbers. On the Spartan side it was a memorable fight, they were men who understood war, pitted against an inexperienced enemy.'

There were other factors, too. The Greeks were fighting on or near their home soil and for them the fight was a matter of survival, not just for the soldiers but for their women, children and homes. On the other hand, the Persians and their allies were far from home.

The Greeks also saw the fight in terms of a defence of civilization, as a contest between their own enlightened men, who freely chose to fight to defend their liberties and way of life, and the 'barbarians' of Persia, who fought out of fear and compulsion. The Persian wars, indeed, played an important part in the consolidation of a pan–Hellenic consciousness, a process in which being Greek was as much about who you were not – that is, not a Persian or a barbarian – as about who you were. This pride, arrogance even, in being Greek was reflected in later writings about the Persian wars – an early reminder that it tends to be the victors who write history.

For example, the Greek Herodotus often emphasized the cruelty of the Persians, even though his accounts are not always one–sided and also contain swipes at other peoples, too. One story involves a wealthy man by the name of Pythius from the legendarily rich land of Lydia in western Anatolia. Pythius entertains the king and his troops on the eve of their departure for Greece. At first we are shown Xerxes' generous nature. Pythius has offered to devote his large fortune to the Persian cause, and the king is so delighted at this show of support that he not only declines the offer but instead promises the old man some of his own fortune. Then, however, the king's mood takes a different turn when

Pythius – whose five sons are all in the Persian army – observes an eclipse and fears it is a bad omen for the fate of the invasion. Thinking that he is on such good terms with Xerxes that the king will grant him a favour, the Lydian asks that his eldest son be excused from military service 'to take care of me and my property'.

According to Herodotus, Xerxes flew into a terrible rage at the suggestion, which he considered 'impudent' – presumably he was most angry at the implication that the Persian invasion might not be a success. Furiously, Xerxes tells Pythius that the old man's life and those of his other four sons will be spared, but 'you shall pay with the life of your fifth, whom you cling to most'. The king then orders that the eldest son be seized and cut in half, and the two parts of his body placed either side of the road, so that the departing army would march between them. As Herodotus grimly notes, 'The order was performed'.

Elsewhere in his narrative, Herodotus relates Xerxes' extraordinary reaction when the first attempt at bridging the Hellespont was wrecked by a sudden storm. Not only did the king have the Phoenician and Egyptian engineers responsible for the bridge beheaded, he also ordered that men with whips give the very waters themselves 300 lashes. It is hardly a flattering portrait of a supposedly great warrior king.

However, despite their common language and culture, the Greeks never wholly united against the common foe. A number of Greek leaders sided with the 'barbarian' Persians over the years, usually as an extension of their internal Greek squabbles, and Greek mercenaries also fought alongside the Persians. Even the hero of Salamis, Themistocles, later found service with Xerxes' son Artaxerxes I after being forced out of Athenian politics, and worked for a number of years under Persian rule in Asia Minor until his death in around 460 BC. (One account suggests that he died after an illness, another that he took his own life rather than be part of a new invasion against his native Greece.)

Internal Greek Disputes

The differences between Sparta and Athens, barely eclipsed by the need to fight off invasion from Persia, lay behind much of the war and disharmony that were to engulf Greece in the century and a half that followed the Battle of Salamis. Ultimately, this conflict would lead to the weakening of both city–states, along with others such as Corinth. This left the Greek world vulnerable to subjugation from the north, and thus led to the end of 'classical' Greece and the start of the Hellenistic period.

The reasons for these conflicts, notably the First Peloponnesian War of 460–446 BC and the Second or Great Peloponnesian War of 431–404 BC, are various. The Spartan oligarchy (and those of other city–states) mistrusted and feared Athenian democracy, and envied Athens its status as the pre–eminent Greek state after the defeat of the Persians. For its part, Athens feared tyranny and oligarchy in other states and arrogated to itself the leadership of Greek civilization. There was conflict, too, over lands outside mainland Greece – for example, Corinth dominated Syracuse in Sicily – and over Athens' desire to use its naval power to control access to grain supplies through the Hellespont and the Black Sea. For, though it espoused democracy, Athens too had a short-lived empire.

The Greeks also squabbled over the northern area of

BELOW: Pericles (495–429 BC), a key figure in Athenian history, was a champion of democracy and believed that the city-state should have its own empire. He supported the arts and encouraged public buildings. In many ways, Pericles symbolizes the cultural greatness of Athens. Roman marble copy after an original by Kresilas, c.440 BC. Berlin, Pergamon-Museum.

Thessaly, which, besides possessing good agricultural land, sat across the main route to Macedon, Thrace and the Hellespont, as well as to other northern lands seen as sources of grain and timber.

On top of these ambitions, domestic affairs were complicated by age-old rivalries among all the various Greek states, as well as by the involvement of outside powers such as Persia – no longer a real threat to mainland Greece but still a power in Asia Minor and the object of various pragmatic alliances for Greek states. Throughout this period, various Greek city-states would come to dominate for periods: Athens and Sparta, of course, but also Thebes and even, briefly, Thessaly. None, however, could hold sway for long or even come close to unifying the Greeks under one power; and eventually, divided and weakened, the Greeks lost their political and military independence.

One of the key figures in the rise – and eventual decline – of Athenian power was Pericles (495–429 BC). A champion of democracy and yet a proponent of empire, Pericles pursued a determined campaign of public building in the city, supported the arts, befriended writers and philosophers, and led Athens to the height of its political and military power. He was a military leader and a democrat, and was liberal and cultured. As such, perhaps more than any other individual, Pericles embodies the greatness of classical Athens and so, by extension, classical Greece. But while his support for democracy, architecture and the arts may have had lasting effects, his city's rise to political power was short-lived. Removed from his position as *straegos* (military commander) soon after the start of the Great Peloponnesian War in 431 BC, Pericles was reinstated but died of the plague soon afterwards.

Perhaps fortunately, he did not live to see the continuation of a drawn-out conflict with Sparta that would reduce Athens to a depleted if not quite spent force by 404 BC.

One of the biggest blows to Athenian dominance came, ironically, well away from the mainland of Greece. In 415 BC, during a pause in the Great Peloponnesian War, the Athenians were persuaded to launch an attack on Syracuse, the powerful city in Sicily founded by Corinth, itself an ally of Sparta. The attack was doomed from the start. One of the young generals and instigators of the invasion, Alcibiades, was quickly recalled from the force to answer charges that during drunken revelries he had damaged and desecrated images of the god Hermes. Instead, the former pupil of Socrates defected to the Spartans. His inside knowledge and advice ultimately helped Spartan-backed Syracuse to a crushing victory in which the entire Athenian expeditionary force was killed or enslaved, while the image of Athenian naval supremacy was swept away. (Alcibiades did return to the Athenian cause against Sparta during the ensuing war, but was never fully trusted and ended his life in exile in Asia Minor.)

Sparta's victory over Athens in 404 BC – achieved with the help of Persian finance – heralded a brief era of Spartan dominance in Greece. But this lasted no more than three decades, and was followed by an even shorter period during which Thebes gained ascendancy. A few voices among the Greeks warned that while they fought endlessly they were simply making each other weaker and more vulnerable to takeover by an outside force – which is exactly what happened in the 4th century BC.

The Democratic Legacy

Though Athens' empire was short-lived, its rise to prominence coincided with one of the most important developments in the ancient world – Athenian democracy.

A key figure in the emergence of democracy was the celebrated law-maker Solon (c. 638–559 BC), who was the city's chief magistrate in 594 BC. Among his achievements, Solon revised and codified laws which extended rights to many, though by no means all, Athenians, and, crucially, gave new power and force to the existing but under-used citizens' assembly. In particular, he abolished the rule by which debts were secured on the individual who borrowed money, so that a man who failed to repay and became a debtor could become enslaved. This iniquitous custom had fallen especially heavily on farmers, who were obliged to pay wealthy landowners a percentage of their crop – a practice called share-cropping – in return for the right to work their land.

Solon did not invent democracy or the rule of law; both evolved through gradual processes involving a balance of competing powers, self-interest and populism, plus a degree of idealism and altruism. This was, nevertheless, a society in which the ruling classes, who included theorists and philosophers, thought carefully about the nature of government and how to accommodate the competing rights of members of its society (even if this consideration did not extend to women, foreigners or slaves).

Nor was the process irreversible. Even after Solon, tyranny reappeared under the ruler Pisistratus. In fact, though Pisistratus (c. 600–527 BC) was a tyrant, he ruled the

ABOVE: This idealized image shows Solon (c. 638–559 BC), the great law maker of Athenian history. While chief magistrate of the city in 594 BC, he both codified and revised its laws and helped pave the way for democracy. Painting, 1699, by Noël Coypel (1628–1707). Paris, Musée du Louvre.

growing city–state with a degree of enlightenment, reducing some of the burdens on the poor, for the most part respecting the laws and rebuilding the city. He also encouraged a sense of pride and identity among the people of Athens and Attica, feelings which in later years would attach also to the city's laws and democratic traditions. So, although Pisistratus was a tyrant in the early Greek sense of having gained absolute power, his rule was not 'tyrannical' in the modern sense of being irrational, dictatorial and malevolent.

The process of involving more and more citizens in government continued again under Cleisthenes (570–c. 508 BC), who is often described as the founder of Athenian democracy. Against a backdrop of Spartan meddling, continuing and progressively worse tyranny, and a people's revolt, the nobly born Cleisthenes established a political structure that for the first time paid real attention to the rights of ordinary male citizens (again excluding women and slaves) rather than just the aristocratic and wealthy. Though men such as Pericles and Ephialtes would extend the system further, giving more power to the citizens' assembly, the balancing act created by Cleisthenes between the competing sections of society was to endure as long as Athenian democracy lasted.

At the heart of the developed system – at least in theory – was the popular assembly of all the adult males eligible to take part and vote: the *ekklesia*. There was also a smaller body, called the *boule*, made up of 500 people, whose job was to discuss topics of interest and choose what was to be discussed at the main assemblies. In theory it was the servant of the *ekklesia*, though in practice a great deal of real day–to–day power resided in it.

For all its shortcomings, Athenian democracy was a bold and radical form of government of which the citizens became extremely proud and which for the most part they

guarded with great care. This system of government was both influenced by and influenced many of the great Greek thinkers, and fostered an intellectually and culturally stimulating environment. Moreover, when, in centuries to come, people in western societies were looking for systems of government other than monarchy or dictatorship, they had to look no further than Athens for inspiration.

Even at the peak of its power, however, Athens had been unable to extend its control over the whole of Greece, and certainly not to neighbouring lands. This meant that Greek influence, though growing through trade and settlements, only indirectly affected much of the eastern Mediterranean. This was soon to change, though, with the arrival on the scene of a new and powerful state.

ABOVE: One of the many legacies of Alexander the Great was the founding of the great city of Alexandria which took his name, and whose theatre is shown here. The now-Egyptian city became one of the most important centres of learning and culture in the ancient world.

Philip and Alexander

While the name and achievements of Alexander the Great (356–323 BC) rightly dominate the period of Mediterranean history from the 4th century BC to the rise of Rome, his father, too, was a remarkable man. Philip II of Macedon (382–336 BC) was a great general and military technician as well as a skilled diplomat, who understood how to make strategic alliances through both political agreements and marriage.

At the start of Philip's rule, Macedon was in some disarray. The kingdom was under threat of attack from the north-west, and while its people were Greek-speaking (they spoke the Doric dialect) the Macedonians were looked down on by other Greeks. Indeed, many regarded the people of this tough, rather uncouth northern land as barbarians rather than Greeks. Under Philip, however, Macedon began to flex its

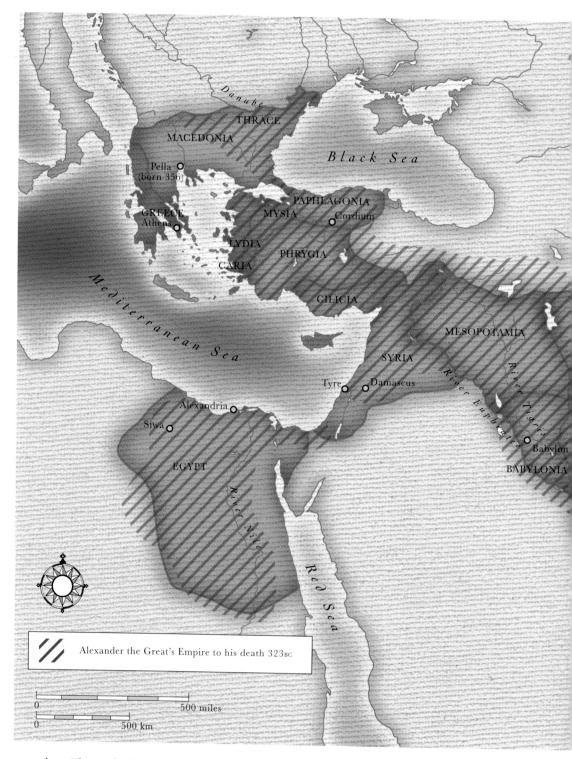

THRACE

MACEDONIA

Pella
(born 356)

Black Sea

PAPHLAGONIA

GREECE
Athens

MYSIA

Gordium

LYDIA

PHRYGIA

CARIA

Mediterranean Sea

CILICIA

MESOPOTAMIA

SYRIA

Tyre Damascus

River Euphrates

River Tigris

Alexandria

Babylon

Siwa

BABYLONIA

EGYPT

River Nile

Red Sea

▨ Alexander the Great's Empire to his death 323BC

0 _____ 500 miles

0 _____ 500 km

muscles. Through his expert tutelage, the army became a well-drilled force that employed a devastatingly effective tight formation from which the soldiers' long spears stuck out menacingly in all directions – rather like the spines of a hedgehog. Soon he had acquired the Athenian colony of Amphipolis in Thrace, which was not just an important trading city but also, because of its proximity to gold mines, a source of significant gold reserves; the king used this wealth to fund his expansionist policy.

Some Greeks were already beginning to warn that Philip and Macedon posed a threat to their independence every bit as great as that of the Persians in previous years. In a famous attack on Philip, the Athenian orator Demosthenes declared that 'he is not only no Greek, nor related to the Greeks, but not even a barbarian from any place that can be

THE EMPIRE OF ALEXANDER THE GREAT

Aral Sea

Caspian Sea

River Oxus

○ Samarkand

BACTRIA

PARTHIA

MEDIA

ARIA

○ Kabul

DRANGIANA

ARACHOSIA

SUSIANA

CARMANIA

Indus River

PERSIS

Persian Gulf

GEDROSIA

MUSICANI

Arabian Sea

LEFT: Though the Macedonian Alexander the Great started his conquests in the eastern Mediterranean his influence and power spread far beyond the sea, to modern day India and Afghanistan. However, his short-lived empire quickly broke up after his death.

named with honour, but a pestilent knave from Macedonia, whence it was never yet possible to buy a decent slave.'

After listing a series of incidents to demonstrate Philip's 'insolence' and menace, Demosthenes goes on to castigate his people for failing to stop the advance of the Macedonian. 'Yet the Greeks see all this and suffer it. They seem to watch him just as they would watch a hailstorm, each praying that it may not come their way, but none making any effort to stay its course.'

The Greek resistance, when it came, was too little. After crushing combined Greek forces at the Battle of Chaeronea in 338 BC, this 'barbarian' was effectively master of the Greeks.

The great irony of the Greek dislike of Philip, which in any case was not universal, was that through his efforts and those of his son Alexander one of the great ambitions of Greek

ABOVE: Alexander the Great and two griffins. Section from a floor mosaic, 1163-66, from the Mosaizisten Pantaleon. Otranto (Puglia, Italy), S. Maria Annunziata cathedral.

foreign policy was achieved – the destruction of the Persian Empire. It had been Philip's own intention to attack the Persians, but before he could act he was murdered in 336 BC. It is sometimes suggested that Alexander connived in the killing, yet, though father and son were not close – the youth sided with his mother Olympia after Philip married again – there is no hard evidence for this.

Alexander was more than just a great soldier and leader of men, though he was certainly both of these. As a youth he was taught by the great Aristotle, no bad tutor for a man who would rule half the known world, and he was undoubtedly intelligent as well as brave.

However, it is for his military exploits that Alexander is chiefly remembered. They followed rapidly from his accession to the Macedonian throne. To the delight of most Greeks – Alexander's hero was Achilles, and he saw himself as very much part of the Greek world – he soon turned his attention to the Persian Empire. First in 333 BC at Issus, then two years later at Gaugamela, Alexander defeated the troops of Darius III; the Persian king was later murdered, bringing the empire that had dominated the region for so long to an end. In between, the Macedonian conquered the main cities of Phoenicia and absorbed Egypt into his empire. But this was just the start. Over the course of the next ten years Alexander took his men across what is now Iran into Afghanistan (Bactria) and across the Indus into India. Only the weariness and homesickness of his men stopped him from going further still. His return journey was difficult, however, and Alexander himself only got as far as Babylon, where he died in June 323 BC.

Alexander's achievements were astonishing, especially for the king of a relatively small nation with a modestly sized, if well-armed and well-motivated, army. Along his route he founded great cities, the greatest of which became Alexandria in Egypt. More surprisingly, given the prevalent view of Alexander as a strong, uncompromising military leader, he helped establish democracies in those Greek cities in Asia Minor that he had freed from the Persians.

Yet perhaps his greatest achievements came after his death. Through his conquests Alexander spread Greekness – Hellenism – across vast areas. The Greek language and culture were able to spread far further than they had done during the classical period. Though Alexander had no heir, and his vast empire was quickly split up, the kingdoms that emerged were Macedonian/Greek kingdoms. One of the most important of these was the new dynasty in Egypt, launched under one of his generals, Ptolemy, which would last until the death of its last monarch, Cleopatra, in 30 BC. The crowning achievement of this kingdom was the development of Alexandria, which, with its fabulous library, became the vital centre of Greek thought. Another vast empire, which inherited much of the Persian Empire's lands, was the so-called Seleucid kingdom, named after and first ruled by Alexander's friend Seleucus. Among its achievements was the founding of the great city of Antioch in Syria.

Alexander's conquests thus helped ensure that Greek culture, language and ideals would flourish far beyond the borders of mainland Greece and that they would in turn be passed on to later generations, right down to our own time. One of the chief recipients of this cultural baton was another Mediterranean civilization that would absorb much of Greek culture, add its own touches, and ensure that both influences were spread across an even wider stage.

The rise of the Romans

Romans and Etruscans

The Romans always had a great reverence for tradition, and no matter what new direction the Roman state and later empire would take, it was usually justified and explained in terms of the past. Just as with the Greeks, the Romans' tales of heroism from the past were more than mere stories: they contained messages and lessons for later generations.

The traditional story of the founding of Rome emphasized a certain wildness and brutality which perhaps reflected how many Romans saw the world. Romulus and Remus were the abandoned sons of Mars, the god of war. They were suckled and raised by a wolf and later cared for by a shepherd. The brothers decided to build a settlement but quarrelled, and Romulus killed his brother. He became king of this new town, which he named Rome after himself and populated with runaways, the homeless and vagabonds. Romulus also abducted women from the Sabine people to breed future generations.

Although the story of Romulus and Remus is arguably the more well-known version of the founding of Rome, in the days of the Roman Empire the story of Aeneas was the more popular founding tale. According to the *Aeneid*, by the Roman poet Virgil, Aeneas, son of the goddess Venus, was a hero who fought the Greeks at the siege of Troy. After escaping the burning city and enduring a long and testing journey, Aeneas and his men fulfilled their destiny and the destiny of the future empire, when they landed in Latium and founded Roman culture, if not Rome itself. This legend's popularity in Roman times was due to the historical legitimacy it gave to the new empire; Aeneas was a hero who exemplified the Roman virtues of a strong sense of duty and reverence to the gods. It is no coincidence that Virgil's epic poem relating the tale was closely modelled on those great legends of Greek heroism and history, the *Iliad* and the *Odyssey*.

Another early story is that of the Roman hero Horatius who single-handedly fought off an Etruscan army as it sought to enter Rome across an old wooden bridge. He faced the Etruscan army alone, taunting them and astonishing them with his bravery until he was finally forced to leap into the Tiber in full armour when the bridge gave way. The city had been saved. (Accounts vary as to whether he survived or not.) As with the story of Aeneas, this story summed up to many later citizens what it meant to be Roman: to show outstanding physical courage, military acumen and, perhaps above all, readiness to sacrifice oneself for the greater good of Rome. It also raises an important theme of early Roman history – the story of their struggle with the Etruscans.

BELOW: A double portrait (marble relief) showing Romulus and Remus. The traditional myth of how Rome was founded involves the two abandoned brothers, who were famously kept alive by a she-wolf. Romulus eventually became king of the settlement they both founded.

KING PYRRHUS (318–272 BC)

King Pyrrhus of Epirus in north-west Greece was urged by the citizens of Tarentum, a Greek city in Italy, to destroy the growing power of the Romans. Sensing a chance to build an empire, Pyrrhus invaded Italy in 280 BC. A brilliant general, Pyrrhus twice defeated the Romans, first near Heracleia and again, in 279, at Asculum. However, on each occasion he suffered heavy losses, while the Romans were bowed but unbroken by their setbacks. It was after this second battle that Pyrrhus reportedly said: 'One more victory against the Romans and we will be ruined'. Since then, a victory that comes at such great cost that it is not worth winning has been described as a 'Pyrrhic victory'. After trying his luck in Sicily, Pyrrhus returned to Italy and was this time beaten by the Romans at Beneventum, an outcome that demonstrated their power to a nervous Greek world. Pyrrhus returned to Greece, where he was eventually killed in fighting in Argos. The Carthaginian general Hannibal was said to have been a great admirer of Pyrrhus, who also used elephants to fight against Roman troops.

Early Rome grew out of a collection of villages that established themselves at a strategic crossing-place over the Tiber in central Italy. The Romans themselves dated this settlement back to the 8th century BC. The early inhabitants were Latin peoples from the region (Latium), while the dominant culture in Italy at the time was the Etruscan. Rather like the Hittites, the Etruscans were for a long time reduced to the margins of history, even though part of their old homeland – Tuscany – is now a popular tourist destination.

No one is sure where the Etruscans came from, or indeed whether they were the original inhabitants of that part of Italy. They spoke a non-Indo-European language, and were deeply religious and artistic. The Greeks – from whom the Etruscans learnt a great deal, including writing – called them Tyrrhenians (hence the Tyrrhenian Sea). In fact, there seem to have been two groups of Tyrrenhians/Etruscans, one in Italy and the other in the Aegean, the latter soon disappearing from history. This idea fits – rather too neatly, perhaps – with the Greek tradition that the Tyrrhenians came from Lydia (western Turkey), and that after a severe drought half the population went off in search of a new life in Italy. Perhaps the truth is that the Etruscans in Italy were an indigenous people strongly influenced by a later influx, conceivably from western Turkey. In any event, by the 8th century BC Etruscan society had developed a strong identity, and was certainly influenced by the Greek colonies that were being established in Italy and Sicily at this time. In turn, the Romans borrowed a great deal from the unsung Etruscans.

According to Roman tradition, the last kings of the city before the monarchy was thrown off and the Republic was established were all Etruscan, the last of them being Tarquinius Superbus (ruled 534–509 BC). Even after these dates – which are uncertain – the emergence of Rome as an imperial centre was a gradual process as it slowly gained control over its neighbours. Nor was it a story of unending success. In around 390 BC, Rome was sacked by Gauls from the north, a foretaste of what would happen to the Roman Empire many centuries later. There is a story that the inhabitants, who took refuge in the Capitol (Rome's central meeting place and centre of power), were saved from a surprise attack only by their geese, who heard the attackers and starting honking in warning.

Gradually, the Romans, by a mixture of absorption and war, extended their control over neighbouring lands and towns, and by the start of the 3rd century BC they controlled much of the Italian peninsula. This expansion brought them into contact, and sometimes conflict, with the Greek cities of the south, for example at Tarentum (now Taranto) and Cumae (near Naples). The Greek cities were not prepared to give way to the barbarian upstarts of Rome without a fight, and in 280 BC they supported Pyrrhus, the Greek king of Epirus, in his plans to attack the Republic. His eventual defeat (see box) made inevitable the subjection of the Greek cities to Roman control. It also made the Greeks, back in their Aegean homeland, very aware that a new power was emerging in the Mediterranean.

Rome and Carthage

Meanwhile the Romans themselves were already well aware of the main power in the central and western Mediterranean – the city of Carthage in modern–day Tunisia. The Carthaginians, descendents of the Phoenicians, had already fought with the Greeks over control of Sicily. Now that the Greeks were off the scene, it was perhaps inevitable that the Romans and Carthaginians would come to war, and they did so, twice in the 3rd century BC and then again, conclusively, in the 2nd century BC.

Carthage initially held the upper hand. It had dominated the western Mediterranean, impatient of any encroachment on its activities as it traded, for example, in Spain. The Carthaginians were great merchants and excelled at agriculture; and, above all, their fleet was thought to be invincible.

The first Punic War (the name comes from the Latin for Phoenician) lasted from 264 to 241 BC, and ended in victory for Rome. Though Carthage survived the defeat, the outcome

BELOW: One of the most famous stories in military history is how the great Carthaginian general Hannibal led his army, elephants and all, across the Alps to attack his bitter enemy the Romans in Italy. Fresco, early 16th century, by Jacopo Ripanda (active 1490-1530). Rome, Palazzo dei Conservatori, Sala della Lupa.

was an enormous blow, depriving it of Sicily and ultimately Sardinia, too. Moreover, the Romans, who had no great naval tradition, now matched the Carthaginians at sea, exploding the myth of their maritime supremacy. The Romans had assiduously built up their fleet for the war, and it is said that they copied the design of a stranded Carthaginian warship while adding a few design elements of their own that would enable them to board their opponents' vessels and attack their crews.

Defeat forced Carthage to look elsewhere to extend its influence, and some of its leading citizens sailed west to Spain. Here at New Carthage – Cartagena – they established a new colony under Hamilcar Barca, who still hoped for revenge against Rome. Soon Carthage's expansionist policies in Spain unnerved Rome and renewed conflict became inevitable.

It was sparked by an attack by Hamilcar's son Hannibal on Sagantum, a Roman ally near Valencia. This was the beginning of the Second Punic War (218–202 BC), which saw one of the most daring and famous attacks in military history when Hannibal led his army – elephants and all – up through Spain and France and across the Alps into northern Italy to attack Rome.

Hannibal's hope was not just that he could take Rome by surprise – no one would have considered such a trek remotely likely – but also that he could persuade Rome's allies on the Italian peninsula to change sides and help defeat it. Though Hannibal met with considerable success – he stayed in Italy for 15 years – ultimately he failed in his main aim. The people of Italy did not revolt against Rome, at least not in the numbers Hannibal required. Eventually, isolated and starved, the Carthaginians had to return to Africa, where the great Roman general Scipio (later Scipio Africanus) defeated Hannibal's forces at Zama in 202 BC.

BELOW: When the great Roman general Julius Caesar defiantly led his army across the Rubicon river in northern Italy in 49 BC, in contravention of ancient laws, it made civil war among the Romans inevitable. Woodcut, Coll. Archiv f.Kunst & Geschichte.

This war appeared to have settled the matter conclusively: Rome was now master of the western Mediterranean. Yet Roman concern about Carthage persisted. Urged on by the politician Cato – who infamously and persistently called for its destruction – the Romans ultimately confronted the African city once more. The Third Punic war (149–146 BC) was not much in the way of a military contest: Carthage was weaker, Rome stronger than before. The grandson of Scipio by adoption, Scipio Aemilianus (sometimes referred to as Scipio Africanus the Younger), captured and destroyed Carthage amid huge bloodshed. Those who were not killed were enslaved, and the land on which the ruins lay were cursed – it was even later claimed (inaccurately) that salt was ploughed into the ground to make the area barren.

Yet as he surveyed Carthage's destruction – it took ten days to burn the city down – Scipio pondered whether this might be the fate of Rome one day. His former tutor, the Greek historian Polybius, was at the general's side and recorded the sight. Later, he wrote:

At the sight of the city utterly perishing amidst the flames Scipio burst into tears, and stood long reflecting on the inevitable change which awaits cities, nations, and dynasties, one and all, as it does every one of us men. This, he thought, had befallen Ilium [Troy], once a powerful city, and the once mighty empires of the Assyrians, Medes, Persians, and that of Macedonia lately so splendid.

Republican Ideals and Empire

The 2nd century BC saw a huge extension of Rome's lands, even as it deleted Carthage from the face of the earth. Macedon, the source of Alexander the Great's power, was first beaten and then brought to submission. The lands of Asia Minor were also turned into a province when the last king of Pergamum, Attalus, died and bequeathed his kingdom to the Romans. Greece itself was also subjected to Roman control, sometimes brutally. In 146 BC, the same year that Carthage was destroyed, Corinth, one of the jewels in the crown of classical Greece, was sacked by the Romans. It was a scene of utter devastation: walls were smashed down, women and children were enslaved, and Roman soldiers casually played board games on discarded works of art.

The Mediterranean was now rapidly falling under Roman dominion. At the same time, however, the Roman state was creaking under the pressure. For hundreds of years Rome had been a republic. It elected two consuls who ruled for a year, advised by a Senate composed of both hereditary and life members. While Rome was no democracy, the ordinary citizens did have a say in government through an assembly, and their interests were represented (in theory, at least) by elected tribunes. Moreover, though women and slaves were excluded from membership, all other Romans were counted as citizens.

The dynamics of success, however, changed the balance of power from within. The Punic Wars had taken soldiers to serve away from home for long periods. Since these were generally peasants and smallholders – for many years the backbone of Roman society – some of the land fell into disuse. This land was bought up by the wealthy, forcing the peasants to move to the cities and eventually creating a larger urban population. Foreign conquests meant more money coming into Rome but also more competition for the farmers from foreign producers, for example, as well as opportunities for further self-enrichment by the wealthy and powerful.

Expansion brought other changes, too. Roman citizenship was – reluctantly – extended beyond the city and its home territory to other Italians. Conversely, the army, as it became more professional and spent long periods on the road, began to owe its loyalty to its commanders rather than Rome itself: the connection between the soldiers and their homeland was being eroded. The fabulous amounts of money around, the dislocated and shifting populations, an increased 'electorate', independently minded armies, growing personal rivalry and ambition – all these elements were conducive to corruption, intrigue

ABOVE: Cicero was a lawyer/ politician who reached the height of his career as an orator, with his famous denunciation of Catiline before the Roman Senate. The charge of Treason failed due to lack of evidence. Cicero's later years were shadowed by the fear of assassination. He was eventually murdered. From the painting by Maccari, Rome.

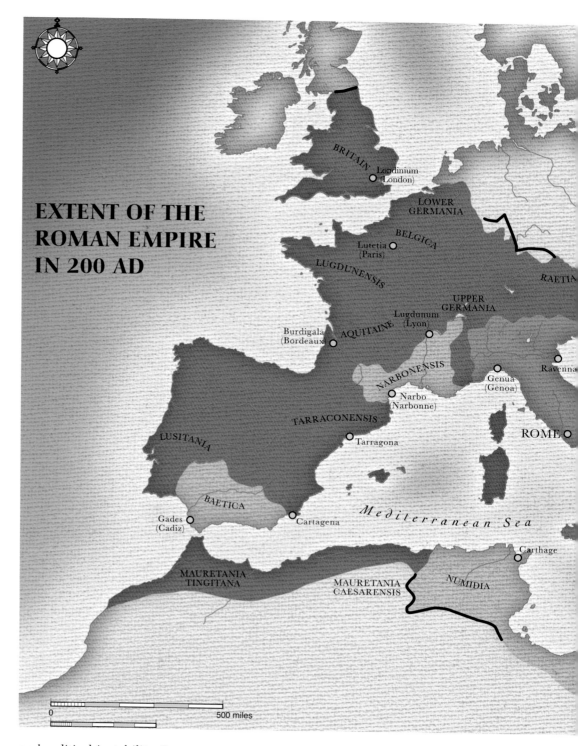

EXTENT OF THE
ROMAN EMPIRE
IN 200 AD

BRITAIN
Londinium
(London)

LOWER
GERMANIA

BELGICA

Lutetia
(Paris)

LUGDUNENSIS

RAETIA

UPPER
GERMANIA

Lugdunum
(Lyon)

Burdigala
(Bordeaux)   AQUITAINE

NARBONENSIS

Genua
(Genoa)

Ravenna

Narbo
(Narbonne)

TARRACONENSIS

ROME

LUSITANIA

Tarragona

BAETICA

Gades
(Cadiz)

Cartagena

Mediterranean Sea

Carthage

MAURETANIA
TINGITANA

MAURETANIA
CAESARENSIS

NUMIDIA

0   500 miles

and political instability. Roman commentators at the time blamed the growing crisis on moral degeneracy, a rejection of the selfless service of the state exemplified by men such as Horatius in favour of personal ambition and greed. Even as Rome's glory grew greater, the Republic was slowly crumbling from within.

The result was a period of civil war and strife that eventually led to the establishment of a monarchical system, albeit one that retained many of the trappings of the Republic. There were numerous 'strong men' whose power and actions helped highlight the growing fractures in the Roman body politic from the end of the 2nd century BC. These included the brilliant but flawed Gaius Marius (157–86 BC), whose crucial pay reforms made the army fully professional, and another soldier, Lucius Sulla (138–78 BC), who seized power by force and became dictator for life, though he then curiously 'retired' in 79 BC. Other key figures included the great orator and politician Cicero and the proud

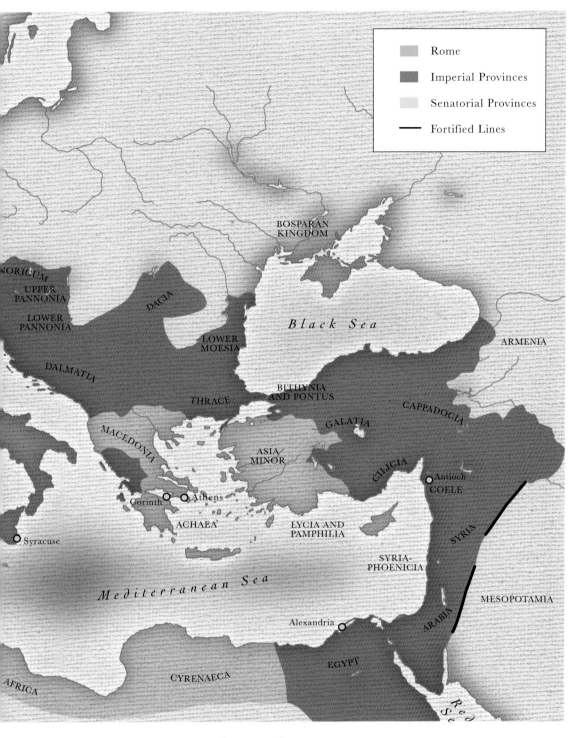

NORICUM
UPPER PANNONIA
LOWER PANNONIA
DALMATIA
DACIA
LOWER MOESIA

Black Sea

ARMENIA

THRACE
BITHYNIA AND PONTUS
CAPPADOCIA

MACEDONIA
GALATIA

ASIA MINOR

CILICIA

Antioch
COELE

Corinth   Athens
ACHAEA
LYCIA AND PAMPHILIA

SYRIA

Syracuse

SYRIA-PHOENICIA

Mediterranean Sea

MESOPOTAMIA

Alexandria

ARABIA

EGYPT

AFRICA
CYRENAECA

Red Sea

LEFT: The sheer scale of the Roman Empire at its peak was remarkable; it was the only empire in history to dominate the Mediterranean Sea from east to west and north to south. This helps to explain why the Romans sometimes simply referred to it as 'our sea'.

and ruthless general Pompey (106–48 BC).

The greatest figure of the time, possibly the best-known Roman of all time, was Gaius Julius Caesar (100–44 BC). By 50 BC Caesar had already earned his place in history by his conquest of the Gauls, his detailed written accounts of his victories, and his voyages to Britannia (Britain) in 55–54 BC. Yet Caesar was more than just a military leader; he was also part of the triumvirate that ruled Rome, alongside Pompey and Crassus. Crassus later died in battle; but not even Rome was big enough to contain the ambitions of both Pompey and Caesar, and the city was forced to make a choice between the two. It favoured Pompey. In 49 BC, Caesar made his move, crossing the Rubicon river from Gaul into Italy with his loyal army – an illegal act. In the inevitable war that followed, Pompey was beaten at the battle of Pharsalus in Thessaly, northern Greece, in 48 BC and soon afterwards was murdered in Egypt. After four years of civil war, Caesar had overcome his

ABOVE: The rule of Caesar Augustus, Rome's first emperor, established a control over the Mediterranean and beyond that was to set the tone of Roman imperial domination of the region for the next 200 years and more. Marble relief, 2nd century BC, Pavlovsk, Imperial Palace.

enemies, though by showing magnanimity to most of them he managed to heal some of the wounds caused by the fighting. He even had time to father a son with the youthful Cleopatra in Egypt before eventually returning to Rome, his power seemingly unchallenged. But after being elected dictator for life, Caesar's rule was short-lived; in the name of preserving the Republic, his opponents murdered him in 44 BC.

If the assassins hoped that Caesar's death would end Rome's shift towards monarchical government, they were badly mistaken. His great-nephew Octavian first helped hunt down the killers and then ruled in another triumvirate with Mark Antony (Marcus Antonius), a trusted ally of Caesar, under whom he had served in Gaul and at Pharsalus; the third member was Marcus Lepidus. For some years Octavian and Antony ruled together, the youthful great-nephew of Caesar concentrating on the west, the military veteran Antony on the east, where he too formed a famous liaison with the Egyptian queen Cleopatra. Such a sharing of power could not last long, and the inevitable clash resulted in Octavian's defeat of Antony's forces at sea off Actium in 31 BC, triggering the suicide not only of Antony but also of Cleopatra, the last of the great Ptolemaic dynasty.

Octavian was now undisputed ruler of Rome and all its vast territories. Though, as Caesar Augustus – Augustus was an honorary title – he was careful to respect the institutions of the Republic, including the Senate; though he was formally elected consul; though his title of 'imperator' technically meant he was a commander of soldiers in battle, and the title 'princeps' simply meant first citizen – despite all this, there was little doubt in Rome about the significance of Octavian's victory. The Roman Empire now had its emperor.

The Imperial Heyday

Augustus is credited with bringing peace and stability to the Roman Empire, valued commodities after the civil strife of the previous decades. When he died in AD 14 at the age of 76, the empire stretched from western France, Spain and North Africa right round the rim of the Mediterranean to Egypt, the Levant and Asia Minor. Over the following two centuries the empire would grow even larger, incorporating much of Britain as well as lands reaching across the Danube to Dacia and eastwards to the Euphrates. In all these areas, for much of the time, Roman law, trade and culture dominated, providing a stable framework within which prosperity – at least for those who were not automatically barred from it – could flourish. A person could sail from one end of the Mediterranean to the other and not leave Roman waters or the Roman rule of law. These truly were the days of *mare nostrum*, 'Our Sea' as the Romans called it: the first and only time that the Mediterranean was united in this way.

The great British historian Edward Gibbon, author of the epic work *The Decline and Fall of the Roman Empire*, had no doubt about the success of Rome at this time. He wrote:

> *If a man were called to fix the period in the history of the world, during which the human race was most happy and prosperous, he would, without hesitation, name that which elapsed from the death of Domitian to the accession of Commodus.*

The vast extent of the Roman empire was governed by absolute power, under the guidance of virtue and wisdom.

The period Gibbon refers to is from AD 96 to AD 180, sometimes called the age of the 'five good emperors'. These were Nerva, Trajan, Hadrian, Antoninus Pius and Marcus Aurelius. It is probably fair to say that these five emperors did display a degree of virtue and wisdom in their rule – a soundness of judgement most clearly shown in the way each ruler adopted an heir to avoid uncertainty and damaging rivalry at his death.

For the problem of succession was one that dogged the empire, both before and after this period of relative tranquillity. There was no generally agreed way of choosing emperors; the hereditary process was hit-and-miss, while competition among different candidates often caused chaos and led to a lack of continuity. In AD 69, for example, after Nero's unlamented demise, there were no fewer than four different emperors competing for power until Vespasian emerged victorious. Later, during the 3rd century AD, there were as many as 24 emperors as Rome battled to preserve its long frontiers; several of them died at the hands of their own soldiers. One emperor, Valerian, who was defeated and captured by the Persians in around AD 259, was skinned (possibly alive), and his skin was then stuffed and treated as a trophy. It was intended as a grisly symbol of Roman subservience to the Persians.

One cannot claim that individual emperors alone could have turned the tide of history and saved the Roman Empire – or at least the western part of it – from its demise in the 5th century. Huge social and economic forces were at work, not least the massive migration of peoples from central Europe and further afield that changed the face of Mediterranean societies, especially to the north and west of the sea.

Yet the success of Augustus, Trajan, Marcus Aurelius and, later, Diocletian showed that

BELOW: One of the favourite stunts of Emperor Commodus was to dress up in a lion skin to copy his hero Hercules and to appear in public as a gladiator; such demeaning behaviour, combined with his greed and corruption, mark Commodus out as one of the worst Roman emperors – a sad end to a golden age of mostly wise rule at the head of the empire. This marble sculpture was found in 1874 on the Esquiline Hill, Villa Palombara. Rom, Palazzo dei Conservatori, Sala degli Orti Lamiani.

the effectiveness of the emperor as head of state often depended on the character and ability of the man who occupied the position. For example, the Emperor Commodus to whom Gibbon refers was as appalling a man as the previous five had been (mostly) virtuous and wise. One of this emperor's favourite acts was to dress in animal skins as his hero Hercules and appear in the arena at the games, where he would kill animals and even other humans in 'combat'. To the Roman public, the appearance of their great leader as a gladiator was both comical and demeaning. It was little wonder that he was eventually murdered in AD 192, strangled in his bed by his wrestling partner, a man called Narcissus.

In the late 3rd and early 4th centuries, two strong emperors helped both to restore some power to the empire and to make changes that would shape Mediterranean and European culture for centuries to come. The first was Diocletian (AD 243–316), an able soldier of modest background from Illyria (the Balkans), who ruled in an autocratic but effective manner. Apart from restoring a degree of stability after years of chaos, Diocletian's most important action was to split the empire into eastern and western sections in AD 285. The north–south line passed between Italy and Greece (significantly, between Latin-speaking and Greek-speaking areas).

Though this division did not last long, there was a clear

See p.56

See p.58

See p.60

See p.72

TIMELINE UP TO THE END OF THE ROMAN EMPIRE IN THE WEST

King Menes/Narmer unites Egypt

Phoenicians found city of Carthage

Possible date for eruption of Thera (or c.1450 bc)

Corinth founds Syracuse in Sicily

End of Minoan society

Chief magistrate Solon lays legal foundations for Athenian democracy

Siege of Troy

Rome becomes republic

End of Mycenaean Empire

Persian fleet crushed by Greeks at Salamis

End of Hittite empire

Phoenicians found Gades, later Cadiz, in Spain

So–called east Mediterranean 'Dark Ages'

BC

c. 3200
c. 1650
c. 1450
c. 1270
c. 1230
c. 1200
c. 1100
c. 1200–900
c. 800
733
c. 594
c. 509
480

See p.69

See p.80

See p.92

Great Peloponnesian War

Rome sacked by Gauls

Birth of Alexander the Great

City of Alexandria founded

Birth of Julius Caesar

Caesar invades Britain

Murder of Julius Caesar

Death of Cleopatra, Egypt under Roman dominance

Augustus becomes Roman emperor

Death of Augustus

Death of Marcus Aurelius, last of the 'five good' emperors

Emperor Constantine inaugurates Constantinople as capital of eastern Roman Empire

Visigoths sack Rome

Romulus Augustulus deposed as last Roman emperor of the west

431–404

390

556

532

100

54

44

30

27

AD

14

180

330

410

476

ABOVE: The end of the weakened western Roman empire was heralded by attacks from Germanic peoples, such as the Goths and also the Huns who came from the east. These peoples were usually described as 'barbarians', and they fought the 'civilized' Romans, as depicted here. Paris, Musée du Louvre.

logic to it. In later years, this would be the fault-line upon which the empire would be permanently divided, leading to the creation of the Byzantine Empire out of the eastern part of the Roman. Diocletian was also remarkable in that he retired from office and then lived in some splendour in a palace in what is today Split in Croatia.

The second key figure was Constantine (AD 285–337), who reunited the empire by force in 324. His main contributions to history lay elsewhere, however. Soon after he gained control of the entire empire, this energetic and brilliant general decided to found a new capital at the old Greek colony of Byzantium. It was a sign that the balance of the empire had shifted to the east, where most of its wealth was located, and also that the power of Rome as a political capital was waning. The new city was called Constantinople.

By this date, moreover, Constantine had taken an even more important step by embracing Christianity. The exact nature of his 'conversion' – the emperor still adhered to a sun cult – and his beliefs are discussed in Chapter Five; but it is clear that it is largely thanks to Constantine that what had once been an obscure Jewish sect gradually took centre stage at the heart of the greatest empire the world had ever known.

The aftermath of Empire

The split between east and west in the Roman Empire proposed by Diocletian finally became reality after AD 392, when the two parts had different emperors. In 476, with the demise of the last emperor of the west, Romulus Augustulus, the western half vanished – though in truth its power had been ebbing away for decades. This, of course, was not the end of the Roman Empire: Gibbon's famous book on its decline and fall continues to the 15th century and the fall of Constantinople to the Ottoman Turks.

Indeed, even in the west, where the empire had disintegrated under attacks from 'barbarians', there was continuity of a sort. The office of the Bishop of Rome – the Pope – kept alive the memory of Rome as an important spiritual and cultural focal point, at least for western Europe. There was even, in later centuries, the slightly curious phenomenon of the Holy Roman Empire in northern Europe – though, as the old joke points out, it was neither holy nor Roman, nor even an empire. But the revival of the name makes an important point: many of the so-called 'barbarians' who invaded and then inhabited western and northern Europe would look back to Rome for centuries to come for cultural and political inspiration. Its laws, boundaries, roads and buildings survived in many areas and were absorbed into later cultures, rather as the Romans themselves had absorbed much from the Greeks in earlier centuries. The Romans had undoubtedly changed Mediterranean society for ever.

Thus, even as the Vandals, Ostrogoths, Visigoths and Huns rampaged across much of Europe in the first centuries AD, links remained between past and present that would continue into the future. Meanwhile, though people would undoubtedly have felt less secure with the erosion of centralized Roman power, for the most part this would have been a slow process. The lives of many ordinary people – for example in Egypt, the Greek states or Asia Minor – would not have changed dramatically.

Byzantium and the barbarians

The invading forces that swept through Europe and the Roman Empire in the 4th and 5th centuries AD involved two main groups. One was made up of Germanic peoples, including the Goths (Ostrogoths and Visigoths), Alans and Vandals; the other was the Huns from the steppes of Asia. The Ostrogoths and Visigoths had migrated to areas bordering the Black Sea, but the arrivals of the Huns from Asia – probably displaced by drought or famine – put pressure on them to move westwards into Europe. Meanwhile, the Vandals from northern Europe began a gradual move southwards. This movement of peoples led to a series of battles and conflicts with the Roman Empire of east and west, as well as conflict between the Germanic

peoples and the Huns. In AD 410, the Visigoths, having previously been in conflict with the eastern Roman Empire, sacked Rome; the year after, Vandals and Alans invaded Spain.

When the Visigoths themselves invaded Spain, the Vandals moved on across the Straits of Gibraltar to Africa. By AD 439, they had conquered Carthage, the new city rebuilt by the Romans soon after they destroyed the old one and which was still part of the western Roman Empire, thus depriving Rome of its main source of grain supplies in North Africa. From this vantage point the Vandals sailed across the Mediterranean to sack Rome in AD 455. Meanwhile, in AD 451 the Huns, who had appeared likely to conquer most of Europe under the ruthless leadership of Attila, were finally checked at a major battle at Châlons in what is now northern France.

The composition of the two armies that met at Châlons shows just how complex the shifting alliances of the time were, and warns against seeing this period of history simply in terms of a contest between Romans on one side and 'barbarians' on the other. The Huns' side included Ostrogoth allies, while the 'Roman' army's main forces consisted of Visigoths, Alans and Franks, plus some Roman troops from Gaul. The Ostrogoths, moreover, who went on to conquer most of Italy at the end of the 5th century, saw themselves as inheritors of the Roman Empire – or at least, their great king Theodoric the Great did. Theodoric had been brought up as a nobleman in Constantinople, and when he had his coins struck they bore the inscription *Roma invicta* or 'unvanquished Rome'. He also

ABOVE: Though the Goths are usually portrayed as barbarians, their leaders often looked to the history of Rome for their inspiration. The Ostrogoth Theodoric the Great, shown here in a 17th century copper engraving, was in fact brought up at court in Constantinople and greatly admired the Roman Empire.

informed the emperor in Constantinople that 'our royalty is an imitation of yours, a copy of the only empire on earth'. For, if the western empire of Rome was dead, the eastern half had still another 1,100 years of life ahead of it.

However, the Byzantine Empire, as the eastern part later became known, showed little imperial brilliance until the arrival of Justinian I (AD 483–565). It was he who, with the help of his exceptional general Belisarius, ejected the Vandals from North Africa and eventually put an end to the Ostrogoth domination of Italy. Just as importantly, Justinian codified the laws of the Roman Empire and, adding some new ones of his own, produced a code that heavily influenced many of the legal systems of Europe down to the present day.

Under Justinian, indeed, the Byzantine Empire reached one of its political and territorial high points. Its main problem at the time was that old foe of Greece and Rome – the Persian Empire.

Something approaching order was, however, restored around the Mediterranean. Much of the east, including Egypt, remained under Byzantine rule; the Visigoths were establishing kingdoms in Spain; and the Franks were dominant in France and Germany. Even though there was still huge disruption in Italy, thanks to the arrival from the north of a new invading group, the Lombards, overall the picture was one of relative calm compared to the confusion and conflict of the 5th century. This was all about to change, however, with the emergence of yet another, utterly unexpected force in the region.

BELOW: The Visigoth king Roderic was defeated and killed in battle defending Spain when Islamic troops invaded from North Africa in 712 and quickly captured the old Visigoth capital Toledo. Copper engraving by M. Merian (1593–1650). Coll. Archiv f.Kunst & Geschichte.

Islamic conquest

The sheer speed at which the forces of Islam conquered massive areas of the Mediterranean still has the power to astonish. Within three years of Muhammad's death in 632 his followers from Arabia had captured Damascus – then under Byzantine control – and by 638 Jerusalem was in their hands. In between, the Byzantine army had been smashed on 20 August 636 at the decisive battle of Yarmuk, a key moment in the history of Europe and the Mediterranean. Many of the Byzantine troops perished when they were driven over the edge of a steep ravine.

The scale of the Byzantine defeat meant there was little to stop the Muslim invaders taking control of much of the eastern Mediterranean and moving into the lands beyond. Having severed links with its Arab allies some years earlier, Byzantium seems to have been totally unaware of the threat emerging from Arabia until it was too late. It was what we would nowadays call a failure of intelligence.

Egypt soon fell to the Muslim forces, who took Alexandria in 642. The Arabs also attacked and defeated the Persian Empire, while at the same time pushing west to North Africa, conquering Carthage in 698. By then, Byzantine dominance at sea had already been challenged when a Muslim fleet defeated the imperial navy off Lycia in 655, and Constantinople itself came under siege in the 670s. The attacking Muslim fleet was defeated on this occasion largely thanks to the use of so-called 'Greek fire', an incendiary liquid that was propelled onto enemy ships, where it burst into flame with devastating results.

ABOVE: The beautiful and evocative Alhambra in Granada in southern Spain remains one of the architectural treasures of Europe and is an example of the influence of Islamic culture in the Mediterranean.

Within a few years, another decisive moment was to occur at the other end of the Mediterranean. After tough fighting against the Berber peoples of North Africa, the Arab forces had reached modern-day Morocco. From there in 711, following a series of exploratory raids, an invasion force of the now subjugated Berbers headed by the Arab general Tariq ibn Ziyad landed on the rocky southern tip of Spain. It was named in his honour 'rock of Tariq' or 'Jebel Tariq': hence the modern name Gibraltar.

A year later the new king of the Visigoths, Roderic, was defeated and killed in battle, and within a few more years the whole of the Iberian peninsula, save possibly a tiny enclave in Asturias on the northern coast, was under Muslim control. In fact, the invaders also took control briefly of the old Visigothic province of Septimania, which stretched from the Pyrenees to modern-day Provence, and was ruled from Narbonne.

By early in the 8th century, much of the Mediterranean was under Muslim control, though attempts to move further north were halted at the battle of Poitiers in 732 by Frankish forces under Charles Martel, grandfather of Charlemagne. It is probably fair to describe it as Arab control, for most Muslims were Arab at this time, though soon many of the conquered peoples, for example the Berbers, Egyptians and Persians, would embrace Islam.

From this point on, the religious divide between Christianity and Islam would be yet another of the fault-lines that run through Mediterranean history. Much of the conflict would inevitably be focused – at least rhetorically – on Jerusalem, a holy centre for both Christians and Muslims (as well as Jews, of course), most notably in the phenomenon of the Christian crusades.

But in many ways a more fascinating meeting-ground of Islam and western Christianity was Spain. Until about 1250, when the Muslims – known in the Spanish context as the Moors – were confined to a narrow area around Granada, the Iberian peninsula was a scene of sporadic fighting between Christians and Muslims, as the frontier between their respective areas of control moved backward and forward, but also

THE NORMANS IN SICILY

The Normans are best known for their invasion of England under William the Conqueror and victory at the Battle of Hastings in 1066. However, they were also responsible for another important 11th-century invasion – this time of Sicily. This strategic island had been settled by Carthaginians, Greeks, Romans and, up until the middle of the 11th century, by Arabs. In 1061, Normans established in southern Italy embarked upon the first of a series of raids on Islamic Messina. By 1072, their leader, Roger d'Hauteville, was accorded the title 'Count of Sicily'. At the time the papacy supported the invasion on two grounds: to re-establish Christian dominion over the island, and to prevent it returning to the rule of Byzantium, who had controlled it before the Arabs. In 1130, Roger's son of the same name was confirmed as King Roger of Sicily. For around 100 years Sicily kept its distinctive identity: a mixture of Latin, Orthodox and Arab/Islamic cultures; religious tolerance was mostly the norm; and a unique form of Norman–Arab–Byzantine art developed. Eventually, though, Sicily became caught up in the dynastic squabbles of western Europe and its insularity came to an end.

BELOW: The emperor Basil II, illustrated here in a Byzantine psalter, was nicknamed the 'Bulgar slayer' for his ruthless treatment of one of the empire's main enemies, but his rule also boosted the prestige and power of Byzantium at the end of the 10th and the start of the 11th centuries. Byzantine illumination, between 1017 and 1025. Venice, Biblioteca Nazionale Marciana.

an environment in which the two faiths lived side by side. Though the so-called *convivencia* ('living together') of the 12th and 13th centuries can easily be overstated, the ability of sections of the two communities (as well as Jews) to live together at times is a reminder that the realities of life do not always fit with the headlines of history. Another reminder comes in the shape of Rodrigo Díaz, better known to us as 'El Cid' ('lord'). This 11th-century military adventurer was later adopted both by the Catholic Church and by Spain as a symbol of their Christian struggle against the 'infidel'; however, it should not be forgotten that he fought against Christian Spaniards as much as against Moors.

Nor was the Islamic world always united. In 750, the ruling Umayyad dynasty in Damascus was overthrown by the 'Abbasids, whose first caliph, al-Saffah – 'The Shedder of Blood' – then proceeded to kill as many of the rival dynasty as he could, while the second caliph, al-Mansur, moved the centre of Islam to a new capital at Baghdad. One Umayyad who escaped was 'Abd al-Rahman, who went to Spain and established a dynasty there that ruled al-Andalus (the Arabic name for the Iberian peninsula, from which we get Andalucia) until the 11th century. It was al-Rahman who fought off an attack mounted on Saragossa in 778 by Charlemagne.

Byzantium, Bulgars and Turks

In the eastern Mediterranean the picture was not just one of the Byzantine army against Islamic forces, but of conflict between Constantinople and the Bulgars too. The Bulgars were people of Turkic or Hun origin who slowly mingled with Slavs and occupied the lands to the north of the Byzantine Empire, roughly where Bulgaria is today. For 200 years up to the start of the 11th century the Bulgars were a constant and aggressive threat to an already beleaguered Constantinople; for their part, the Bulgars were concerned about Byzantine expansion into northern Greece. The ferocity of the conflict is shown by two incidents at either end of this grim period.

In 811, the Byzantine Emperor Nicephorus was defeated in battle by the Bulgar Khan Krum. It was the first time an emperor had been killed in battle for nearly four and a half centuries, and to celebrate his achievement Krum had Nicephorus' skull turned into a drinking bowl.

In 1014, the Emperor Basil II (AD 958–1025) undertook a successful campaign to subdue the Bulgars. Having captured 15,000 prisoners, Basil was enraged when his men came under attack from another Bulgar force and blinded all 15,000 of his captives, save for 100 who were blinded in just one eye so they could lead the mutilated troops back to the Bulgar leader Samuel. Samuel was reportedly so appalled at the sight that he died of a heart attack.

Basil's conquests later earned him the name Basil Bulgaroktonus or 'Bulgar–slayer'. However, his 49–year reign was as important for the land and wealth he brought to the empire as for his defeat of the Bulgars. For the first time in centuries, Byzantium seemed a power to be reckoned with.

ABOVE: The Christian Crusades were launched in 1095 by Pope Urban II, who called for the great and the good of western Europe to reclaim the Holy Lands for Christendom.

Though it had lost its important foothold in the western Mediterranean, Sicily, to the Arabs in the 9th century, the empire controlled Greece, parts of Anatolia, northern Syria and Bulgaria, and had extended its indirect influence over larger areas still. Yet this was to prove one of Byzantium's last great high points.

At the same time there was further division in the Islamic world, with a rival caliphate, the Fatimids, founded by followers of the Shi'ite tradition of Islam in Cairo in AD 969. Yet this did not stop the Byzantine Empire suffering a major defeat in 1071 at Manzikert at the hands of the Seljuk Turks. The co–emperor Romanus Diogenes was himself captured in the battle. Though released, he was blinded by supporters of his co–emperor Michael VII and later died from his injuries.

The Seljuk Turks were part of a group of Turkic peoples from Asia, and had enthusiastically converted to the Sunni tradition of Islam. Their victory over Byzantium heralded the gradual advance of Islam and the Turkish into largely Christian and Greek–speaking Anatolia. Ultimately, this would pave the way for the formation of what became known as the Ottoman Empire. More immediately, the establishment by the Turks of the sultanate of Rum – they saw themselves as the inheritors of the mantle of the empire of Rome, hence 'Rum' – alarmed the world of Christendom and was one of the factors leading to the crusades.

Crusading

It all began with what seems to have been a misunderstanding. When the Byzantine Emperor Alexius I, alarmed by the advance of the Seljuk Turks, sent an appeal for help to Pope Urban II in 1095, he probably had in mind the despatch of a few thousand well-trained mercenary troops. The Pope, however saw a bigger picture. At the Council of Clermont in the same year, Urban argued that it was the spiritual duty of Christians to travel to the Holy Land and bring it back under the 'rightful' control of Christendom. Meanwhile, the more particular needs of the Byzantine Empire were to be rather overlooked. (In 1054 there had been a decisive and final break between the Latin-speaking 'Catholic' Church of Rome and the Greek-speaking 'Orthodox' Church of the eastern empire, and mistrust between the two traditions had steadily grown.) Much of western Christian nobility, inspired by the stark terms in which the fight was portrayed as one between good and evil, heeded the Pope's call, and the First Crusade was launched with Franks and Normans to the fore.

The First Crusade was by far the most successful. After passing through the Byzantine Empire, its knights captured Jerusalem in July 1099, a deed grimly marked by a massacre of thousands of prisoners, including women and children. Four so-called Latin kingdoms, or provinces of 'Outremer' ('Over the Sea') were set up in Edessa, Antioch, Tripoli and Jerusalem itself. From this point on, the main purpose of subsequent crusades was to hold on to or recapture these Latin kingdoms. The Second Crusade (1147–49) unsuccessfully tried to recapture Edessa from the Seljuk Turks, while the fall of Jerusalem in 1187 to the famed Kurdish general Saladin (1138–93), ruler of Syria and Egypt, prompted the ambitious but failed Third Crusade. This was the expedition led by kings from western Europe, including Richard I ('the Lionheart') of England and the Holy Roman Emperor Frederick I (who drowned during the course of it), and it has given rise to countless tales and legends.

During this period, Constantinople looked upon the crusaders with a mixture of mistrust, fear and disdain. During the First Crusade – specifically called to help Byzantium – Alexius refused to let the Crusaders enter newly captured Nicaea except in small numbers for fear they would destroy the city, though he did take advantage of the Crusaders' presence in the region to win back some land from the Turks. To the sophisticated Byzantines, the crusaders were little more than northern barbarians, albeit Christian ones, who understood little of the region, of Islam or of the complex situation in which Constantinople found itself.

This mistrust proved justified when a claimant to the imperial throne ill-advisedly called on troops from the notorious Fourth Crusade (1202–4) to help him. In 1204, 20,000 or so crusaders sacked the city – the first time that a foreign army had done so in its 900-year history. The Latins then established a kingdom in Constantinople that lasted until 1261, though the Byzantine court limped on elsewhere in the meantime and eventually returned to the city. None of the original aims of the Fourth Crusade were accomplished.

BEL:OW: Though their original aim of restoring Christianity to all of the Holy Land ended in complete failure, soldiers of the infamous Fourth Crusade did succeed in capturing Constantinople in 1204, a hitherto unconquered city ruled by fellow Christians. Painting by Domenico Tintoretto (1560–1635). Venice, Palace of the Doge, Sala del Maggior Consiglio.

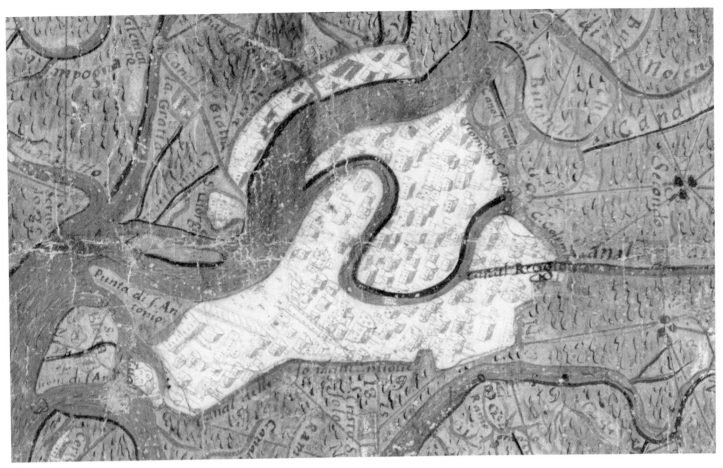

There were later crusades and military adventures, and in 1229 the Holy Roman Emperor Frederick II, despite being excommunicated at the time, even negotiated control of Jerusalem and was crowned king there. However, Islamic forces retook the city 15 years later and in 1291 the final Frankish outpost in the Holy Land, Acre, was captured and destroyed by the new Mamluk dynasty ruling Egypt. The eastern Mediterranean was once more largely under the control of Islamic government, with the weak Byzantine Empire reduced to an isolated outpost: the years of crusading had brought it very little benefit, and a great deal of harm.

In the west a different story unfolded. In Moorish Spain, new invasions from North Africa had strengthened Islamic rule in the 11th and 12th centuries. But at the start of the 13th century, as the Holy Land was falling once more into Islamic hands, the Christian powers in Spain – Leon–Castile, Aragon–Catalonia and Portugal – gained the upper hand. By the middle of the century the Christian reconquerors of Spain, already masters of the important city of Toledo since 1085, had succeeded in taking the main cities of Córdoba, Valencia and Seville. The split between east and west in the Mediterranean was becoming more pronounced.

ABOVE: Early map of Venice. Its primary natural advantage was its lagoon, a priceless defence against land attack. The geography of Venice also forced Venetians to look outwards towards the sea rather than inward. Detail from a map of the lagoon 'Laguna Di Venezia' (west at the top). Drawing, water coloured, 1692, by Antonio Girolamo Vestri. Venice, Archivio di Stato.

Merchant cities

The period of the crusades and the Christian reconquest of Spain saw the emergence of new powers in the Mediterranean: the merchant cities. Influential commercial centres were not new to the sea – the cities of Ugarit, Tyre and Sidon in the ancient world are evidence of that. But thanks in part to growing populations, better shipbuilding technology and – mostly – increasing prosperity, medieval trading states were able to exert enormous power over the waters and the lands beyond. The mightiest of these was to be Venice, closely followed by its arch-rival Genoa, though Pisa, Barcelona, Marseille, Amalfi

ABOVE: The monarchs of Spain, Ferdinand and Isabella, greet Christopher Columbus after his famous voyage to the Americas in 1492. In that same year the Catholic rulers brought an end to the last Moorish stronghold on the Iberian peninsula. Educational poster for schools (colour lithograph, 1914). Dortmund, Westfaelisches Schulmuseum.

and others also loomed large.

From as early as AD 810, Venice had evidenced a clear sense of communal pride and the ability to fight above its weight when its people managed to ward off an attempted invasion by Charlemagne's son Pepin. Its primary natural advantage was its lagoon, a priceless defence against land attack. The geography of Venice also forced Venetians to look outwards towards the sea rather than inward; indeed, for a long time Venetians were forbidden to build up estates on the mainland. Its close relationship with the Byzantine Empire, to whom it was technically subject for centuries, meant that merchants of Venice could take advantage of the wealth in the east, including the routes through to the Black Sea controlled by Constantinople.

This connection brought cultural benefits, too: when St Mark's was rebuilt in the 10th century, the new church was modelled on a basilica in Constantinople. This close relationship, however, did not stop the Venetians profiting at Byzantium's expense. After a falling-out in the 12th century, it was the Venetians who helped divert the troops of the Fourth Crusade to Constantinople, where the Italians benefited from subsequent Latin rule. Venice was eventually to have footholds, if not full-scale colonies, all over the central and eastern Mediterranean, from Crete to Cyprus, in parts of Greece and Anatolia, down the Dalmatian coast and also in the Black Sea.

Though Venice and the other merchant states helped supply the crusades, they had traded with the east long before them and continued to do so long after the expeditions became just wishful thinking. This trade linked east and west, often crossing borders between Christendom and Islam – even if in theory it was forbidden to sell essential goods such as wood and iron to Muslim countries.

It was the merchant states, in effect, that ruled the sea. By 1277, when Genoese ships first sailed past Gibraltar and round to western Europe, the northern kingdoms of Europe were being brought into the Mediterranean world; a world that, for the most part, was growing in prosperity.

A grim interlude: the plague

However, if the 13th and early 14th centuries were prosperous years for much of the Mediterranean – one hesitates ever to describe the political environment there as peaceful – this boom was delivered a crippling blow in 1347 with the arrival of the plague. The Black Death was as devastating to the Mediterranean world as it was to Europe as a whole. Indeed, it is thought to have arrived in Europe in the Mediterranean, via ships from Crimea in the Black Sea, whither the plague had come from Asia.

A contemporary Italian account gives a colourful account of how the Genoese trading port of Caffa (now Feodosiya) in Crimea was the source of the European outbreak. The

THE JANISSARIES

The Janissaries were the household troops of the ruler or sultan of the Ottoman Empire from the late 14th century until the early 19th century. Originally enslaved prisoners, by the early 15th century the Janissary recruits were young, usually Christian, boys, who were brought up in an austere environment and trained as elite troops. Most converted to Islam. Many of the youths were between the ages of seven and 14, and came from Albanian, Bulgarian, Serb and, later, Hungarian and Greek communities, all subjects of the Ottoman Empire, and until the 16th century they were expected to be celibate. In the 17th century, recruitment was abandoned, as the elite group found itself attracting enough volunteers. The troops took part in all the empire's major battles, including the conquest of Constantinople – which became Istanbul – in 1453. The Janissary Corps, which could number 200,000 or more, eventually became a political force, leading to conflict with the sultan. In 1826, Sultan Mahmud II, who wanted a more modern army, had his artillerymen fire on their barracks after a revolt. Those who were not killed were later executed or banished.

story was that when Crimean Tatars besieged Caffa they threw the bodies of their own plague victims into the city to ensure that the Christians would suffer the same grisly fate as they had. Though the Genoese immediately tossed the bodies into the sea, they still caught the disease; so when, as the Tatars left, the merchants immediately set sail for Italy and home, they took the plague with them on board their ships. Though this account may be broadly accurate, it is now thought that the plague spread more generally from ships in the Crimea, and not from one specific source.

The plague hit Constantinople in 1347, and by 1348 had spread to much of the rest of the Mediterranean. One place especially badly affected was Cyprus, which was simultaneously struck by a severe earthquake and tsunami even as the plague took hold. In all, it is estimated that around one-third of the population of areas affected by the plague died, and that large Mediterranean cities took perhaps half a century to recover from this catastrophe.

The appearance of the nation-state

Another, rather more positive development in the 14th and 15th centuries was the gradual emergence of the nation-state. This was a slow process that would not be complete for hundreds of years, but in France and Spain in particular there were clear signs of a national identity taking shape. In Spain this was given a strong initial impetus by the 'reconquest' of the land from the Moors, and was propelled further in 1479 by the marriage of the

Below: The Janissaries were the household troops of the Ottoman ruler and were originally young boys from Christian families recruited and trained to serve the sultan as elite soldiers. They were violently disbanded in the 19th century. Copper engraving. Coll. Archiv f.Kunst & Geschichte.

KINGDOM
OF
FRANCE

BURGUNDY

SAVOY

Paris

Rhine

Danube

Venice

Genoa

Rome

Mediterranean Sea

SICILY

Tunis

MALTA

	Approximate frontier of the Ottoman Empire in 1481
Sarukhan	Turkish Emirate

0   500 miles

0   500 km

monarchs of the rival kingdoms of Aragon and Castile, Ferdinand and Isabella. Under 'Los Reyes Catolicos' ('the Catholic monarchs'), reconquest was completed in 1492 with the defeat of the Nasrid kingdom of Granada and the formal end of Moorish rule in Spain. It is no great coincidence that in the same year a Genoese explorer called Christopher Columbus, who was sponsored by Isabella, sailed across the Atlantic to the Americas. Spain and Portugal, having completed the reconquest of their own lands, were now in effect setting out to extend their dominion to the new world; the age of exploration was well under way.

France, too, was simultaneously gaining a national identity and emerging as a maritime power in the Mediterranean, developments which would see it ultimately look to North Africa and the Near East to extend its influence.

In the eastern Mediterranean, however, Byzantium, the direct descendent of the

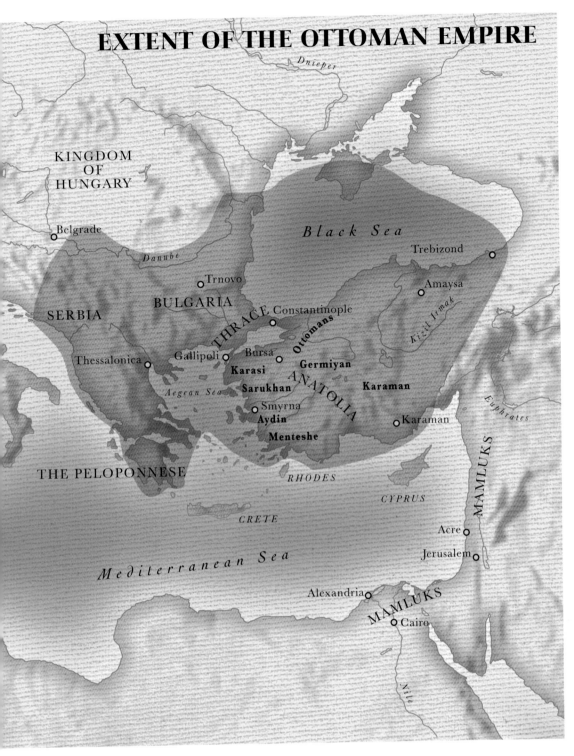

EXTENT OF THE OTTOMAN EMPIRE

Dnieper

KINGDOM OF HUNGARY

Belgrade

Danube

Black Sea

Trebizond

Trnovo

Amaysa

BULGARIA

THRACE

Constantinople

Kizil Irmak

SERBIA

Ottomans

Thessalonica

Gallipoli

Bursa

Karasi

Germiyan

ANATOLIA

Sarukhan

Karaman

Aegean Sea

Smyrna

Aydin

Karaman

Euphrates

Menteshe

THE PELOPONNESE

RHODES

CYPRUS

MAMLUKS

CRETE

Acre

Jerusalem

Mediterranean Sea

Alexandria

MAMLUKS

Cairo

Nile

LEFT: The power base of the mighty Ottoman Empire, the greatest seen since Roman days, was in and around modern day Turkey. By the 16th century, its influence had spread to the Middle East, Egypt and across much of the eastern Mediterranean.

once-mighty Roman Empire, was falling into an ever-weaker state. Its leader was now referred to in the west simply as the 'emperor of the Greeks'. On occasions in the 14th century the empire even had to call on the help of its foes the Turks to fight off Serb attacks on Constantinople. In the end, however, it was the Turks themselves who put the ailing empire out of its misery and built a formidable Mediterranean empire of their own.

The Ottomans

It is unfortunate that the prevalent view of the Ottoman Empire is coloured by its description at the end of the 19th century as the 'sick man of Europe'. For to focus on this image is to ignore the power and influence of an empire that lasted 500 years and unified the eastern Mediterranean in a way not seen since the glory days of the Roman Empire.

Ottoman is the western name for the Osmanli, the followers of Osman: a Turkic people of Asian origins who lived in Anatolia. At the end of the 14th century and the very start of the 15th, Ottoman successes under its fourth ruler Bayezid I included the incorporation of small Turkish emirates, such as those of Karasi and Sarukhan. Such expansion effectively left Constantinople encircled, and the end of the Byzantine Empire seemed inevitable. A belated attempt by the Christian world to stop the Islamic Ottomans from moving further was decisively ended at the Battle of Varna in 1444, when the 'crusading' army of 30,000, including Hungarians, Poles, Czechs and Croatians, was overwhelmed by a force of 120,000 Turks.

ABOVE: The emergence of the Ottoman Empire ensured the extension of Islamic culture to much of the Mediterranean. In 1453, after the Ottomans captured Constantinople, now Istanbul, its famous basilica St Sophia was turned into a mosque – Haga Sophia.

The End of Byzantium

The decisive year was 1453, when, after two months of attacks, the Turkish Sultan Mehmed II took Constantinople and immediately transformed the famous church of St Sophia into a mosque. On that day in May, the Byzantine Empire, the once proud inheritor of Roman supremacy, ended – more than 1,100 years since Constantine had founded the eastern capital in his name. The news inevitably sent shock waves around the whole Christian world, even though the Latin church had until recently done little to protect the Greek torch-bearer of eastern Christianity.

However, for Mehmed the Conqueror, the old empire did not fall, it just changed hands – and he assumed the title of Roman Caesar. The tradition of the Roman Empire took a long time to die.

Mehmed's stunning victory was the launch pad for the Ottoman Empire, which by 1517 had extended its dominion over the Balkans, Syria and Egypt and by 1529 was threatening Austria for the first time. In the meantime, the Ottoman sultan also assumed the title of caliph, making him the leader of the Islamic world. To the west, the Ottomans came into conflict with the Spanish, from whom they took Algiers in 1529, and with whom they were destined to be bitter rivals for decades to come.

The Ottomans' seemingly inexorable advance was jolted in 1571 when Turkish forces suffered a huge defeat at sea. This was the Battle of Lepanto off Greece, in which the Turkish navy, led by Ali Pasha, lost the bulk of its ships and perhaps 20,000 men against a Holy League fleet comprising Spanish, Venetian and Genoese forces. However, the Ottoman Empire quickly rebuilt its fleet and was still able to maintain its hold over Cyprus against the Venetians. The real long-term effect of Lepanto – the last major sea battle fought with galleys – was to confirm an east–west split, with the west broadly under Spanish dominion and Ottoman maritime influence confined largely to the east.

Ottoman rule left its mark in many parts of the Mediterranean, for example in the Balkans, where great cities such as Sarajevo and Mostar were established. The relative peace and stability that Ottoman rule brought to the Islamic world led to a period of extensive building, with many new bridges, aqueducts, baths and, of course, mosques erected. In Jerusalem, the Sultan Suleiman the Magnificent (1494–1566) rebuilt the city walls, and was a noted patron of the arts and philosophy as well as an acclaimed poet himself. He was also known within the empire as the 'law–maker' for his comprehensive overhaul of the Ottoman legal system.

It should be noted, too, that, for the most part, the Islamic rulers of the Ottoman Empire tolerated the practice of other faiths, such as Judaism and Christianity. Indeed, under Ottoman rule the Orthodox Church positively flourished in some areas previously dominated by the Latin Church, as the Islamic leaders continued their centuries–old policy of playing one tradition off against the other.

Threats Within and Without

However, like any empire, the Ottoman Empire faced problems that, over the course of the ensuing centuries, would slowly damage it. Internal weaknesses included poor leadership – the age of Suleiman was often looked back to with nostalgia – and a general tendency towards intellectual conservatism. This latter trend, not unusual in successful but ageing empires, contrasted with the growing intellectual dynamism of some western countries associated – partly as cause, partly as result – with the Renaissance, the Reformation and later the Age of Enlightenment.

Economically, the age of exploration in the west would slowly decrease dependence on the eastern Mediterranean. For example, once the ocean routes round the southern tips of Africa and South America had been discovered, spices could be shipped directly from India and the Far East rather than having to be imported over land. And while the Ottomans encouraged and promoted trade, it was often in the hands of foreign merchants and thus not always in the best interests of the empire's hierarchy. The important west Anatolian trading port of Smyrna (now Izmir) became a popular destination for French, Dutch, British and Italian merchants in the 17th century; however, its rise to prominence owed nothing to any deliberate planning by the Ottoman bureaucracy. Moreover, the

BELOW: Naval battle of Lepanto, 7 October 1571. The Venetian, Spanish and papal fleet under Don Juan d'Austria defeats the Turkish fleet. Painting by Andrea Micheli, called Vicentino (1539-1614). Venice, Doge's Palace.

Ottoman Empire lacked political unity, ranging as it did from North Africa to the Balkans and south-east Europe, and relied upon the support of local leaders for its continuance. As a result, the personal loyalty of individual subjects to the sultan was weakened.

Externally, the empire had to contend not only with the emergence of new and confident nation-states in the west, but to the east with Persia and above all Russia, the new giant with whom the Ottomans fought both on land and in the Black Sea. Thus, after 1683, and the failure of the Turks' second siege of Austria, the empire's story was mostly one of territory lost, albeit with the occasional recovery and counter-attack along the way. Two of the biggest blows were the loss of Crimea to Russia in the second half of the 18th century and the achievement by the Greeks of independence in 1830, after a romanticized struggle that fired the imagination of many in the west – fostered notably by the well-publicized support of the British poet Lord Byron, who eventually died from fever on his way to help distribute money raised to help the Greeks.

The battle for naval dominance

The independence of Greece was made possible by the naval defeat of Ottoman and Egyptian forces at Navarino in 1827 by a combined British, French and Russian fleet under the command of the British admiral Sir Edward Codrington. This victory was symbolic of the new maritime powers in the Mediterranean: France, Russia and, above all, Britain. The ascendancy of the Royal Navy in the sea was really a logical extension for a new world-wide empire whose power largely rested on its ability to control the seas. As early as 1704, the British had captured the strategically vital port of Gibraltar from their long-standing enemy Spain, enabling the British navy to dominate the entrance to the Mediterranean.

By the end of the 18th century, the sea had become a setting – but only one of the settings – for a bitter Anglo-French imperial rivalry that came to the fore when Napoleon Bonaparte (born Napoleone di Buonaparte in 1769 in Corsica, a year after France had bought the island from Genoa) invaded Egypt in 1798. Not since the days of the crusades had the French – at that time the Franks – sent troops to Egypt, and this act was bound to provoke not just the nominal rulers of Egypt, the Ottoman Empire, but the British too.

Notwithstanding Napoleon's successes on land, the decisive conflict took place at sea. A force led by the British admiral Horatio Nelson annihilated a French fleet at Aboukir Bay on 1 August 1798 – a victory that won the naval hero the title Baron Nelson of the Nile and, more significantly, isolated the French forces in Egypt, where – Napoleon having returned to France – they eventually surrendered in 1801. From now on, Britain would be the dominant military force in the

THE BATTLE FOR MALTA

The tiny island of Malta has long been regarded as an important strategic location for anyone wishing to control the passage of ships between the eastern and western Mediterranean. A succession of powerful peoples have occupied the island: the Phoenicians from about 800 BC, followed by Greeks, Carthaginians, Romans, Normans and Arabs. In 1798 the French under Napoleon briefly governed it before Britain took control in 1800; while in the Second World War the island withstood attack from both German and Italian forces. One of the most dramatic incidents in Maltese history came in the 16th century, when the island was home to the military-religious order of the Knights of St John, who became known as the Knights of Malta. In 1565, the Ottoman Turks launched a huge attack, deploying a force of around 30,000 men. By contrast, the knights, who had earlier been driven from Rhodes by the Turks, could muster just 10,000. The stakes were high; even the English queen Elizabeth I claimed the very future of Christendom might be at peril if the knights were defeated. After five months of brutal conflict, reinforcements arrived and the Turks gave up the siege.

Mediterranean, establishing bases on Malta and Cyprus as well as at Gibraltar. The sea had meanwhile become part of a much larger global struggle between the western powers, as France and, to a lesser extent, Spain began to exert their influence in North Africa. As early as 1830 France invaded Algeria, beginning a long and complex association with that country that would not formally end until the second half of the 20th century.

Another key event in the history of the Mediterranean came in 1869 with the opening of the Suez Canal. It began as a French enterprise with Egyptian backing, but the following decade the British bought a controlling interest in it from the Egyptian Khedive Ismail – the viceroy of the Ottomans. The canal was an important development for the sea, encouraging shipping to pass through the Mediterranean en route to the east. Yet at the same time it underlined how the role of this great sea, once the seat of empires, had changed. One no longer had to sail past Gibraltar just to get into, or out of, the Mediterranean. Its political and military importance remained, but now just as one scene on a larger stage of world events.

The long history of the Mediterranean has cast its shadow over events in the 20th and 21st centuries. The continuing issue of Palestine, the momentous Suez Crisis of 1956, the state of relations between the Christian west and Islam, the vexed question of whether Turkey has a place in the European Union: all have their roots in the past. Since the end of the Roman heyday, no one culture or nation has been able to control the Mediterranean politically, even if at times the Ottoman Empire and the British Navy came close. In place of such dominance, there is a diversity of nations and societies, each now able to celebrate its own particular role in the ever-changing history of the Mediterranean. From Lebanon to Spain, and from Italy to Tunisia, the region's many countries and different peoples have all contributed strands to the fascinating and complex story of this sea and the peoples who have lived on and around it. And, as we continue to learn more from archaeology about the many mysteries of the past, we can be sure that that story will get even more colourful and intricate in the years ahead.

ABOVE: The battle of Aboukir Bay, better known as the battle of the Nile, was a decisive moment in the maritime history of the Mediterranean, and established the British Navy as the dominant naval force on the sea until well into the 20th century. Painting, by Louis Francois Lejeune (1775–1848). Versailles, Château et Trianons.

CHAPTER 3
ARTS AND SOCIETY

The artistic and intellectual influence of the ancient world on the modern has been immense. Much modern western art, from the Renaissance onwards, has been inspired by classical themes developed in the Mediterranean. Moreover, the entire tradition of contemporary philosophy is built firmly on the foundations laid down two and a half millennia ago in Athens and elsewhere in Greece. Modern languages, writing and even laws also have their roots in the extraordinarily fertile world of Mediterranean antiquity.

RIGHT: The impact of the ancient world of the Mediterranean on modern art and culture has been profound. In the visual arts, much of the inspiration of the great artists of the Renaissance and afterwards came from classical themes, as here in this riotous painting of the mythical story of how the god of wine Bacchus falls in love with his future bride Ariadne, who has been abandoned by her lover Theseus. Titian, c.1487/90–1576. 'Bacchus and Ariadne', 1522/23. Oil on canvas, London, National Gallery.

Attempts by humans to represent the world around them in paintings, drawings and sculptures stretch back into the mists of time. The best-known ancient examples of such efforts are found in the cave art of Mediterranean countries such as Spain, France, Italy and parts of the Balkans. Here is the beginning of art as we know it.

Painting and sculpture

The Earliest Paintings

The oldest date from as far back as 30,000–35,000 years ago, to what is called by archaeologists the Aurignacian period – named after a rock shelter found at Aurignac in the French Pyrenees. Many of the most striking examples, however, date from the later Magdalenian period (c. 17,000–10,000 BC), which is named after another rock shelter found at La Madeleine in France's Dordogne region. The images were created in various ways, ranging from the use of fingers to make simple impressions in clay walls to engravings on rock made with flints, or sometimes stone tools, to elaborate paintings on cave walls.

The main colours available to these early painters were red (from ochre), black, white, yellow and brown, though they also mixed up the pigments in containers. In at least one example a painter used a human skull as a container. The paint was bound with animal fats and applied with rudimentary brushes.

In many cases the results are stunning. In particular, the depiction of animals is impressive even for a modern audience that has easy access to all of the world's best art via books, television or websites. For example, at Lascaux in the Dordogne the so-called Chamber of Bulls contains a marvellous series of paintings, the oldest of which is thought to date from around 17,000 years ago. They include the Great Bull, which measures more than 5 metres (16 feet) long and whose features are beautifully illustrated. Elsewhere in these caves, which were discovered by chance by a group of schoolchildren in 1940, there are mysterious paintings of red cows and horses, as well as abstract shapes. Some of the images are so high they must have been painted using scaffolding.

Another astounding example of cave art is at Altamira in northern Spain. In 1879 archaeologist Don Marcelino de Sautuola and his five-year-old daughter Maria were

BELOW: The cave art of prehistoric society in the Mediterranean, such as this painting from Lascaux in France from around 17,000 years ago, continues to amaze experts; to this day, no one is quite sure what the exact purpose of the paintings was.

exploring the caves when the girl looked up and noticed the extraordinary images on the ceiling; it was the first time modern humans had seen this prehistoric art. Indeed, for a number of years no one could really believe that such supposedly primitive peoples could have produced such wonderful art, and the images were widely assumed to be a hoax or practical joke until experts finally authenticated them.

Unfortunately, no one knows the purpose of these magnificent paintings. It has been variously suggested that they were designed to teach hunting, or that they formed part of a religious ritual and that the caves were regarded as sacred sanctuaries.

ABOVE: Though Egyptian art is fascinating and gives us a real glimpse into the culture of Ancient Egypt, one of its most remarkable features is how little its stylized format changed over the centuries.

Egyptian and Minoan Art

The gap between the end of Magdalenian art, *c.* 10,000 BC, and the next well-known genre of Mediterranean art is a long one: some 7,000 years stretch between the cave paintings and the work of Egyptian artists.

One of the most remarkable features of Egyptian art is how little it changed over thousands of years. The standard style for their paintings is what is called 'frontalism': the heads of the characters are in profile, as are the arms and legs, yet the eyes, shoulders and rest of the body are shown front on, giving the distinctive and stylized angles of Egyptian paintings. Another feature was that pharaohs and gods were painted larger than people considered less important.

The Egyptian style of sculpture also adhered to a strict format: again the images face to the front, while a figure's face is often slightly upturned. Among the many figures sculpted by Egyptians were animals important to their religious beliefs, including cats. One of the best-known images of Egypt is, of course, that of the sphinx. Many of these were sculpted, though the one most widely known today is the huge Great Sphinx of Giza; the exact purpose of these images is unknown.

The painting style of the Minoans, examples of which survive on palace walls in Crete in the form of frescoes, shares some similarities with that of Egypt. Here, too, we find the heavily stylized depiction of the human body, notably in the shoulders and eyes. Yet there is a greater fluidity to the Cretan human images. They portray movement better, and it is perhaps fair to say that there is an energy and dynamism in their art that one does not readily associate with the Egyptians.

When one thinks about Minoan art, the form that usually takes precedence is that society's wonderful pottery. The famed Kamares ware is well-known for its eggshell-thin sides, decorated with fine images on a black background. These pieces were highly prized, not just in Crete but in the Levant and Egypt, to where they were exported. One important detail of Minoan art is shown in the Harvest Rython, a stone ornament dating from between 1650 and 1450 BC, which depicts human faces displaying emotion. While this may seem unremarkable to us now, this is the first known instance in ancient art in which human emotion is shown. The slightly later Mycenaean culture also produced some interesting sculpture, though their pottery was generally inferior to that made by the Minoans.

The Hittites, whose society flourished at about the same time as the Mycenaeans, drew on a number of different influences in their art, including Mesopotamian and local Anatolian culture. As noted in Chapter Two, the Hittites were almost lost to history, but their rediscovery in the 19th century was accompanied by an appreciation of their artistic talent, notably in their carving and metal-work. Especially impressive is a series of scenes from Hittite mythology carved in rock near the empire's capital of Hattusa (now Bogazköy in modern-day Turkey), which shows lions, sphinxes, gods and goddesses.

Greek and Roman Art

Greek art was to have a huge influence on art in the modern world, thanks partly to the fact that artists in the Renaissance drew such inspiration from classical Greece.

Greek sculpture evolved considerably over the hundreds of years between the start of the classical period in the 5th century BC and the 2nd century BC, by which time Roman dominance was established. Early images were frontal and stylized, recalling Egyptian art. Yet at the high point of classical Greece – the time of Pericles (c. 495–429 BC), the rise of democracy and the defeat of the Persians – sculpture was transformed into something far more confident, dynamic and idealized. The representation of human anatomy is far more accurate. Even figures at rest – for example, the wonderful *Discobolos* or *Discus Thrower* by Myron, captured at the moment just before a throw – imply movement even if they do not show it. Indeed, Myron's bronze statue of a heifer was considered sufficiently lifelike to be mistaken for a real animal. Among other famous Greek sculptors of this period were Polyclitus, who created a statue of the goddess Hera at Argos and who wrote about how to create symmetry and the ideal mathematical proportions of the human body in his book *Canon*.

BELOW: This wonderful figure of a discus thrower Discobolos *by Myron (Greek sculptor, 5th century BC) is a good example of classical sculpture in which a sense of movement and dynamism is expertly captured. Marble statue, Roman copy after a bronze statue by Myron. Rome, Vatican Museums.*

Later Hellenistic Greek sculpture – from the period after Alexander the Great (356–323 BC) – is generally considered to be less idealistic, more sentimental and inferior to that of the classical period. Nonetheless, this period saw the creation of one of the most famous works of art in history, *Aphrodite of Melos*, better known as the *Venus de Milo*. The sculpture that now stands in the Louvre in Paris is not, however, the original Greek work but is thought to be a Roman copy. Originally the sculpture had arms which held a shield and a mirror, the latter enabling the goddess of love and beauty to admire herself.

Though there was a school of painting in Athens from the 5th century BC, the only Greek painting that has survived is found on pottery. Most of this is realistic in nature and depicts the myths, legends and life of the Greeks.

Arguably, the chief importance of Roman art is as a transmitter of Greek art. The *Venus de Milo* is just one of many Greek works that are known to us only through Roman versions. Other examples include the marble sculpture of the Trojan priest Laocoön and his two sons, who were attacked and killed by giant snakes, and the sculpture of Apollo Belvedere. As in many areas of culture, the Romans were impressed by most of the Greeks' artistic achievements and, by incorporating them (albeit with adaptations) into their own practice, helped make them available to later generations.

Yet the Romans had their own style, too. Initially this was heavily influenced by the Etruscans, but came to be characterized by a distinctively Roman approach – that of realism. As one might expect from a society that had an intensely practical outlook on life, the Romans liked to see portraits and busts of individuals, which were among their favourite art forms, rendered in realistic mode. Images of Julius Caesar do not try to depict him as a graceful youth but portray him as a powerful, battle-hardened man who has learnt from experience. Unlike the Greeks, who favoured idealized images of famous people, the Romans generally liked to see their leaders as they really were.

This is not to say that Roman art could not be propagandist. In the Augustan age, for example, the great Altar of Augustan Peace (*ara pacis augustae*) juxtaposes a real event – Augustus' homecoming after a successful visit to the provinces – with allegory and scenes from Roman legends, such as the founding of Rome. Another magnificent piece of art with propaganda as its aim was Trajan's Column, which commemorated the emperor's military victories in Dacia, now Romania.

Much of what we know about Roman art has come to us through the tragedy of Pompeii, when the eruption of Mount Vesuvius in AD 79 buried not only the town's citizens but also its buildings and their contents, leaving all well preserved.

In time, and as the Roman Empire in both east and west came under threat, the style of art moved away from the naturalistic towards stylization, as shown for example in a bust of the eastern Emperor Theodosius II from the 5th century AD, which is now in the Louvre, Paris. The survival of the eastern empire at Constantinople, the old Greek colony of Byzantium, later led to the development of a separate school of art known as

ABOVE: The intricate work of the 30-metre high Trajan's Column in Rome, shown here, depicts the Dacians retreating from the battlefield with their eyes turned back, and the successful military exploits of the Emperor Trajan (AD 53–117) in Dacia, now Romania. Art often had a propaganda role in ancient times, where a leader's image was every bit as important as it is today. Rome, Museo della Civilta Romana.

Byzantine. One of the key forms of Byzantine art was the mosaic, which reached a peak in the late 11th and 12th centuries, when Byzantine artists were in great demand among Norman kings and in the Venetian Republic. Indeed, through Venice, Byzantine art had an influence on Italian art more widely.

Islam, too, developed its own tradition of art. One of the great legacies of the Islamic presence in the Mediterranean has been its architecture, though other art forms have been important too. As the religion forbids representation of natural images, Islamic artists developed a tradition of beautiful abstract decoration known as arabesque. This can take either geometric or what is called 'flowing' form. Traditionally, the most important form of Islamic art is calligraphy; texts from the Qur'an are often to be found beautifully inscribed on ceramics and buildings.

Renaissance Art

Nowhere did the culture of the ancient world make a greater impact than in Renaissance art. The world of ancient Greece especially was the inspiration for much of the unparalleled beauty created by artists in Europe and especially Italy from around the 14th century AD. Here the world of Christian art and the classical world were fused. Among the best-known works are Raphael's frescoes in the Stanza della Segnatura in the Vatican in Rome, one of which, known as *The School of Athens*, represents Greek philosophers such as Plato and Aristotle. The great Michelangelo's early sculpture *Sleeping Cupid*, meanwhile, was so imbued with classical feeling – as well as being artificially aged – that it was sold as a work of antiquity. The remarkable engraving *Battle of the Nudes* by the Florentine Antonio Pollaiuolo is another work directly influenced by classical depictions

BELOW: The influence of classical themes on Western art over the centuries is well illustrated in the wonderful Sleeping Venus, *which was painted by the talented young artist Giorgione in around 1510, and completed by Titian after Giorgione's death. Dresden, Gemaeldegalerie, Alte Meister.*

of the human body. The widespread use of nude figures in classical sculpture helped encourage Renaissance artists to depict the human form in nude and idealized form. Further examples of how the classical world influenced Renaissance artists can be seen in the great Titian's *Bacchus and Ariadne* and in the wonderful *Resting Venus* by Giorgione. The classical themes of the ancient world have continued to inspire great art to this day.

Architecture

Bronze Age Architecture: The Pyramids

Some of the most instantly recognizable architecture in the world is also some of the earliest – the pyramids of Egypt. The first of these was built for King Djoser at Saqqara, the burial place of the ancient Egyptian capital Memphis, around 2700 BC. It is a step pyramid, rather than the more familiar smooth–sided design, and was designed by an architect called Imhotep, who rejoiced in an array of wonderful titles. These included 'Imhotep the Builder, the Sculptor, the Maker of Stone Vessels', 'Treasurer of the King of Lower Egypt', 'First One Under the King' and even 'Chief Carpenter'. Imhotep was certainly an extraordinary figure; as well as being responsible for the world's first pyramid, he was also a priest, a scholar, an astrologer and an expert on medicine. His wide range of abilities and learning led, much later in Egypt's history, to his being elevated to the status of a god, and the rather more dubious honour of being portrayed in Hollywood movies as a bad guy – for example, in the 1999 film *The Mummy* starring Brendan Fraser and Rachel Weisz.

The most famous of Egypt's 97 known pyramids is the Great Pyramid at Giza, near Cairo, also called the Pyramid of Khufu (Cheops to the Greeks), which was built around 2560 BC. The Great Pyramid, built as Khufu's tomb, was originally 145.75 metres (478 feet) high, though as a result of erosion its current height is 138.75 metres (455 feet), and consists of around two million stones; for four millennia it was the tallest man–made

ABOVE The first-known pyramid built in Egypt was at Saqqara and was a step pyramid rather than the more familiar straight-edged form. It was designed in around 2700 BC by the great architect, priest and medical expert Imhotep.

ABOVE: The great Parthenon in Athens remains one of the architectural treasures of the ancient world and its beautiful proportions still entrance visitors. It was completed in 432 BC and was dedicated to the goddess Athena, though much later it became a church and then a mosque.

structure anywhere. The building that finally overtook the pyramid in the 14th century AD was Lincoln Cathedral in England, whose spire reached 160 metres (525 feet). The only surviving monument of the Seven Wonders of the Ancient World, the Great Pyramid was built over a period of 20 years with astonishing precision – the base was made level to within 2.1 centimetres, less than an inch.

As with all pyramids, there has been much speculation about the Great Pyramid's 'true' purpose. The most likely explanation remains the most obvious and simplest – that it was the final resting place for an immensely powerful ruler with a strong belief in the afterlife.

Though the Egyptian pyramids are not the oldest large-scale stone buildings in the Mediterranean – that distinction belongs to the mysterious temples of Malta, mentioned earlier – they remain among the most impressive. Yet other Bronze Age societies created fine buildings too. The Hittites, for example, developed an impressive porticoed entrance hall, incorporating a stairway with pillars on either side, while the Minoans built large palaces with intricate passages and staircases.

Greek Architecture: the 'Three Orders' and the Parthenon

Notwithstanding the awe-inspiring magnificence of the pyramids and the mystery of the Maltese temples, undoubtedly the most influential architecture in the ancient world was that of Greece and Rome.

It is thought that the early buildings of Greece were made of wood, using posts and lintels. Naturally, any such wooden buildings have long since vanished. But plentiful local supplies meant that many later buildings were constructed from the far more durable and elegant marble.

Right from the start, a variety of architectural styles were used. There are three main styles or 'orders' of Greek architecture: Doric, Ionic and Corinthian. The Doric order is named after the Dorians, the Greek–speaking farmers and soldiers who were dominant in the west and south of Greece (the notoriously tough Spartans were Dorians). As one might expect of such people, their style of building was bold, with limited ornamentation. Columns – a crucial feature of Greek building – in the Doric style were undecorated at the top and bottom.

The Ionic style takes its name from the style of the people of Ionian Greece, who lived in Attica, the eastern Aegean and Asia Minor, and who are generally regarded as being more highly cultured than the Dorians. This style is more ornamental and decorative, and Ionic columns were taller than their Doric counterparts. The bases of the columns were moulded, and the top was usually decorated, albeit with a fairly simple scroll design

The third order is the Corinthian, which takes its name from the city of Corinth, an early rival to Athens as the cultural capital of Greece. Corinthian columns were the most decorative of all, with the top or 'capital' of the shaft usually bearing a leaf motif. Its greater use of ornament made the Corinthian column very popular with the Romans.

A good if small example of a classical Ionic building is the Temple of Athena Nike ('Athena bringer of victory') on the Acropolis in Athens. It was completed around 424 BC and housed a wooden statue of the goddess Athena. An intriguing example of Corinthian style is the Tower of the Winds in Athens, which was built around 50 BC. Inside were placed a sundial, a water clock and a bronze weathervane in the form of the sea god Triton, who pointed the direction of the wind with a wand.

By far the most famous Doric-style construction – indeed, possibly the best-known building in the world – is the Parthenon in Athens.

This astonishing construction, dedicated to the patron goddess of Athens, Athena Parthenos, was completed in 432 BC and is regarded by many as the world's most beautifully proportioned building. Its creation was initiated by the great Athenian Pericles and overseen by the sculptor Pheidias. It was built on the Acropolis, the 'sacred rock' of Athens and the most important

ABOVE: The Pantheon in Rome has a stunning dome at the top with a small opening or oculus, which allows sunlight to flood the space below. The opening is also part of the engineering design that strengthens the structure.

part of the city. In later years, the Parthenon kept its religious purpose by being used first as a Christian church – when some of the 'pagan' images were defaced – and then as a mosque in the 15th century, when the Ottoman Empire controlled Greece. In 1687, when it was being used more prosaically by the Turks as a gunpowder store during a siege by Venetian forces, it caught fire during a bombardment; the resulting explosion badly damaged the building.

Some of the most famous parts of the building – a number of sculptures and a part of the magnificent frieze that once adorned it – were removed from the site in the early 19th century by a British ambassador and aristocrat, Thomas Bruce, seventh Earl of Elgin, and eventually placed in the British Museum. These Parthenon Marbles – better known as the Elgin Marbles – have since been the cause of a long-running dispute between the Greek and British governments. Part of the frieze, whose full significance is still unclear, depicts the Procession of the Panathenaea, the ancient and most formal religious festival of Athens, while another shows the gods seated as if meeting in council.

Roman Architecture: the Pantheon

If the Greeks excelled in architecture, they were matched, arguably even surpassed, by the Romans.

The Romans did not invent the architectural use of the arch – they seem to have got that idea from the Etruscans – but they did develop its use in conjunction with Greek practice to produce a whole new form of architecture. The combined use of vaults, domes and arches meant that the Romans could create huge buildings with large interior spaces. This new approach to architecture, coupled with their invention of concrete (see Chapter Four) led to an exciting new era of building in the ancient world. It can be seen in many famous buildings of the Roman period, including the Triumphal Arch of Constantine and the Colosseum in Rome, as well as in many structures all over the vast Roman Empire. Another hallmark of Roman building was lavish ornamentation.

One of the undoubted glories of Roman architecture is the Pantheon in Rome itself, a striking structure with an extraordinary central dome. The dome is in the form of a perfect hemisphere, 43.3 metres (142 feet) in diameter. At the top is the oculus, a circular hole that epitomizes the ingenious nature of the building. The light provided through the oculus adds colour, depth and movement to the interior of the building, and so enhances its beauty. But the hole is also intensely practical, too. The dome was cast in one single piece of concrete and designed in such a way that it gets lighter in weight the higher it rises. At the very top, the existence of the hole removes the need for a heavy section of concrete weighing down the middle of the dome. Instead, the gap acts as a form of compression ring. Thus the feature that perfects the building's great style also enhances its structural strength.

There was an earlier Pantheon – the name means 'a temple to all the gods' – on the site, but that was destroyed. The replacement was completely rebuilt under the expert eye of the Emperor Hadrian in the 2nd century AD. Hadrian, who gave his name to the defensive wall across the north of England, was a noted patron of the arts and architecture.

The fact that the Pantheon has survived so long is partly a testament to the ingenuity of the design, the quality of the engineering and the strength of the materials. It is also partly attributable to the fact that its 'pagan' origins were overlaid with Christianity when that faith became the dominant religion of Rome. At the start of the 7th century AD, the Byzantine emperor Phocas the Tyrant gave the former temple to Pope Boniface IV and the Pantheon became a Christian church dedicated to Mary and all the Christian martyrs.

Its marvellous original form survived, however, and it was this design that prompted the great Michelangelo to note that the building was of 'angelic and not human design'. Another great painter, Raphael, was buried in the Pantheon in 1520.

Later Influences: Neoclassicism, Byzantium and Islam

The classical styles of Greece and Rome have had a significant influence on architecture not just in the Mediterranean but across the whole world. In northern Europe, for example, an 18th–century reaction against what some considered to be the excesses of

LEFT: A good example of how classical architecture has influenced more modern building, through what is known as neoclassicism, is shown in the familiar form of the White House in Washington, the official residence and office of American presidents.

POMPEII AS AN INSPIRATION FOR ARTISTS

The unearthing of the ruins of Pompeii, buried since AD 79 by volcanic debris, inspired artists and writers alike. The buildings of neoclassical architect Robert Adam, for example, were influenced by the style of buildings and decoration found in the Roman town. Also in the 18th century, the British potter Josiah Wedgwood used dancing figures modelled on bas-reliefs found at Pompeii to decorate his pottery. In his book *Pictures from Italy*, Charles Dickens described the 'strange and melancholy sensation' of standing in the ruins of Pompeii and looking up at Mount Vesuvius, and of 'seeing the Destroyed and the Destroyer making this quiet picture in the sun'. Other writers who visited the site include Mark Twain, Johann Goethe and Henry James; the British author Edward Bulwer-Lytton wrote a novel *The Last Days of Pompeii*, which became popular in the 19th century. In the 1970s, the oil billionaire J. Paul Getty had a replica of the Villa dei Papiri (near Herculaneum) built in Malibu, California to house his collection of classical art.

baroque and rococo styles heralded a return to the simpler, straighter lines of the ancient world, a style known as neoclassicism. This movement was aided by interest in discoveries at Herculaneum and Pompeii (see box). An excellent example of this kind of architecture can be found at Stourhead House in Wiltshire, England, one of the first neoclassical or 'Palladian' houses to be built in the country. Perhaps the most famous of all neoclassical buildings is the White House in Washington DC, office and residence of the US president.

Another descendant of Roman architecture was the style of building adopted by the Byzantine Empire, though it evolved into a distinct and different eastern form. An early example is the 5th-century basilica of St John of the Studion, the oldest surviving church in Constantinople and now a mosque (a basilica was originally a Greek or Roman secular building of a kind later adapted for use as a religious building).

The renowned St Mark's Basilica in Venice is a powerful example of Byzantine architecture in a city that spent much of its history involved in the affairs of Byzantium. In Constantinople itself, the chief feature of the famous Hagia Sophia basilica – built at the command of the Emperor Justinian in the 6th century AD – is its main dome. Again, this building, whose name means 'holy wisdom', was later converted into a mosque and is now a museum.

Mosques have been at the forefront of an Islamic architectural movement that has left its mark throughout the Mediterranean. Beautiful domes, arches and courtyards, and intricate mosaic patterns are the hallmarks of this movement. The Great Mosque of Córdoba in Moorish Spain, begun in the 8th century AD, was rightly regarded as one of the wonders of Mediterranean architecture, and reflected Córdoba's status at that time as one of the wealthiest and most sophisticated cities in the region. Among its most striking features are the distinctive striped arches that run through the building. In the 13th century, after the city was reconquered by the king of Castile, Ferdinand III, the mosque was consecrated as a cathedral, and in the 16th century a gothic chapel was built inside the structure of the mosque.

Also in the 16th century, the greatest of the Ottoman architects, Mimar Koca Sinan (see box opposite), set about creating numerous buildings and mosques, the greatest of which was probably the Selimiye Mosque in Edirne, Turkey, a breathtaking building full of light and intricate patterns. To give his mosques interiors that were as light and open as possible, Sinan used buttresses on the outside of, rather than within, the building.

Back in Moorish Spain stands the magnificent Alhambra Palace of Granada. No one knows who designed this spectacular and profoundly moving building, completed in the

THE ARCHITECT SINAN

Mimar Koca Sinan (AD 1489–1588), the greatest architect of the Ottoman Empire, was born in Anatolia to Christian parents. As a child he joined the Janissary Corps – where he was taught, among other skills, building and carpentry. At first Sinan's talents were put to work in a military context, building bridges and ships to assist in the expanding empire's aggressive campaigns. Eventually his skills and ability to work well under pressure were recognized and he was appointed Chief Architect to the Sultan. It is said that in his long career Sinan was responsible for designing or restoring some 400 buildings. He became wealthy and was admired by the great Suleiman the Magnificent. Suleiman was regarded within his empire as the second Solomon, and was thus expected to possess buildings as impressive as those of the biblical king who built the great Temple in Jerusalem. Sinan designed many of his mosques as part of larger complexes that included schools, hospitals, guest rooms and baths. In the splendour of the Selimiye Mosque at Edirne, Sinan felt he had at last surpassed the achievement of Hagia Sophia in Istanbul, a building that had always inspired him.

ABOVE: The fabulous mosque in Córdoba in southern Spain was an early mark of Islamic culture in the Iberian peninsula. Over the centuries the Moors enlarged and enhanced La Mezquita into a vast, magnificent house of worship. They creatively used a variety of architectural styles including Persian, Mid Eastern Islamic, Roman and Gothic that together helped define Moorish architecture. One of the most striking design elements of La Mezquita is the double-tiered 'candy stripe' arches supported by sculptured pillars.

14th century, but its serene courtyards, wonderful arches and extraordinarily detailed design enthral visitors to this day, and ensure that this Moorish building remains one of the architectural treasures – indeed, one of the great symbols of civilization – of the Mediterranean.

Language and writing

A key sign of sophisticated civilization is the ability to make records in written form. The use of writing is essential in the communication of rules and laws, and thus helps in the development of government.

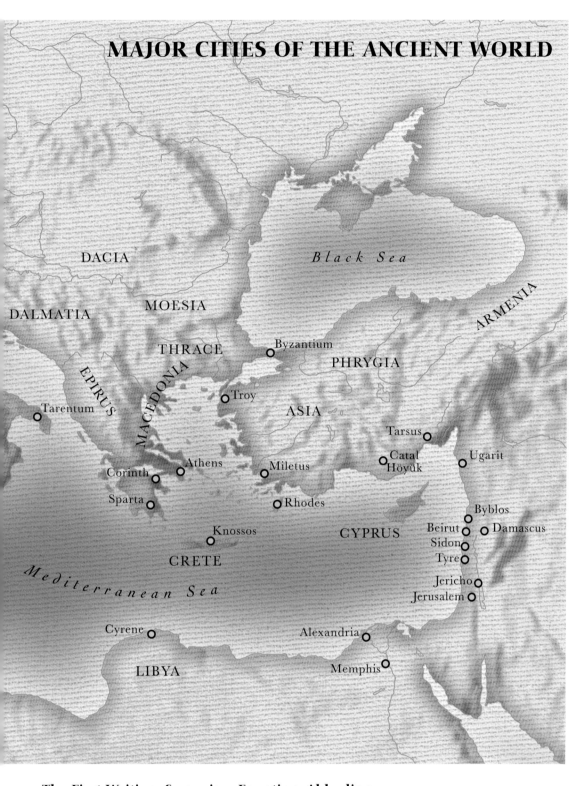

MAJOR CITIES OF THE ANCIENT WORLD

DACIA

Black Sea

MOESIA

ARMENIA

DALMATIA

THRACE

Byzantium

PHRYGIA

EPIRUS

MACEDONIA

Troy

ASIA

Tarentum

Tarsus

Catal
Höyük

Ugarit

Corinth
Athens

Miletus

Sparta

Rhodes

Byblos

Knossos

CYPRUS

Beirut
Damascus

Sidon

CRETE

Tyre

Jericho

Mediterranean Sea

Jerusalem

Cyrene

Alexandria

LIBYA

Memphis

The First Writing: Sumerian, Egyptian, Akkadian

The origin of writing is a complex and controversial issue. We cannot yet be quite sure where writing first began, when, or even for what purpose. One theory is that the use of written symbols grew out of the need for merchants and traders to record and codify their complex transactions – in other words, that writing grew out of accountancy. Another view is that it developed slowly out of the visual arts as images of real objects became more and more abstract and evolved new and different meanings.

Writing probably began in Mesopotamia, where it was developed by the Sumerians in the 4th millennium BC. By around 3100 BC the first hieroglyphics had appeared in

ABOVE: Luxor (Upper Egypt), Amon Temple, Court of Ramses II (New Kingdom, 19th dynasty, built under Ramses II c.1260 BC). Entrance pylon and obelisk seen from the court of Ramses II.

Egypt, and thus the civilization of the Nile was the first in the Mediterranean to evolve writing. The term 'hieroglyphics' comes from the Greek for 'sacred carved writing', because the Greeks who came across this script assumed it was of religious significance. Many of the inscriptions were, and the Egyptians themselves referred to the writing as *mdju netjer* or 'words of the gods'. But hieroglyphics were simply their form of writing and could be used for all kinds of purposes, from prosaic accounts to recording the dramatic deeds of the pharaohs.

The Egyptian language was not, however, written exclusively in hieroglyphics. A later written form of the language was 'hieratic', a simplified form of hieroglyphics that made it quicker to write and was used for business and bureaucratic purposes. Yet another written form evolved out of hieratic and is known as 'demotic', a term meaning 'popular script'. By the time of the Ptolemaic dynasty in the 4th century BC, demotic was the everyday script in use. There was also a later written version of the Egyptian language known as 'coptic', though this was based on the Greek alphabet with some characters

added from demotic. By the 13th century AD, the ancient Egyptian (or coptic) language had been replaced in Egypt by Arabic; however, it still survives in the rituals of Coptic Christians, who today make up about 5 per cent of the Egyptian population.

The Sumerians had meanwhile developed the cuneiform script, their equivalent to hieroglyphics, to record their language. This format was also adopted by other peoples, notably in the influential Akkadian language. The Akkadians of Mesopotamia came to prominence some time in the 3rd millennium BC; their great king and founder of the city of Akkad was Sargon I. Akkadian is a Semitic language that lived on for centuries to become the first true international language of its time, and was for hundreds of years the language of diplomacy in the Near East – rather as, much later, French became for a time the language of diplomacy in Europe. (Other examples of Semitic languages include Arabic, Hebrew, Aramaic and Syriac.) Official communication between dignitaries from different cultures, for example between a Hittite king and a lesser ruler, might be written in Akkadian.

ABOVE: Detail of a wall covered in hieroglyphs at the Amon Temple in Luxor (Egypt). The temple was built under Amenophis III c.1400 BC, and enlarged under Ramses II. Other forms of Egyptian writing evolved from this, including what is known as 'hieratic', a simplified version that was easier and quicker to write and was used for business transactions.

The Phoenician Alphabet

Akkadian's role as an international language was later assumed by two tongues of the type that we call Indo-European – a vast group of languages with a distant common origin. These were Latin and, first of all, Greek.

There are signs that the earliest written Greek developed from contact between the Mycenaeans and the Minoans. It is clear from archaeological discoveries that the Minoans had developed a form of writing by the middle of the 2nd millennium BC. This conclusion followed from the discovery of a script called 'Linear A' in a language which is still not fully understood. A similar script was also used to produce writing that we call 'Linear B'. In 1952, a British linguist, Michael Ventris, demonstrated that the language of Linear B was an early form of Greek, the language that would have been spoken by the Mycenae, the people who took over Minoan society on Crete. This suggests that they adapted the Minoans' script for their own language.

Intriguingly, however, it appears that between the peak of the Mycenaean civilization around 1250 BC and the end of the so-called Mediterranean Dark Ages around 900–800 BC, the inhabitants of Greece somehow lost the art of writing. It seems likely that the Greeks, whose ancient language is today virtually synonymous with writing and education, rediscovered this vital art thanks to the Phoenicians, who themselves spoke a Semitic language. This is what the ancient Greeks themselves believed. The historian Herodotus, writing in around 450 BC, noted:

'The Phoenicians… introduced into Greece… a number of accomplishments, of which the most important was writing, an art till then, I think, unknown to the Greeks.'

BELOW: In the 1950s, a British expert discovered that a mysterious writing known simply as Linear B used an early form of Greek, shown here on a writing tablet from Mycenae. It is believed that the Mycenaens, the forebears of the Greeks, may have learnt the script from the Minoans.

The earliest evidence of the Phoenician alphabet and script come from the trading port of Byblos, and it is often claimed that the Phoenicians, who were among the most active traders in the Mediterranean, adapted and developed their alphabet to simplify the recording of their commercial transactions. The Greeks adapted this alphabet of 22 letters, all of them consonants, to their own language, adding vowels, for example alpha (which became our 'a') and iota ('i'). The names were also adapted, though many of them only slightly, from the Phoenician: the Greek names alpha, beta, gamma and delta come from the Phoenician aleph, beth, gimel and daleth. (Aleph was a consonant in the Phoenician alphabet.)

Thanks in part to its adoption by the Greeks, the Phoenician alphabet has had a huge impact on the written languages of the modern Mediterranean. The Romans adapted the Greek alphabet (via the Etruscans) to Latin, which in turn has had a huge impact on the development of many modern western languages, including Spanish, Italian, English and Portuguese. Indeed, Latin remained the official language of Portugal until the late 13th century.

Latin also became the language of the Roman Catholic church and of science. It was, for example, used by the 18th-century Swedish scientist Carl Linnaeus as the language for his classification of the plant kingdom into different categories such as genus and species – the basis for all modern scientific naming of the natural world.

The Phoenician alphabet also influenced the alphabet and writing of two other major Mediterranean languages: Hebrew and Arabic. The latter dominated an area from Spain to Turkey at the height of Islamic influence in the region and is still one of the major Mediterranean languages.

Literature

Greek Narrative and Poetry

It is ironic that while the Phoenicians gave the Greeks their alphabet and probably taught them writing, virtually nothing of Phoenician writing remains, while the Greeks have left us a vast and impressive body of literature. These writings have had a profound effect on subsequent western civilization.

When one considers ancient Greek writing and poetry, the dominant figure is, of course, Homer; and the dominant works are those two epic poems of early Greek literature, the *Iliad* and the *Odyssey*. It must be admitted that we cannot be sure who Homer was, or even indeed that one person wrote both those poems, though most experts assume that he is their author. Both works date in written form from the 8th century BC; both are based on the ancient tradition of oral storytelling, which began to decline with the advent of Greek writing at some point in the 9th or 8th century BC.

As we saw in the previous chapter, the *Iliad* tells part of the story of the siege of Troy, the city on the Dardanelles attacked by the Mycenaeans some time in the 13th century BC. It is a powerful and immensely moving story in which one of the main characters is Achilles, the heroic warrior of the Greeks. Yet for Homer it is not just Achilles' prowess as a warrior that matters, but his reactions to events around him. Much of the story centres on Achilles' rage at the Greek king Agamemnon's taking of a woman as 'spoils of victory' from under Achilles' nose. While the proud Achilles sulks in his tent, his great friend Patroclus is killed in battle by the hero of the Trojans, Hector. Overcome by grief, remorse and anger, Achilles then takes on Hector in single combat and slaughters him, dragging the dead man's body through the dirt for good measure. There follows one of the most moving scenes of the poem, when Hector's father, the great but aged king of Troy, Priam, risks his own life to beg Achilles for the return of his son's body so he can be given the appropriate funeral. A weeping Achilles takes pity and agrees.

Homer used a number of literary devices that were to become standard features of such epic poems in the future and have thus helped to shape the history of literature. One is the epic simile, which appears frequently. A simile is the description of a person or object by likening it to something else, introduced by the word 'as' or 'like'. An epic simile is simply an extended and more elaborate form of this figure. One of the most beautiful in the *Iliad* comes at the start of Book Three, when Homer is describing the imminent clash of the two armies. He writes:

'As when the south wind gathers a mist around a mountain's peaks – no joy to the shepherds, but better than night for the thief, and a man can see only as far as a stone's throw – so a thick swirl of dust arose under their feet as they marched; and they came on at speed over the plain.'

ABOVE: This 2nd-century Roman bust of the great Greek poet Homer is based on imagination, as no one can be sure what he looked like or even exactly when he lived, though the great 8th-century BC poems attributed to him, the Iliad *and the* Odyssey, *continue to inspire succeeding generations. Paris, Musée du Louvre.*

Another key element of Homeric writing is the description of the pantheon of Greek gods and how they become intimately involved in the affairs of men. In the *Iliad* the gods take sides, with Apollo and Aphrodite favouring Troy while Athena, Hera and Poseidon are with the Greeks. Herodotus credits Homer with being one of the two poets who described the Greek gods and 'gave them all their appropriate titles, offices and powers'. The other is the 8th-century BC poet Hesiod who wrote *Theogony*, an account of the origin of the gods and of the world.

Homer's second great work, the *Odyssey*, is an epic sequel to the *Iliad*, describing how one of the Greek heroes, Odysseus, makes his way home to Ithaca after the 10-year siege of Troy; his journey takes him another 10 years, and on the way he has a series of colourful adventures. What holds the story together is Odysseus' love for his loyal wife Penelope and hers for him: the poet uses a device familiar to modern TV and film watchers, a 'split screen', first describing events affecting Odysseus, then moving to those concerned with Penelope, then back again. Its compelling story and timeless themes have led some to describe the *Odyssey* as the greatest story ever told. Certainly the impact of both Homeric poems on subsequent literature has been immeasurable.

Another important and influential Greek poet was Sappho, who lived on the island of Lesbos in the late 7th or early 6th century BC and who provides us with the rare and very welcome voice of a woman from ancient times. Perhaps inevitably, she is best known for the female eroticism of her poetry, which has led to the words 'lesbian' and 'lesbianism', from the island on which she lived, plus the adjective 'sapphic'. The focus on her sexuality has rather overshadowed comment on her poetry, the surviving fragments of which show a delicacy and tenderness coupled with a sense of playfulness that continue to delight readers. Sadly, comparatively little of her work has survived, perhaps in part because during the early Christian era her works were considered neither seemly nor important, and thus were not copied and preserved.

BELOW: The hero of Homer's Odyssey, the Greek warrior Odysseus, with the goddess Athena. Odysseus faced an epic journey to return home after taking part in the siege of Troy, though with the help of Athena he returned safely eventually. Detail of an amphora, found at Vulci. Munich, Staatl. Antikenslg.& Glyptothek.

HESIOD

The Greek poet Hesiod is thought to have lived just after the time of Homer and was probably writing around 700 BC. His two great works were *Theogony* and *Works and Days*. In contrast to the obscurity of Homer, we do know a little of Hesiod's life: he came from Boeotia in Greece, though his father was from Asia Minor, and he may have had a brother called Perses. The importance of Hesiod is that he gives us much of our knowledge of Greek mythology, including the names and origins of the gods, and the Greek view of the origin of humankind. According to Hesiod, time was divided into five Ages. The first was the Golden Age under the time of Kronos, father of Zeus; a time of peace and serenity. This was followed by the Silver Age of Zeus, who usurped his father. Then came the Bronze Age (a time of war), the Heroic Age (the time of the Trojan War), and finally the corrupt times in which Hesiod lived, the Iron Age. This 'myth of the ages' has had a profound impact on western thought, notably in the idea that there was at one time a Golden Age to which we look back with longing and regret. A similar theme is found in the story of the Garden of Eden.

Greek Drama

If the Greeks, through Homer, can be said to have invented the epic poem, they can also be said to have invented drama. The figures most strongly associated with the development of Greek drama are Aeschylus (525–456 BC), Sophocles (496–406 BC) and Euripides (c.485–406 BC), the so-called three great tragedians. Drama existed in Greece before these three, but earlier works were performed by a single actor with a chorus, a group of people who sang and also entered into dialogue with the actor, setting the mood for the performance. The innovation of Aeschylus was to add a second actor, and this extra relationship inevitably increased the dynamism of the work. Aeschylus, who was fêted in his time by fellow citizens, took a full part in the dramatic real-life events of Athens of his day – fighting against the Persians at Marathon in 490 BC and 10 years later at Salamis, taking part in the victory that helped to end the Persian threat to the Greek mainland. Out of the 90 or so plays he wrote, one that has survived is called *The Persians* and deals with those decisive events at Salamis. His masterpiece, however, was his only surviving trilogy, *The Oresteia*, a powerful work which explores the enduring themes of suffering and the meaning of justice.

Sophocles, a younger contemporary, went one step further than Aeschylus by adding a third actor to his plays, an innovation the older dramatist himself later adopted. Another of Sophocles' contributions to the genre was his great emphasis on making sure the scenery was better painted and arranged to enhance the theatrical effect.

Drama in Athens was intensely competitive, and the plays, which were performed at festivals, were judged by a panel of 10, with awards going to the best tragedy and the best comedy. There was great rivalry between the young Sophocles and the established Aeschylus, and the older man was said to have been less than happy when, in 468 BC, the precociously talented Sophocles beat him to the prize with his first production. On his own admission, Sophocles led a rather dissolute life in his youth. 'I thank old age for delivering me from the tyranny of my appetites', he is reported to have

said later. He wrote at least 120 plays, possibly more, and won many first prizes, though only seven tragedies survive. These are *Antigone, Electra, Ajax, Women of Trachis, Philoctetes, Oedipus at Colonus* and *Oedipus the King*. This last play is Sophocles' best-known work and is one of the most famous and influential dramas in history. The chief character of the play, Oedipus, discovers that, thanks to cruel twists of fate, he has unwittingly not only killed his own father but also married his own mother. The themes of the play include the role of fate but also human pride, and it is rightly considered one of the most powerful works in the canon of world drama.

The last of the three great tragedians is Euripides, who died within a few months of Sophocles in 406, and among whose surviving works are *Alcestis, Andromache* and *Medea*. A less overtly popular dramatist in his lifetime – though his genius was nonetheless appreciated – Euripides is now regarded by many scholars as the most influential of the three great writers in the development of the dramatic form. He introduced more realism to the stage and the role of the chorus was further limited; his plays often dealt with social issues rather than the endless machinations of the gods, putting the 'common man' centre stage. Euripides spent his last years in self-imposed exile for reasons that remain obscure, and his death had more than a touch of tragedy about it. A guest of the Macedonian king Archelaus, the dramatist was supposedly torn to pieces by the king's pack of hounds.

Greece had its great comic playwrights too. The works of Aristophanes (c. 445–380 BC) apply a biting satire to many of the great issues facing Athens at the time of the writer's life, including the seemingly endless Great Peloponnesian War and the weakening of Athenian democracy. Aristophanes also poked fun at eminent Greek individuals, including the great philosopher Socrates and his fellow writer Euripides. His 11 surviving works include *The Acharnians, The Wasps, The Frogs* and *Lysistrata*; in the last of these the women of Athens, tired of war and the loss of their sons, refuse sex to their husbands until Athens makes peace with her rival Sparta.

Roman literary genius

Although Roman drama may not have the same high reputation as its Greek counterpart, Rome nevertheless produced many outstanding writers, including the early poet Ennius (239–169 BC) and the great playwright Plautus (c. 250–184 BC), who was immensely popular in his own time and whose works reveal a writer of comic genius. His two plays about twins and the confusion they can cause, *Menaechmi* and *Amphitruo*, helped shape Shakespeare's *The Comedy of Errors*.

Two later Roman poets, Horace (65–8 BC) and Ovid (43 BC–AD 17) have been central to the story of modern western literature. Horace came to prominence during the long and peaceful reign of the first Roman emperor, Augustus, and his work is often associated with that regime, which he certainly celebrated in his work. But Horace was far more than simply a court poet, and his clever satire and, particularly, his beautiful poetic *Odes* mark him out as one of the most accomplished writers of the ancient world.

The work of Ovid is still widely read and highly regarded. A complex, self-absorbed and ironic character, Ovid explored themes including love, mythology and exile – of

ABOVE: One of the most influential of the great Greek tragedians was Euripides, whose many plays dealt with the more everyday issues faced by ordinary people rather than being concerned mainly with the actions of the gods and lofty themes. Sculpture, Roman copy, 2nd century BC after a Greek original from the 5th century BC. Copenhagen, Ny Carlsberg Glyptothek.

PREVIOUS PAGES: The oracle of Delphi, in the temple of Apollo on the slopes of Mount Parnassus in Greece, attracted people from all over the Mediterranean world who came to ask for guidance about the future.

which he had personal experience after he was banished by Augustus from Rome in 8 BC, eventually dying at Tomi on the Black Sea (a place he professed to hate but about which he, frustratingly, tells us very little). His great works include *Fasti* and *Metamorphoses*. The simple but captivating story of Pygmalion appears in the latter; the sculptor Pygmalion, a misogynist, makes a statue of a beautiful girl and then prays to Venus that he might have a wife just like her. The goddess takes him at his word and brings the statue to life. This was the story that inspired George Bernard Shaw's play *Pygmalion*, which in turn was the basis for the popular musical and film *My Fair Lady*.

The greatest Roman poet, however is Publius Vergilius Maro (70–19 BC), better known to us as Virgil and perhaps the most influential writer of the ancient world. (His main rival for this accolade is Homer.) Virgil's great achievement was the *Aeneid*, an epic poem on the scale and in the style of Homer's two great works, and rivalling them in popularity and influence.

The story starts with the sacking of Troy and follows the exploits of the young Aeneas, a cousin of the Trojan Priam. Aeneas escapes the destruction and sets out with a band of compatriots to find a new land in which they can start a new society. Along the way Aeneas meets and falls in love with the Carthaginian queen, Dido. When Aeneas is reminded of his destiny – to found Rome – he leaves, and a grief-stricken Dido kills herself, with the sword given to her by Aeneas, atop a huge funeral pyre she has had built. (This episode alone has inspired many artists, writers and musicians through the centuries.) Though the poem ends before the new city is founded, it is clear that this event is what this great saga is heralding. It is explicitly the (mythical) story of the founding of Rome, and can be described as the 'national poem' of the Romans; Augustus himself liked to trace his family's lineage back to Aeneas.

Yet though the *Aeneid* can be seen in 'nationalistic' terms, intended in part as praise for Augustus and the new-found Roman peace of his reign, the poem is more than that. Its sheer poetic beauty and its universal themes of love, the human condition and destiny are the reasons why Virgil's masterpiece has withstood the tests of time and has continued to be read and understood by different nations and generations.

Virgil's other great works were a series of poems called collectively the *Eclogues* and the *Georgics*. Virgil grew up in a farming family in northern Italy, and these poems centre on the theme of farming and the land, though in their many digressions they

BELOW: The story of the Carthaginian princess Dido's desperate love for Aeneas, the legendary founder of Rome, has long inspired artists. This ceiling fresco is by Felice Giani (1758–1823), after Virgil's Aeneid. Bologna (Emilia Romagna, Italy), Palazzo Marescalchi, Sala di Enea, Hall of Aeneas.

range more widely. The *Georgics* includes a beautiful version of the story of Orpheus and his descent into Hades, the underworld, to bring back his wife Eurydice, and the awful moment when, in defiance of Hades' condition, the hero looks back to check his beloved wife is there and she is lost to him for ever.

The poem *Eclogue 4*, meanwhile (written in about 40 BC), tells of the coming of a child who will rule the world, a world made peaceful by his father. This work inevitably attracted the attention of Christians, whose claim that the poet was thereby heralding the birth of their saviour Jesus Christ helped to ensure that Virgil's reputation survived the sometimes narrow critical judgements of the Middle Ages. In fact, the child in *Eclogue 4* was either a reference to the hoped-for offspring of Mark Antony and Octavia, sister of Octavian (later Augustus), or to a more abstract concept such as the 'spirit' of the age.

Ancient historians

ABOVE: One of the outstanding characters of 5th-century Greece was the widely travelled historian Herodotus, whose lengthy Histories *about the Persian wars and their background still make fascinating and lively reading, even if they are not always entirely reliable.*

Though it is convenient to slot ancient writers into categories, for example, poet, dramatist, essayist, and so on, we must guard against assuming that this is how those writers necessarily saw themselves. This also applies to those ancient writers we describe as historians. For example, the 'father of history', the Greek Herodotus (c. 484–c. 424 BC), might well have seen himself as performing a similar role to that of Homer, that is, recording and explaining the past, or recent events, for the sake of contemporary and later society.

Herodotus' lengthy nine-book *Histories* tells the story of the fateful Persian–Greek rivalry and the wars between them at the start of the 5th century BC, set against the backdrop of the many different cultures of the region. The *Histories* are certainly a wonderful read, full of engrossing stories and descriptions of those many peoples – the 'barbarians' – who surrounded the Greek world. Herodotus was brought up in Asia Minor, lived for a time in Athens and settled in southern Italy, while in between he travelled a good deal. Therefore he had a good personal knowledge of the Aegean world and beyond, as well as an excellent eye for detail, and based his work as much on what he had been told or had seen as upon traditional sources.

The accuracy of his accounts is another matter. Clearly it would be wrong to accept all that Herodotus wrote at face value. He was prone to bias and exaggeration; for example, he describes the Persian invasion force under Xerxes as containing a staggering 1.7 million men, which seems incredible. Above all, one has to be aware that Herodotus saw the world in terms of the Greeks against the rest – the barbarians – and that this black-and-white view coloured his judgement, as did his opinion of certain Greek states. The biographer and essayist Plutarch (c. AD 46–120) described Herodotus as the 'Father of Lies', possibly because of Herodotus' views on Plutarch's native land, Boeotia. Yet it is clear from Herodotus' writings that he attempted to sort out fact from fiction, and he often gives the reader alternative views or explanations of events. Certainly, our understanding of the Greek world and its neighbouring peoples would be far poorer without his fascinating work.

A younger contemporary of Herodotus who took a very different approach was the Athenian Thucydides (c. 455–400 BC), who wrote the *History of the Peloponnesian War*, an account of the great conflict between principally Athens and Sparta, in which he himself took part – though not successfully: he was exiled in 424 BC for failing to save the

Athenian city of Amphipolis in Thrace from a Spartan attack. It is clear from Thucydides' account that not only did he know of Herodotus' work, but he was determined to distance himself from it, to be far more careful of the information he used and how it was checked. At one point he writes tellingly:

> *The absence of romance in my history will, I fear, detract somewhat from its interest; but if it be judged useful by those inquirers who desire an exact knowledge of the past as an aid to the interpretation of the future, which in the course of human things must resemble if it does not reflect it, I shall be content. I have written my work, not as an essay which is to win the applause of the moment, but as a possession for all time.*

This was a clear reference to the colourful nature of Herodotus' accounts and his ways of collecting information. Thucydides' self-imposed rigour and his interest in the theory and techniques of history have earned him the epithet 'the historian's historian' and a reputation as the father of historical method.

Another fascinating Greek historian is Polybius (c. 200–c. 118 BC), who through chance of circumstance came to be an eye witness of one of the most symbolic moments in Roman history, the destruction of Carthage in 146 BC. Polybius was one of 1,000 Greeks forcibly removed to Rome as punishment for the Greeks' lack of support in Roman campaigns against Macedon. His misfortune is our gain, for as a result Polybius was able to examine at first hand the power of Rome – an insight enriched by his friendship with Scipio Aemilianus (Scipio Africanus the Younger). The historian was with Scipio when the general captured Carthage in 146 BC and ordered its complete destruction. Polybius also took the trouble to retrace the route that Hannibal had taken across the Alps into Italy in the previous century so that he could given an authentic account of it.

The outcome was Polybius' *Histories*, only parts of which survive, in which he described the history of Rome from his own Greek vantage point. Polybius was clearly a great admirer of Scipio, and he also had a great respect for much of Roman society and the Romans' rapid rise to prominence. Part of his mission as a historian was to explain to the Greeks – who considered themselves a more cultured and sophisticated people – just how and why this rise had occurred. Writing of the period from 220 BC, before the start of the second Roman war with Carthage, to 168 BC, when the Romans defeated Perseus of Macedon, Polybius declared:

> *There can surely be nobody so petty or so apathetic in his outlook that he has no desire to discover by what means and under what system of government the Romans succeeded in less than fifty-three years in bringing under their rule almost the whole of the inhabited world, an achievement which is without parallel in human history.*

Another historian close to the action was Julius Caesar (100–44 BC). He is obviously best known for his own role in history: for his conquest of Gaul, his role as dictator of Rome and his own fateful assassination. Yet he was also a prolific writer, producing notably his commentaries on the

BELOW The Roman general Scipio Africanus the Younger captured Carthage in 146 BC and had it ruthlessly levelled to the ground. However, according to his companion and friend the Greek historian Polybius, Scipio wept for the fate of this and other great cities, believing that such destruction would one day be inflicted upon Rome herself. Chalk lithograph, coloured, by R. Weibezahl. Coll. Archiv f.Kunst & Geschichte.

BELOW: Though the most famous Greek philosophers are those of Athens in the 5th and 4th centuries BC, earlier great thinkers such as Anaximander (c. 610–546 BC) had a major impact on the development of classical philosophy. Anaximander was from Miletus, a Greek city in Asia Minor. Roman mosaic, 3rd century AD. Trier, Rheinisches Landesmuseum.

Civil War and more famously on the *Gallic War*. His writing is clear and bold, one might also say a little plain, and his prose style was much praised by contemporaries.

Though one has to accept that Caesar's accounts of events in which he was a key player are inevitably coloured by his own judgement and perceptions, his works give invaluable insight both into Roman politics in the last days of the republic and also into the important campaign against the Gauls.

The greatest of all Roman historians, however, was Tacitus (c. AD 56–c. AD 120). In his two major works, *Histories* and *Annals*, the historian charts the first century of the Roman Empire from the death of Augustus to the death of Domitian. Tacitus, himself involved in politics, does not paint a flattering picture of Roman political life and leadership in this period. His portrayal of its corruption and moral degeneration was to strike a chord in many later generations. His work was a favourite of Machiavelli (1469–1527), author of *The Prince*, a pragmatic, almost cynical 'how to rule' guide for Italian princes, and Tacitus' disdain for tyranny made him popular with revolutionaries in France in the 18th century – though Napoleon despised him as an 'unjust detractor of mankind', possibly because the French dictator felt Tacitus was judging him down the centuries. The Roman's clear, pithy prose is an excellent vehicle for his generally realistic, if gloomy view, of Roman history, and makes him one of the most readable of all historians of the ancient world; among his great admirers was the famous 18th–century British historian Edward Gibbon.

Philosophy

Among the best–known legacies of the ancient world – and almost certainly the most important – were the intellectual achievements of the Greeks, which laid down the foundations for the framework of western civilization. In the beginning was philosophy.

Nowadays, there is a relatively clear distinction between philosophy and science (even if areas such as the science and philosophy of the mind blur the debate). This categorization does not always apply to the ancient world so neatly: many philosophers were also what we would call scientists, and vice versa. The best example is that of Aristotle (384–322 BC). We will look at science and the attempt by Aristotle and others to explore the boundaries and workings of the physical world around them in the following chapter. Here we consider how humans pondered their place in the universe and its ultimate meaning – the origins of philosophy.

The Early Greek Philosophers

The word 'philosophy' comes from the Greek, meaning 'love of wisdom'. Traditionally, when we think of philosophy our minds automatically turn to Athens and the great figures of Socrates (c. 469–399 BC), Plato (c. 427–347 BC) and, later, Aristotle. Yet the love of wisdom flourished earlier, too, in the Ionian cities of Asia Minor, and especially in the city of Miletus in the 6th century BC. (It is worth pausing to note that this was a wealthy trading city. As has often been remarked, the main luxury that wealth can provide is the time and freedom to think.)

The three main Milesian philosophers of this time were Thales (*c*. 624–*c*. 547 BC), Anaximander (*c*. 610–*c*. 546 BC) and Anaximenes (*c*. 585–528 BC). Their precise theories about the world – Thales, for example, thought that everything derived from water; Anaximander talked about the world emerging from what he called the Boundless – are perhaps less important that the fact that they were searching for rational explanations for the world around them.

Their theories did not come out of a vacuum, of course. They were influenced by eastern thought and religion, including ideas and beliefs from Babylon, Egypt and the Near East – a reminder that the Greeks did not invent intellectual curiosity. But the attempts by the Milesians to produce systematic, reasoned explanations of the world represented a clear move away from simply describing the world in terms of gods and faith, and in this they laid down the foundations for later Greek thought. Aristotle considered Thales, who left behind no writings, to be the first true philosopher.

Other philosophers from the bold, dynamic world of early Greek philosophy included Xenophanes, who wryly noted that humans create gods in their own image; Heraclitus, who maintained the world was created by neither humans or gods; and Parmenides, who suggested that the physical world of the senses was but an illusion.

Next, however, the story shifts to Athens, the city associated with the three greatest names of Greek philosophy.

Socrates

It is hard to disentangle Socrates from his equally famous pupil Plato. This is because Socrates left no writings, and so to discover the great man's philosophy and learn about his life we have to rely on Plato's works, along with those of the historian Xenophon.

In his early days, Socrates was a sculptor and also performed his military duties as a soldier, distinguishing himself with bravery. He enjoyed going to parties and indulged in bouts of heavy drinking, apparently being able to stay relatively sober while everyone else around him became intoxicated. He was married, too, though his wife Xanthippe has unfortunately gone down in history as being 'shrewish' – how unfairly, we do not know – and he had three sons. Socrates' views about tyranny, democracy, the gods and morals in general led him into conflict with the authorities in Athens, and eventually to his demise in 399 BC. Accused of denying the city's gods and of corrupting the city's young,

ABOVE: Two of the great names of classical philosophy are the Athenians Socrates and Plato. Socrates, whose ideas survived through the writings of his pupil Plato, was sentenced to death in 399 BC and forced to commit suicide by drinking a cup of the poison hemlock.

the philosopher was found guilty. Though he could still have avoided death by showing contrition, Socrates insisted he had done nothing wrong and suggested he should be rewarded rather than punished. Infuriated by the philosopher's obduracy, the Athenian jury sentenced him to death. Socrates died, as was the custom, by drinking a cup of the poison hemlock.

One of Socrates' main contributions to philosophy, as shown in Plato's writings, was his approach to the subject. He was by inclination a teacher, a 'midwife of knowledge' as he himself put it, and he sought to encourage people to work out answers and to seek the truth for themselves, chiefly by the means of dialogue and systematic questioning. This 'Socratic dialogue' forms the basis of Plato's writings, through which Socrates' ideas are communicated to us.

From this process of self-examination, Socrates believed, people could discover underlying truths and true knowledge. He held that all bad acts arose from a lack of true knowledge. In his view, Socrates' awareness of his own ignorance made him, paradoxically, wiser than those who claimed possession of knowledge; he maintained that we have to accept how little we know, our own ignorance of the true nature of things, in order to learn more about who we are and what life truly is. He famously remarked: 'The life which is unexamined is not worth living.'

It is Socrates' relentless and rational approach to the quest for philosophical truth – which he applied to issues such as justice, piety, courage and wisdom – rather than the content of his philosophy, that has most influenced western civilization. He lived, and in a sense died, for philosophy, and thus became the model of what a philosopher should be. For him, the main concern of philosophy was the examination of a person's place in the world and personal morality – ethics – rather than cosmology, the origin and physical nature of the world. Socrates and, more explicitly, Plato to an extent turned their back on the latter, and in this choice one may see emerging the growing distinction between natural philosophy – science – and moral philosophy.

Plato

Our view of Socrates is naturally shaped by Plato and his writings, but the pupil was far more than just a recorder of his teacher's sayings. Born into an aristocratic Athenian family, Plato rejected a career in what he considered to be the overly aggressive politics of the city–state and instead devoted his life to philosophy, eventually becoming Socrates' star pupil. It was in his copious writings that Plato developed his own influential philosophy. In these, Plato, for the most part, used the dialogue format that Socrates had so successfully employed orally; but it becomes clear that, as his writing progressed, more and more the voice of the 'teacher' is in fact that of the pupil.

Plato's most famous idea was what is called the theory of 'Forms'. Plato argued that beyond the physical world of sensations in which we touch, feel and see things, there is another realm. This is the realm of perfect Forms, such as Good, Beauty and Justice. These are permanent, fixed and unchanging, in contrast to what exists in the physical world, which is subject to decay and any element of which is but an imitation of the perfect Form.

To illustrate this argument Plato used what is called the allegory of the cave, in which one is to imagine a group of humans chained in a cave with their backs to the entrance. All they can see in the darkness is the cave wall, on which are the shadows of passing objects cast by a fire behind them. Outside the cave and beyond the fire is the sun. Plato's point is that, for the prisoners, the shadows they see on the wall are 'real', whereas in truth they are just images – imperfect reflections – of reality. In the same way, he argues, what we consider to be 'real' in the world are but shadows or imitations of the ultimate nature of reality, the unchanging Forms. Of all the Forms, the supreme one was Good – which in this allegory is represented by the sun.

Plato's most famous work is the *Republic*, in which he depicts an ideal society and concerns himself primarily with an investigation of the nature of justice. Like Socrates, Plato mistrusted democracy and is doubtful about any form of government that is not carried out by the enlightened. Quoting his teacher, he famously states in the *Republic* that either philosophers should become kings or existing kings should become like philosophers in their search for wisdom and truth.

The aristocratic Athenian is also important for the foundation of his Academy in the city around 387 BC. It was supposedly called the Academy because it was built on land once owned by a legendary hero called Academus (or Academos). It survived as a place of learning until the 6th century AD, when it was closed by the Byzantine emperor Justinian because of its 'pagan' origins.

Though Plato looked down on the natural sciences, he valued the purity of mathematics highly and saw it as an aid to understanding philosophy. Indeed, tradition has it that written above the entrance to the Academy were the words: 'Let no one ignorant of geometry enter.'

Aristotle

The most famous pupil of the Academy and of Plato was Aristotle (384–322 BC). Aristotle was born in Macedon and

BELOW: *This depiction of Aristotle (384–322 BC) as a wise bearded man shows the sort of classical image with which we associate this great philosopher and observer of the natural world. His works as both scientist and philosopher had a huge impact on Western thought. Engraving, drawn by Joachim von Sandrart (1606–1688), engraved by Philipp Kilian, after antique bust. Coll. Archiv f.Kunst & Geschichte.*

came to Athens to study. In later life he travelled widely and was himself a teacher at the Academy. For three years Aristotle tutored a teenager and fellow Macedonian called Alexander – better known as Alexander the Great. He also established his own school in Athens, called the Lyceum. Unlike Plato, Aristotle took a deep interest in the natural sciences as well as moral philosophy, and his voluminous body of writing covered subjects as diverse as astronomy, physics, biology and meteorology, as well as politics and literary criticism.

As a philosopher, Aristotle's work on logic was to have an impact for centuries to come. For example, he championed the use of a system of reasoning known as the 'syllogism'. This is made up of three sentences: two premises, and a conclusion drawn from the combination of them. To take a simple example: 'If all humans are mortal; and if Athenians are human; then all Athenians are mortal'. Above all, the philosopher emphasized the central importance of reason in human life, both in understanding the world and in achieving happiness and virtue.

Aristotle's views on both philosophy and science were largely lost to the west for hundreds of years, as early Christianity turned its back on systems of thought based on 'pagan' thinkers. Eventually, however, thanks to Islamic scholars and a growing intellectual curiosity in the west, Aristotle became a crucial influence in medieval European scholarship and theology.

The Roman world

A school of philosophy and ethics, originally Greek, that had a deep and lasting impact on many Romans was Stoicism. Stoicism was a product of the Hellenistic period in Greece, and was founded by Zeno of Citium in about 300 BC. Many prominent Romans were attracted by it, including the playwright Seneca and the emperor Marcus Aurelius. Stoics believed that the universe was governed by an immutable, absolute law, and that the essence of humanity was reason (in this there was a similarity with Aristotle's thinking). For Stoics, the ultimate achievement was to lead a virtuous life, and this meant living according to reason, resisting selfish thoughts and deeds and the tyranny of one's passions. With its robust ethics and emphasis on virtue, Stoicism has attracted a considerable following through the centuries. Indeed, even today the word 'stoical' is part of everyday speech to describe a person bravely putting up with misfortune.

A philosophical approach usually contrasted with Stoicism is Epicureanism. Developed by Epicurus (341–270 BC), it is often misrepresented as conferring licence to pursue a life of selfish pleasure and luxury. In fact, Epicurus, who himself lived in great austerity, taught that the pleasures of the mind and intellect were far more important than the transient pleasures of the body, and that the avoidance of pain and anxiety was more important than the pursuit of pleasure. Ultimately, Epicurus believed in moderation in all things – a very modern philosophy.

Epicurus also followed Democritus (c. 460–c. 370 BC) in holding that the world is made of atoms (see Chapter Four). The Roman poet Lucretius (99–55 BC) developed Epicurus' thoughts on atoms and the nature of the world, and his epic philosophical poem *De rerum natura* (*On the Nature of the Universe*) later became influential among scientists and philosophers.

BELOW: One of the schools of Greek philosophy to have a lasting effect on the Romans was Stoicism, founded by Zeno of Citium in about 300 BC, which appealed to prominent figures in Rome over a number of centuries. Paris, Musée du Louvre.

The Roman world produced other original thinkers, too. One was Plotinus (c. AD 205–c. AD 270), who was born in Egypt and moved to Alexandria, one of the cultural capitals of the world, where he became a devoted student of philosophy. Later he moved to Rome, where he set up his own school.

Plotinus is usually considered the father of neoplatonism which, as its name suggests, was heavily influenced by Plato's philosophy. It is often described as the last of the great pagan (i.e. non–Christian) philosophies of the ancient world, though in modified form it influenced Christian and Islamic thought in later centuries.

This philosophy built on Plato's works to develop a complete cosmology of the world. It proposed a divinity that manifested itself in three aspects. The first was the One, transcendent and indivisible, which flowed into the second, the Divine Mind; the third manifestation was the World Soul, which linked the realm of the intellectual with the material world. The chief work of neoplatonism was Plotinus' *Enneads*, published after his death by his pupil and fellow philosopher Porphyry.

Plotinus held that it was possible for the soul to achieve a kind of ecstatic 'union' with the One, something the philosopher was said to have achieved several times in his own life. This inward–looking approach has strong echoes of some eastern religions and struck a chord in later Christian mysticism and the contemplative approach of the monastic movement. Neoplatonism was a major influence on St Augustine of Hippo (AD 354–430), who was a bishop in Africa and an important voice in the development of the early Christian church.

ABOVE: *The Greek thinker Epicurus (341–270 BC) is one of the most misunderstood of classical philosophers. His work is sometimes portrayed as encouraging hedonistic, selfish, physical gratification when in fact he lived a simple life, taught the virtues of moderation and elevated the pleasures of the mind over those of the body. Paris, Musée du Louvre.*

Ancient laws

Another area in which both the Romans and the ancient Greeks have influenced the shape of the modern world is the law. Neither invented the idea of having rules that govern how society operates – one of the prerequisites for a civilization – as we know that the Egyptians, Babylonians and Hittites, for example, all had their own arrays of laws and set punishments for crimes. But it was the Greek and especially Roman laws that helped set the framework for modern legal systems.

One of the best-known names in the history of law is the 7th–century Athenian Draco, who around AD 620 was responsible for a code of laws so severe that we still use the word 'draconian' for rules or other measures we consider harsh. From what we know of them, Draco's laws do seem very tough: for example, according to later writers they stipulated the death penalty in even the most minor of offences, such as stealing a cabbage or an apple. Yet, in one very important sense, Draco's code marked an advance. For the first time laws were written down: thus there was an impersonal authority to refer to, instead of justice being left to more arbitrary oral rules or meted out by aggrieved parties in disputes and feuds.

In 594, the newly elected chief magistrate of Athens, Solon, completely overhauled the system of law, partly perhaps to reflect what was happening in practice in departure from the strict letter of Draco's laws. One element that was preserved from Draco's code was

RIGHT: In Athens, citizens used to write on shards of pottery – called ostraka – the name of the person they thought should be exiled from the city state. These ostraka bear the name Themistocles, the hero of the Battle of Salamis against the Persians, who was nevertheless ostracised in around 471 BC. Athens, Agora Museum.

the notion of involuntary homicide – which in English law broadly equates to manslaughter – as distinct from intentional homicide or murder.

The chief court in Athens was the Areopagus, an ancient institution traditionally made up of Athenian aristocrats, though its composition and powers were to evolve over the centuries. Initially it seems to have dealt with all homicide cases, though by the 4th century BC it handled mainly murder (intentional homicide) cases. Other crimes were dealt with by other courts. There was even a special seashore court for citizens who had already been exiled but who were later accused of murder or intentionally wounding an Athenian. The defendant had to wait in a boat moored offshore at Phreatto while his case was heard by judges on the shore.

According to Aristotle, it was thanks to Cleisthenes (570–*c.* 508 BC), the man usually credited with founding Athenian democracy, that the famous practice of ostracism was instituted. This was originally designed as a way of stopping powerful men

CICERO

Marcus Tullius Cicero (106–43 BC) was among the most influential men of his age, which in itself was one of the most turbulent and important in Roman history. As a young man, Cicero made his name as a lawyer, though he was also, by turns, philosopher, administrator, orator, writer and politician. He was certainly a first-class writer, though he regarded politics as his most important activity. A staunch defender of the Republic, he fell out with the triumvirate of Caesar, Pompey and Crassus, and was exiled. On his return he concentrated on writing and the law, until Caesar crossed the Rubicon and provoked civil war. Cicero took Pompey's side, but was forgiven by the victorious Caesar. Cicero later witnessed Caesar's own murder in 44 BC and this time he backed the right man – Octavian rather than Mark Antony. In a famous series of speeches known as the *Philippics*, Cicero denounced Antony in forthright terms. He was at this time one of the most powerful men in Rome, effectively defending the Senate and the Republic against what he foresaw (correctly) was a move to create a monarchy. The two rivals were soon temporarily reconciled and Antony swiftly and bloodily had his revenge. Not only was Cicero stabbed to death, but his hands and head were cut off and displayed in the Senate.

from destabilizing society or from trying to seize power. Each year, the city's popular assembly voted to decide if there should be a vote on ostracism that year. If they opted for one, it was held two months later, at a gathering of the citizens in the *agora* (marketplace). Here they wrote on shards of pottery (*ostraka* – hence ostracism) the name of the person they thought should be sent abroad – ostracized – for up to 10 years. As a safeguard, the vote was valid only if at least 6,000 people took part in it. (The ancient sources disagree on this point – some claim that the individual had to receive at least 6,000 votes to be ostracized.)

The first known case of ostracism was that of the Athenian Hipparchus, exiled in this way in 487 BC. Some of the shards bearing names of 'victims' of ostracism have survived, for example, one with the name of Aristides, who was banished around 483 BC.

The Romans' legal system stretched back to the early days of the Republic, and unlike some other aspects of their society was very much their own creation rather than an adaptation of the Greek system. In around 450 BC the existing Roman laws were codified for the first time in what are known as the Twelve Tables, which were not formally abolished until the 6th century AD, though Roman law changed and adapted to new circumstances long before that.

Out of the Roman system of criminal and civil courts there arose two roles that seem familiar to us even now. One was that of advocate, in other words someone who spoke in court on behalf of another: the orator and politician Cicero (see box opposite) and Pliny the Younger were both advo-

ABOVE: The great Byzantine emperor Justinian I (483–565) not only restored many lands to the empire, but was a patron of great buildings and also oversaw a crucial codification of Roman law. Mosaic, 6th century. Ravenna, San Apollinare Nuovo.

cates. The other was that of independent legal expert, a person whose views on the correct interpretation of the law were sought by others. These opinions became one of the varied sources of Roman law. The others included popular laws, decisions made by the Senate and the emperor, and earlier decisions of magistrates. This led to a bewildering array of different sources. When the Byzantine Emperor Justinian had the Roman legal system codified in AD 530 it drew on no fewer than 2,000 books. From the Middle Ages, the Roman system of law started to form the basis of many legal systems in Europe; it remained the main source of laws in Germany until the start of the 20th century. A notable exception was the English legal system, which never accepted Roman legal principles as binding in its laws.

Yet, despite the importance of Roman laws in shaping modern legal jurisprudence, we cannot assume that in the days of the empire they extended to everyone: for, though Rome's laws were applied to its own citizens, they did not always protect non-citizens in areas governed by Rome. So, for example, when Pliny the Younger was governor of Pontus-Bithynia (Turkey) from AD 111 to AD 113, he wrote to the Emperor Trajan describing how he had executed a number of local Christians. He added: 'There were others possessed of the same folly; but because they were Roman citizens, I signed an order for them to be transferred to Rome.'

Interestingly, Trajan's reply, in which he commends Pliny, also warns the governor against stretching the limits of justice in deciding who should be condemned. 'Anonymously posted accusations ought to have no place in any prosecution,' writes the emperor. 'For this is both a dangerous kind of precedent and out of keeping with the spirit of our age.'

Women in the ancient world

If foreign subjects of the empire lacked the rights of Roman citizens, much the same can be said about the position of most women in the ancient Mediterranean as compared to that of their male contemporaries. They lacked formal power, too – very few women feature in the headlines of history in Rome or Greece. This did not mean women had no influence in such societies; evidently, many could and did have enormous influence as wives, daughters and mothers of men in prominent positions. But their formal rights and influence, as allowed in law and custom, were generally curtailed.

An exception to some degree was Egypt, where a woman could hold the 'top job' of pharaoh and where the ordinary woman in the street was regarded as more nearly equal to a man than her counterparts in many other Mediterranean societies. Women in ancient Egypt could own and dispose of property, receive the same rate of pay as men, become warriors, musicians and bureaucrats, and steer ships. The Greek historian Herodotus was clearly somewhat taken aback when, in the 5th century BC, he declared that the Egyptians had 'reversed' the normal habits of humankind. He says: 'For instance, women attend market and are employed in trade while men stay at home and do the weaving.'

Cleopatra is of course the best-known female ruler, not just in Egypt but possibly in the world. But before her there had been Neithikret (ruled *c.* 2148–2144 BC), Sobeknefru (*c.* 1787–1783 BC) and Hatshepsut (*c.* 1473–1458 BC). Hatshepsut is an intriguing figure. The widow of pharaoh Tuthmosis II, she had acted as regent for her stepson, the future Tuthmosis III. However, rather than remaining as regent, she soon had herself crowned as pharaoh. The queen seems to have enjoyed a peaceful reign, marked by considerable building work, yet after her death she was virtually wiped out of history. Tuthmosis III, who was brought up to be an able scholar and soldier, acceded to the throne after her

and many buildings associated with the queen in her lifetime were vandalized or destroyed – more likely because she was seen as an usurper than because of her gender.

Cleopatra

Cleopatra (69–30 BC) was not only the most famous of the female Egyptian pharaohs, she was also the last of either sex. With her death ended the Greek/Macedonian Ptolemaic dynasty that had lasted since the death of Alexander the Great, and after her demise the country was effectively ruled by Rome. Though Macedonian by culture and language, Cleopatra VII – she was not the first queen to bear the name – apparently learned Egyptian, probably the first in her dynasty to do so.

Cleopatra was propelled into fame when her brother Ptolemy XIII, who co-ruled with her, imprudently decided to get involved in Roman internal politics. He first welcomed the great general Pompey as a guest but then connived with his adviser Pothinus in the

Roman's murder. The aim was to win favour with Pompey's great rival at the time, Julius Caesar. However, Caesar could hardly take pleasure in the death of a fellow Roman at the hands of an Egyptian – it is reported that Pothinus even presented Pompey's head to Caesar as a 'gift' – and the former conqueror of Gaul was genuinely outraged. In the ensuing war, Caesar sided with Cleopatra and Ptolemy eventually died, apparently by drowning while trying to cross the Nile.

Meanwhile, Cleopatra, who then co-ruled with another brother, Ptolemy XIV, had captivated the ageing Caesar to such an extent that they became lovers and had a son, called Caesarion. She also went with Caesar to Rome and was in the city when he was murdered in 44 BC.

If Rome had been unimpressed with Caesar's relationship with the foreign queen, they were even less so when the 'sorceress', as she was sometimes called, became involved with his great ally Mark Antony. The couple eventually had three children. Antony based himself in Alexandria and may even have married the Egyptian queen, despite having an existing wife, Octavia, sister of his fellow Roman ruler Octavian, the future Emperor Augustus. The relationship between the glamorous, exotic Cleopatra and the rugged general Mark Antony has since inspired many artists, writers and film–makers. Whether she was as beautiful as was claimed on her behalf one cannot be sure; some suggest that it was her style, grace and above all her great intelligence that attracted men such as Caesar and Mark Antony.

Certainly her ability to regain and maintain power suggests a woman of considerable political skills, while her relationships with those two powerful men show her ability to think ahead and look after the interests of herself, her children and Egypt. She was far from a model of moral virtue: Cleopatra probably had a hand in the deaths of two of her siblings. Yet her scandalous image is probably as much a product of a stereotypical reaction to the idea of a female ruler of a powerful eastern country as of moral revulsion at behaviour that hardly differed from that of her male contemporaries.

Another society in which women seemed to have a degree of equality with men was Minoan Crete. The existence of art depicting women among the spectators at events, and even taking part in the notorious activity of bull–vaulting, points to a higher status enjoyed by females in that culture.

Women in Ancient Greece

If Minoan and Egyptian society had a comparatively egalitarian view of women, the same could not be said of ancient Greece, and certainly not of Athens. True, in Athens a woman could be a citizen; but she had few other rights, including very limited ability to own property – unlike women in Sparta, who could at least inherit land. With the exception of Plato, the standard Athenian view of women, even among 'enlightened' philosophers, was that they had strong emotions and weak minds. Aristotle, the greatest mind of his and many other generations, said that in women the ability to reason was 'inoperative'.

We should not be too shocked at the

BELOW: One of the very few women to play a visible role in Athenian society was Aspasia, the lover of the statesman Pericles. She was highly regarded as an orator and a writer and was admired by the philosopher Socrates. Woodcut, undated, c.1880.

Athenian attitude towards women; after all, it is only in very recent times that women in any society have achieved anything like equality with men. Perhaps it is simply more surprising that a city-state so pioneering in many other areas – in drama, philosophy and political organization – could be so illiberal in its attitude to half the human population.

This did not mean it was impossible for a woman in Athens to exercise any influence in the public domain, however.

A woman called Aspasia (c. 469–406 BC), who lived in the city but had been born in Miletus, certainly had a degree of informal power. Her status as a foreigner meant she could never be an Athenian citizen, nor could she legally marry one. However, Aspasia was well known in Athens, not simply because she was the long-time lover of the city's hero Pericles, but because of her skills as both orator and writer. The great Socrates is said to have admired her mind.

When Pericles' two sons by his wife died, he petitioned to have his son by Aspasia made legitimate – in defiance of a law the great man himself had brought in many years before. After his own death, the Athenians, who had generally denigrated Aspasia as variously a foreigner, a prostitute and an enemy of the state, relented in their disdain for her and granted their dead hero's wish.

Slaves

ABOVE: Slavery in ancient Greek society varied considerably; undoubtedly one of the worst forms was the use of slaves to mine silver near Athens, in which the unfortunate victims lived and often died in appalling conditions. Assyrian relief, 705–681 BC.

A class of person even more disadvantaged in early Mediterranean societies than women was slaves. The existence of slavery was the norm rather than the exception. Greeks, Romans, Hittites, ancient Egyptians, Christian Europeans, the Ottomans – all these and many other cultures used slave labour. Slaves were big business too, bought and sold around all parts of the Mediterranean. In much of Mediterranean history – as in the rest of the world – it was often the fate of any conquered people to suffer enslavement.

It was long assumed that slave labour was used to build the Egyptian pyramids. Now experts believe that much of this demanding work was done by farmers during the annual flooding of the Nile, when they could not work on the land. This does not mean that slavery did not exist in ancient Egypt. Thutmose III (c. 1479–1424 BC) is thought to have brought back some 90,000 prisoners from a successful military campaign in Canaan, most of whom would presumably have been co-opted as soldiers or slaves in some capacity. Estimates vary, but it may be that 10 per cent of the Egyptian population were slaves of some form, many of them foreigners. There is evidence, however, that the lot of the slave in ancient Egypt may have been less grim than that of slaves in other parts of the Mediterranean.

In Greece, Athens included, slavery was as commonplace as elsewhere. There may have been as many as 100,000 slaves in Attica – the land around and including Athens – in the 5th century BC. Slaves had few rights and were essentially treated as their masters' property; they worked in houses as domestic servants, as farm labourers or as craftsmen. Their living conditions varied enormously according to the positions they held and the households in which they worked; it would be wrong to imagine all Greek slaves in

ABOVE: One of the most famous revolts in Roman history was led by the gladiator Spartacus in the 1st century BC. He is presumed to have died in the brutal Roman suppression of the revolt though his body was never found. Woodcut, 19th century.

chains. Many of them seem to have worked alongside free people living broadly similar lives – except for the obvious fact that they were not allowed to travel freely. It is also worth reminding ourselves that because of poverty and the need to continue working as long as possible to support oneself and one's family, many 'free' people in the ancient world and even later were not, in practice, free to come and go as they pleased. Nevertheless, some slaves lived and worked in appalling conditions – as, for example, in the silver mines of Attica, where thousands, including young children, were put to work in a terrible environment.

A damaging aspect of Athenian and other Greek slavery was the influence it had on people's attitudes to slaves for centuries to come. Just as Athens transmitted great and enduring concepts such as democracy and philosophy to the rest of the Mediterranean world, so it passed on its own justification of slavery as the natural order of things. Aristotle, who had so great an influence on medieval thought, pondered the question of the morality of slavery. He believed in the hierarchical nature of the universe, and came up with an opinion that has prevailed until comparatively recent times. Having asked: 'But is there any one thus intended by nature to be a slave, and for whom such a condition is expedient and right, or rather is not all slavery a violation of nature?' he continued: 'There is no difficulty in answering this question, on grounds both of reason and of fact. For that some should rule and others be ruled is a thing not only necessary, but expedient; from the hour of their birth, some are marked out for subjection, others for rule.'

Roman Slaves and Revolt

One of the few voices in the ancient world – and probably the first – to speak out against the idea of slavery was that of the followers of Stoicism, the Greek philosophy that so influenced Roman thinking. However, this did not stop the Romans being large-scale owners of and traders in slaves. For the Romans, as for others in the ancient Mediterranean world, slaves were a precious commodity. It was, for example, considered noteworthy that the Gauls were so fond of Roman wine that they were prepared to hand over a slave in return for one large jar of the precious drink. Slave markets existed all over the empire: in Rome itself, on the Greek island of Delos and in Side (Turkey), for example. Delos, which was made a free port in 166 BC, was said by the Greek writer Strabo to be able to handle the buying and selling of 10,000 slaves every day at the start of the 1st century BC.

People became slaves in a variety of ways. They might be kidnapped and sold into slavery by criminals or pirates; be enslaved after being taken prisoner during a military campaign; be born into slavery or fall into it through debt. Tens of thousands of women and children from Carthage were sold into slavery after the Romans destroyed the city in 146 BC. A little more than 20 years before that, the Roman general Aemilius Paulus had attacked the Greek state of Epirus, which the Roman Senate wanted to punish for having sided with the Macedonians. The Romans took as many as 150,000 people captive to be sold into slavery, leaving the area virtually deserted.

Slavery had some curious by-products. Because many slaves were brought to Rome from the Greek-speaking world, a large number of people in the empire's capital spoke Greek rather than Latin as their main language. And the movement of slaves around the Mediterranean from ancient to medieval times brought about a great mixing of races, cultures, languages, faiths and practices.

Some people actually volunteered to become slaves, hoping that in this way they might escape the drudgery of their existing lives and that through their intelligence (and in some cases learning) they could become well-placed as a slave and ultimately earn freedom in better conditions. Slaves could in certain circumstances achieve freedom, usually through the action of their masters, and some attained considerable influence or fame. The noted Roman Stoic philosopher Epictetus (c. AD 50–130) was a former slave, born in Phrygia in Asia Minor. No matter how repugnant the concept of slavery may be, such stories should caution us against assuming that the lives of all slaves at all times in the ancient world were ones of unremitting misery.

Nevertheless, for most slaves life was grim and they lived under the constant fear of ill-treatment or worse from capricious owners – Epictetus himself is said to have been beaten badly as a slave. It is little wonder, then, that on occasion slaves revolted against their masters. The most famous example involved the slave gladiator Spartacus.

Spartacus had been born free in Thrace and had probably fought in the Roman auxiliary forces; later – possibly after deserting – he was captured and sold into slavery. In 73 BC, he and a group of 80 other gladiators armed with kitchen knives broke free from their quarters at Capua in southern Italy and fled to the slopes of Mount Vesuvius. Along the way Spartacus picked up other disgruntled slaves and slaves who had already fled captivity and who were hiding in the countryside. At its peak the revolt attracted up to 120,000 followers, and this band resisted the Romans, who were slow to realize the scale of the rebellion, for more than two years. Eventually, after several Roman defeats, legions under Marcus Licinius Crassus destroyed Spartacus' forces at a battle in southern Italy in which thousands of slaves died. Around 6,000 captured slaves were then crucified along the Appian Way from Capua to Rome. Many others fled for their lives.

One of the bitter tragedies of the story of Spartacus is that he had intended to take his followers to the relative safety of the Alps. The idea was that from there everyone could return to their former homelands. Yet too many of the slaves preferred instead to stay in Italy and make their fortune in plunder; and it was this that ultimately sealed the rebellion's fate.

Slavery and the slave trade continued for centuries in the Mediterranean after the failed revolt of Spartacus and the demise of the western Roman empire. For example, for many centuries the Slavs were a major source of slaves for the rest of Europe: many of them were enslaved by their German neighbours and transported from the Adriatic by merchants. Indeed, it is from the name 'Slav' that we get our word 'slave'. In the 15th century, Venetian merchants still traded in servant girls bought at slave markets in the Black Sea ports and in the Balkans. In the 17th century, the Knights of Santo Stefano in Livorno (Leghorn) in Italy were notorious for their raids against Turkish and North African targets and their capture of Muslims to sell as slaves. Such activity was common among Christian and Islamic pirates, who were not always fussy about whom they sold into slavery.

ABOVE: The Mamluks were a caste of warrior slaves in Islamic society made up of men who were originally prisoners, most of them of Turkic origin. They eventually became a force in their own right and took power in Egypt in the 13th century. Arabian illumination, 15th century. Paris, Bibliothèque Nationale, Add. 18866, fol.140.

The Mamluks

One group of slaves who came to prominence en masse were the Mamluks. These were prisoners, most of them Turkish in origin, who became the personal slaves of Islamic rulers and formed a warrior caste of their own. In Egypt the Mamluks became so powerful that in 1250 they seized power, and the Mamluk sultanate ruled there until the arrival of the Ottoman Empire. It was the Mamluks who dealt the final blow to the already doomed Christian crusaders by taking their last territory in the Holy Land, Acre, in 1291.

Slavery and Entertainment

The relationship between slavery and entertainment in the Mediterranean world was unfortunately often a close one. As we have seen, the great slave rebel leader Spartacus was himself a gladiator. Gladiatorial combat is one of the most famous – and infamous – features of Roman culture. Another legacy of the Etruscans, it had its origin in funeral rites, a personal combat held to mark the passing of someone already dead. The contest was typically fought to the death unless mercy was shown to the vanquished. As mass entertainment it dates from the 3rd century BC, after which it slowly grew in scale and ambition. Most gladiators were slaves, prisoners of war and criminals. They were paid for their performances, and *if* a captive gladiator survived three to five years of combat he might be freed. They trained for the events like any athletes and wore body armour, though they were not allowed to wear Roman armour.

The gladiatorial combats usually took place in the afternoons of the games, after a morning devoted to the *venationes*, in which specially trained fighters fought with and

RIGHT: The concept of gladiatorial combats was originally, like so many Roman practices, an Etruscan concept and sprang out of funeral rites to mark the death of an important person. Most gladiators were slaves or criminals, though occasionally there were volunteers. Roman, 4th century mosaic. Madrid, Museo Arqueologico Nacional.

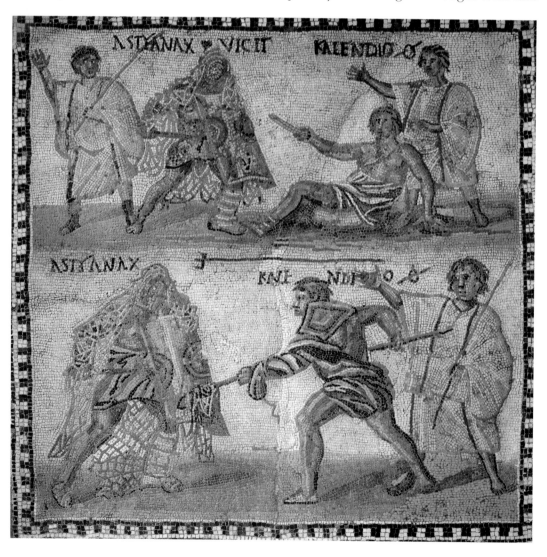

usually killed an assortment of wild animals. Lions, tigers, elephants – all kinds of animals from far-flung parts of the empire were used. As many as 9,000 animals were killed in just one games held by the Emperor Trajan.

Though to us such sport seems cruel and barbaric in the extreme, to the Romans it was on the contrary a symbol of the imperial triumph over the cruel and barbarous forces of nature. As for the gladiatorial contests, Romans had to confront and deal with death on a daily basis, and needed to know how to kill someone in combat. In a militaristic empire in the ancient world, life and death were always close companions.

Another no less energetic but rather less bloody ancient form of sport was the original Olympic Games. The first known games took place at Olympia in 776 BC, though they were almost certainly held before then. At first there was just one event, the foot race or *stadion*, but gradually more and more events were added as the games, held in honour of the gods, became more prestigious and attracted more competitors. Typically, athletes took part naked, often covered in oil, and originally competitors had to be male, free men – in other words, not slaves – and of Greek origin, though, after the Roman subjugation of Greece, Roman and other nationals competed. The games reached their height in the 5th century BC, and their prominence dwindled under the influence of the Romans. The arrival of Christianity as the official religion of the Roman Empire doomed the 'pagan' Olympics, and in AD 393 the Emperor Theodosius banned the 1,000-year-old games. They were revived at the end of the 19th century, with the first of the modern Olympic Games being held, appropriately, in Athens in 1896.

The Mediterranean still remains at the cultural heart of Europe and the rest of the world. For many, it is true, the area is simply a holiday destination, a place to sample (virtually) guaranteed sunshine, fine beaches and a place to get – and show off – that all-important tan.

Yet the Mediterranean has been, and still is, appreciated for far more than just its climate. Its ancient sites of past glories, its food, wine and stunning diversity of peoples and cultures have long attracted visitors. In the past, the mysteries of Etruscan art, for example, captivated the British author D. H. Lawrence, while the unique light and landscape of this stunningly beautiful area have brought artists from all parts of the globe. Literature, music, drama; all have their roots in the history and melting pot of Mediterranean civilization. On a more populist note, Mediterranean-style gardening and Mediterranean cuisine are just two of the trends that have caught on in northern Europe in recent years.

Meanwhile, studies of the languages, cultures and art of the region continue and often throw up new and exciting discoveries. For example, just as the Hittites – once the forgotten society of the Mediterranean – were found to have been a major force in the region, so too has Etruscan culture. the Etruscans, who were for so long overshadowed by the success of the Roman world, have come to be seen as increasingly important.

Just as our perception of the modern world is constantly changing, our view of the unique contribution of the Mediterranean world to modern culture also continues to evolve. In many ways, the modern world is constantly re-inventing the Mediterranean to suit its needs.

ABOVE: The revival of the Olympic games was a conscious attempt to recreate some of the perceived nobility of the classical world. Appropriately enough, the first modern Olympics, at which medals were awarded to the victors, as well as olive branches as a symbol of the old games, were held at the Greek capital Athens in 1896.

CHAPTER 4

ADVENTURE AND INNOVATION

Innovation and adventure have been two important characteristics of the Mediterranean world. Early humans had to adapt to the sometimes challenging conditions of the climate and geography. The sea itself was both an obstacle and an opportunity – to be faced with courage and ingenuity. Out of this struggle were born many inventions and discoveries that were to change the world.

RIGHT: The politics and geography of the Mediterranean have often worked hand in hand to produce new chapters in cultural development. When Islamic society came to dominate the eastern part of the Mediterranean, the Christian West searched for new sea routes to the east, which, for example, resulted in Portuguese sailors sailing to India. Portuguese ship with Indian crew. Coloured copper engraving, by Joannes Doetechum after drawing by Jan Huygen van Linschoten (1563–1611). Paris, Bibliothèque Nationale.

Mocadaon

et transportandis
ses Malabares.

Fusten welcke die Portugeesen ēn haer vianden die Malabaren
gebruycken ter oorloch, ēn om coopmanschap te voeren.

B.

It is hard to overstate the physical, geographical fact of the sea and its effect on the peoples who lived around it. Nowadays we think little of taking a flight across the Mediterranean in just a few hours and consider a boat journey on its waters as a leisurely pleasure to be savoured. Yet to the ancient world the sea was a formidable barrier, a potential foe to be treated with respect – and a challenge that had to be confronted. Great rivers such as the Rhône and the Nile were useful routes of communication and transport, of course, but for really effective travel and trade humans needed to conquer the sea.

Grappling with the sea

The Beginnings of Maritime Trade

It was not only the sea itself that was to be feared. For centuries – and this trepidation lasted until the late Middle Ages – there was always the nagging fear: what nameless terror might lie over the horizon?

It is likely that the earliest boats were craft such as reed rafts, dugout canoes and vessels kept afloat with inflated animal skins. Rafts made from papyrus reeds were still used on the Nile up to the 20th century. In 1988, a contemporary version of a Corfu reed boat was used to travel successfully from Laurion to Melos in the Aegean Sea, showing that such a feat was possible. Its crew of six propelled the vessel with oars, and the voyage took seven days. It is now thought that quite extensive sea routes were established by 6000 BC in parts of the eastern Mediterranean.

There were a number of reasons for putting to sea, among them to fish, to trade and to seek new lands in which to settle. Through such journeys people spread new techniques, for example in pottery making and farming, to other communities. Through sea travel, too, knowledge became diffused through the region.

When it came to technological breakthroughs with boats, the Egyptians were once more in the lead. The earliest known image of a sail dates from Egypt around 3100 BC, and the Egyptians were definitely using oars to propel boats by around 2500 BC. By then, Egypt, the east Mediterranean superpower of its day, was already trading regularly with its neighbours, especially along the coast in the Levant where the Egypt–Byblos axis became an established and enduring trading route.

BELOW: The first known people to use sails to propel boats in the Mediterranean were the ancient Egyptians and they quickly established local trade routes. This Egyptian papyrus (11th/10th century BC) is from the Book of the Dead of Amon priest Khensumose, showing the deceased sailing through the underworld. Vienna, Kunsthistorisches Museum.

One of the earliest insights into what we might grandly call 'international trade' comes from the long reign of the Fourth Dynasty pharaoh Seneferu (c. 2597–2547 BC), who, it is recorded, imported 40 ships laden with cedar wood – almost certainly from Byblos – with the probable aim of making yet more ships. Egypt had little of its own timber, whereas Lebanon had a plentiful supply of cedar. The journey from the Nile delta could apparently take between four and eight days by sea, and was not a voyage to be undertaken lightly.

ABOVE: One of the first great trading peoples to travel throughout the Mediterranean sea were the Phoenicians, who took their ships not just around the eastern part of the sea but to the far west, to Spain and even ventured beyond to the Canary Islands and the British mainland. Beirut, National Archeological Museum.

It is not surprising that one of the first seafaring 'powers' in the Mediterranean was the island of Crete, whose future would inevitably be limited without ships and trade. Cretans were trading with neighbouring islands and areas as far apart as Sicily, Egypt and the Levant from around 3000 BC, and the Minoans took their goods as far west as Malta, Sardinia and even Spain by the 2nd millennium BC, showing that by this time, while humans may not have conquered the Mediterranean, they were certainly able to cover significant distances across it.

One of the main shipping routes in the east of the region was a circular one, starting in the Aegean and going first to Crete, then down to Egypt, across to the Levant, west and north to Cyprus and Anatolia, then back across to Crete, finishing up back at the Aegean islands and mainland. Such a route kept the periods for which a ship had to be on the open sea as short as possible.

The Minoans, who made use of this route, did not just trade with their home-produced and celebrated pottery, though this has been found as far away as Egypt, Syria and Cyprus. The Egyptians seem to have developed a taste for their coloured fabrics as well, and the Minoans also sold and bought weapons, jewels, semi-precious stones and copper.

Another key trading society from around 3000 BC would probably have been the ancient city of Troy, which from its position close to the Dardanelles controlled an important route between the Aegean and the Sea of Marmara and, ultimately, the Black Sea.

Early Trading Posts: the Emporia

One of the most fascinating aspects of early trade in the Mediterranean was the establishment of what were called emporia. These were founded by the Phoenicians, the supreme trading people of the Mediterranean in the 1st century BC, and were small settlements set up on distant shores from where the merchants could do business with local people.

Even though they were on 'foreign' soil, emporia were built around sanctuaries dedicated to the Phoenician gods; the sanctuary was a place where a person could enter and do business without (at least in theory) any risk of being harmed. In this way

religious beliefs from the east spread all around the sea, with shrines established in such far-flung places as Sardinia and Spain. At Gades (now Cadiz), for example, there was a shrine to Melqart, the Phoenician equivalent of Hercules. The Greeks, trading rivals of the Phoenicians, quickly adopted the idea and set up their own emporia, with shrines to their own gods, all around the Mediterranean. Thus the observance of religion and the practice of trade went hand in hand in both the Greek and Phoenician worlds.

One emporium that developed into a large and unusual settlement was that of Naukratis on the Nile delta. This was the only trading centre that the Egyptians allowed the Greeks to establish on their territory, and was founded in the 6th or possibly the 7th century BC. Normally, individual Greek cities set up their own settlements, but Herodotus

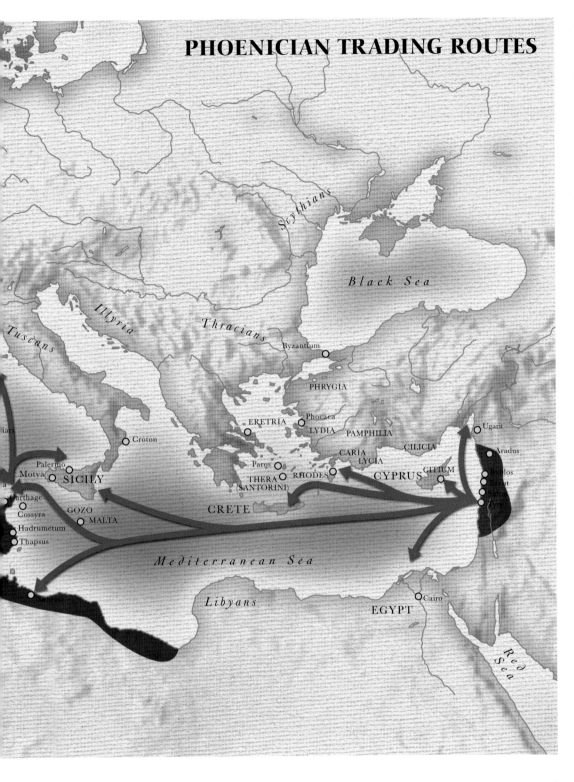

PHOENICIAN TRADING ROUTES

Scythians

Black Sea

Illyria

Tuscans

Thracians

Byzantium

PHRYGIA

ERETRIA

Phocaea

LYDIA

PAMPHILIA

Croton

CARIA

CILICIA

Ugarit

Aradus

Paros

LYCIA

Byblos

Palermo

RHODES

CYPRUS

CITIUM

Berout

Motya

SICILY

THERA
(SANTORINI)

Sidon

Carthage

Tyre

Cossyra

GOZO

CRETE

Hadrumetum

MALTA

Thapsus

Mediterranean Sea

Libyans

Cairo

EGYPT

Red Sea

LEFT: Though the original Phoenician homeland in the Middle East was relatively small, the influence of the Phoenicians was great thanks to their huge trading empire, which may have spread as far as Cornwall and perhaps even the Canary Islands.

tells us that Naukratis involved all three main Greek peoples, Ionians, Dorians and Aeolians, from no fewer than nine city–states.

Navigation

To begin with, sailors would venture out only on short voyages and only in daylight, remaining in sight of land and using familiar landmarks to guide them on their way. This coast–hugging style brought with it the risk of running aground on rocks or sand beds – particularly in large rivers, estuaries and shallow coastal waters – and so two different devices were developed to test the depth of water in which a boat was floating. One was the sounding pole, used by Egyptian mariners as early as the 3rd millennium BC. The other was the sounding weight, typically made of lead (hence also called a sounding lead), which was attached to a line that was then lowered to the sea bed. Sounding leads were used from at least 2000 BC in Egypt and were an important tool of maritime safety for many centuries to come. The Greeks and Romans put soft tallow at the bottom of their weights so they could bring up samples of the sea bed. This told them if they were sailing over rocks or sand or other potential underwater hazards.

One of the biggest problems for sailors, however, was how to find their way on longer voyages when reassuring landmarks were no longer visible. Sailing from Crete to the Nile delta, for example, could mean sailing out of the sight of land for days and nights on end. The solution was to use what is called 'environmental navigation'. This involves observing natural phenomena such as the position of the sun or the stars, the direction of the wind or the sea swell, or the direction in which migrating birds were flying. The Greeks knew how to find the North Pole using the constellation of the Great Bear (Ursa Major), while the Phoenicians used Ursa Minor. Such techniques – which were widely used in the Mediterranean until the end of the 1st millennium AD – could produce surprisingly accurate navigation. This was especially true on familiar routes in known waters, where experienced mariners learned the subtle variations of local conditions.

It was harder when one was journeying into unknown waters, which for east Mediterranean sailors usually meant travelling west. There was, for example, huge suspicion of what lay through the Pillars of Hercules out in the Atlantic Ocean beyond – the so-called Dark Ocean. There were tales of strange and terrible monsters and deadly whirlpools that could spell disaster for the unwary mariner.

One of the few ancient peoples who did venture into the Atlantic were the

BELOW One of the greatest trading people in the history of the Mediterranean were the Phoenicians who voyaged all over the sea, and possibly much further too, and were skilled seamen and navigators. Wood engraving, c.1880.

Phoenicians, who had an established settlement at Gades (Cadiz) beyond the Straits of Gibraltar. It was the Phoenicians who sailed round Portugal and Spain to reach Cornwall in search of its tin, hundreds of years before Julius Caesar crossed the English Channel from Gaul to Britain with his expeditionary force.

The Phoenicians may also have visited the Canary Islands off the west coast of Africa, traversing waters unknown to and potentially perilous for most Mediterranean mariners. There is even a theory that the Phoenicians deliberately encouraged rumours of the dangers of the Atlantic in order to dissuade other people from voyaging there and competing with them for trade.

The widespread use of navigational instruments seems to have started with Arabs in the Indian Ocean in the 9th century AD, when they developed the *kamal* to find out the altitude (the vertical angle) of the North Star – and thus their latitude. (The angle at which you see the North Star above the horizon tells you your latitude – in simple terms how far north or south you are.) This tool consists of a small wooden board with a hole drilled through the middle of it; a piece of knotted string passes through the hole. Before leaving his home port the sailor held the end of the string in his teeth and held the wood up so that the bottom edge lined up with the horizon. When, after adjusting the length of the string, the top edge of the wood lined up with the North Star, the sailor could take a fixed reading for its altitude and thus his latitude – to be marked by a knot on the string. Knowing the latitude on which his port lay helped the sailor find his way home. The different knots on the string corresponded to the different latitudes of known ports. The *kamal*, which means 'guide', may have been based on knowledge Arabs had gleaned from the Persians or Greeks.

ABOVE: Although the use of astrolabes goes back many centuries, as this 11th-century Arabic version shows, they were not properly adapted to use for maritime navigation until the 15th century. Kassel, Staatliche Museen.

The theoretical concept of an astrolabe, a more sophisticated tool for solving problems to do with time and the position of the stars and the sun, dates back to ancient Greece. The actual instrument was probably in use by the 4th century AD, and the invention was further developed by Arab scholars. However, it was not used as a navigational aid by seamen until the early 15th century, when a simplified version, known as the mariner's astrolabe, was used by Iberian and Genoese sailors.

Another important advance for navigation came with the invention of the compass. Though first used by the Chinese in the 11th century AD, compasses were being employed by Arab sailors in the Mediterranean by the following century and may well have been independently invented by them. The earliest device was a water compass in which the magnetic material floated on the water and pointed in the direction of magnetic north. The compass was a major breakthrough for sailors. Though it could not tell you where you were, it was ideal for telling you in which direction you were heading.

Soon Arab and other mariners were using sandglasses to help measure their speed – by helping them see how long it took to travel a fixed distance – and by the 13th century they were consulting rudimentary navigational charts.

Another welcome development for sailors was the arrival of the lighthouse. The very earliest attempts to warn seamen off dangerous rocks or stretches of coast were fires or beacons lit on headlands. However, in the 3rd century BC, a dedicated building with a light

ABOVE: One of the seven wonders of the ancient world was the lighthouse built on the island of Pharos near Alexandria in the 3rd century BC. Sadly, it was destroyed by a powerful earthquake at the start of the 14th century. Woodcut, 19th century.

was built on the island of Pharos, near Alexandria, one of the busiest harbours in the world at the time. This lighthouse was sufficiently unusual and noteworthy for it to be reckoned one of the Seven Ancient Wonders of the World. The name of the island has even come into modern language – *la phare* is the French for lighthouse. Unfortunately, an earthquake destroyed this unique structure in August 1303.

After the Romans built a lighthouse at Ostia, Rome's port, in AD 50 the use of these life-saving constructions spread even further around the Mediterranean world. In all, the Romans built more than 20 and perhaps as many as 30 lighthouses.

Much later, the navigation of the Mediterranean was transformed by the arrival of much more powerful and less weather-dependent forms of propelling vessels – above all, the steam ship.

Security and Piracy

As navigation and the safety of shipping improved, so trade became more widespread throughout the Mediterranean.

In the late 13th century the Genoese opened up the route into the Atlantic and around to western Europe, and so started a new and lucrative trading pattern with that area. In the Mediterranean itself, vast convoys of merchant ships used to ply their way along established routes that crisscrossed the sea from north to south and from east to west. For example, Venetian merchants sent at least seven large galleys (ships with oars and usually sails) to Alexandria and Beirut each year in the late 15th century, trading in exotic spices and cotton.

In the following century the growing population of the Ottoman Empire's new capital at Istanbul needed a substantial supply of food. It therefore began to import vast quantities of grain from one of the traditional breadbaskets of the region, Egypt. A western traveller in Istanbul at the time noted with some surprise that though eight large ships laden with grain had just arrived from Alexandria, such supplies would not feed the city for much more than a day.

Often the merchant ships sailed in convoy and with armed protection to defend themselves against one of the great scourges of the Mediterranean from ancient times to the 18th century – piracy. At various times in the ancient world, attempts were made to reduce this menace. A notable example was the short but remarkably effective campaign by the Roman general Pompey in 67 BC. In just three months, with a massive force of ships and men, he virtually ended the phenomenon of serious piracy in the Mediterranean for many years.

Curiously, the man who was to become Pompey's great rival, Julius Caesar, was reportedly captured by pirates in Asia Minor in 75 BC. The story goes that when the pirates asked for a ransom of 20 talents for his release Caesar insisted that it be raised to 50 talents – a sum more in keeping with what he felt he was worth. Upon his release,

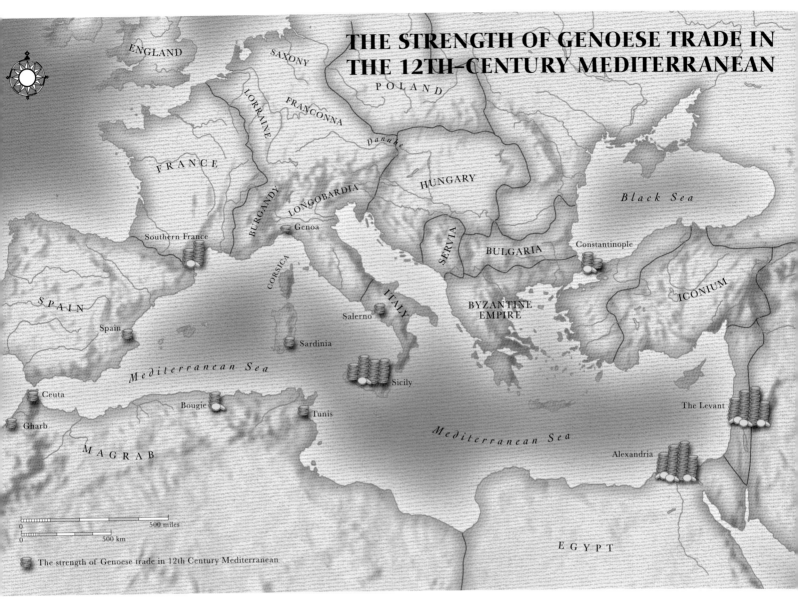

THE STRENGTH OF GENOESE TRADE IN THE 12TH-CENTURY MEDITERRANEAN

ENGLAND

SAXONY

POLAND

LORRAINE

FRANCONNA

Danube

FRANCE

BURGANDY

LONGOBARDIA

Genoa

HUNGARY

Black Sea

SERVIA

BULGARIA

Constantinople

Southern France

CORSICA

ITALY

BYZANTINE EMPIRE

ICONIUM

SPAIN

Salerno

Spain

Sardinia

Sicily

Mediterranean Sea

Ceuta

Bougie

Tunis

The Levant

Mediterranean Sea

Gharb

Alexandria

MAGRAB

500 miles

500 km

EGYPT

The strength of Genoese trade in 12th Century Mediterranean

Caesar, as he had warned them, captured the pirates and they were subsequently crucified. However, as they had treated him well during his captivity Caesar is said to have cut their throats first to reduce their suffering.

Despite Pompey's cleaning-up operation, piracy eventually returned to the sea and once again became a constant threat, especially once the power of the Roman Empire had begun to decline. Pirates were attracted by rich cargoes, not just of goods but of people, too. Captives could be sold into slavery or ransomed, as in the case of Caesar. From the start of the 14th century the Venetian authorities helped establish what was called the *mude* or convoy system, in which armed galleys carried the most precious cargoes around the pirate-ridden seas.

The Route to India and the Suez Canal

Arguably the most important development in Mediterranean maritime history was the building of the Suez Canal. This 160-kilometre (100-mile) waterway stretching from Port Said in Egypt to Suez in the Red Sea was opened in 1869 as a French project with Egyptian support. Within a decade, the British prime minister Benjamin Disraeli had intervened to buy a majority shareholding from the khedive of Egypt in order to guarantee British interest in the strategically vital waterway. In 1888, the Convention of Constantinople opened the canal to all nations. Its existence meant that European shipping did not have to use

ABOVE: In the Middle Ages the waters of the Mediterranean were dominated by the fleets operated by powerful merchant cities such as Venice and Genoa. The merchants traded not just with Christians in the north and west of the region but with Muslims to the south and east of the area too.

CHRISTIAN AND MUSLIM PIRATES

One of the worst periods for piracy in the Mediterranean Sea was the 17th century. Attacks broadly followed religious lines. The Christian pirates and privateers operating out of Malta, such as the Knights of St John, preyed mostly on shipping from the Islamic Ottoman Empire. They targeted the wealthy and goods-laden convoys that moved between Egypt and Istanbul. During one attack in 1644, the Knights of Malta managed to capture Turkish ships that were carrying part of the sultan's harem. Muslim prisoners were usually sold into slavery. The knights saw themselves as protecting Christian interests and counter-balancing the activities of the Barbary Coast pirates. These pirates, named after the coast of North Africa that was home to the Berbers, were for the most part Muslims or Muslim converts operating out of ports such as Algiers, Tunis and Tripoli. They usually preyed on Christian shipping, including the Dutch and British ships that were beginning to appear in ever greater numbers. Barbary corsairs sold thousands of British sailors into slavery, and often sailed to British waters to capture them. Yet the religious divide was far from absolute; pirates were happy to raid any ship if the cargo was attractive enough.

the long and sometimes dangerous route right round the Cape of Good Hope in South Africa to reach India and the east, but could instead use the more tranquil Mediterranean – which by this time was once more relatively free of pirates.

The story of that route to India and the initial struggle to find it was a long and colourful one, and it started with Mediterranean sailors. Indeed, it may go back as far as the time of the Phoenicians, who were perhaps the first to try to discover a route round Africa, both from west to east and from east to west.

In the 2nd century BC, meanwhile, a Greek sailor, Eudoxus of Cyzicus, became convinced that such a route existed. While sailing in the Arabian Sea and Indian Ocean he had found the wreck of what he was sure was a ship from Gades in Spain. This persuaded him not only that Africa could be circumnavigated, but that it already had been. He tried twice himself; the first time ended in failure when he was driven ashore in Morocco – and during his second attempt Eudoxus vanished altogether.

Centuries later, in 1291, the Genoese brothers Ugolino and Vadino Vivaldi set sail from Morocco in search of the route. This was the year when the last Christian stronghold in the Holy Land, Acre, fell; a time when the Christian west in the Mediterranean felt cut off from the Islamic east. Unfortunately, the brothers shared the fate of Eudoxus and were never seen again.

The route was eventually found by the great Portuguese navigator Vasco de Gama in 1497, five years after the Genoese Christopher Columbus had reached the Americas.

Exploration of the mind

If the sailing of the Mediterranean and the waters beyond was evidence of people's eagerness to explore the outside world, then the development of science and mathematics shows an equally strong desire to explain it. In science, the classical world had an

LEFT *Among the great traders in the Mediterranean were the Venetians, whose ships ventured as far east as the Levant and who established settlements throughout the region; their major trading rivals were the Genoese.*

VIKING RAIDS

Viking raids are usually associated with the British Isles and with the Atlantic coast of western Europe. But the Vikings travelled further afield, to north America and east to what is now Russia, and they also made it as far as the warmer waters of the Mediterranean. In AD 844, Viking ships went up the river Tagus in Portugal and attacked Lisbon. They were beaten off, but instead of returning home they continued round the coast and attacked Seville, where they were eventually defeated by Moorish troops. Still undeterred, they attacked a settlement in North Africa and ended up wintering back in Aquitaine in south–west France. Some 15 years later, Vikings attacked settlements in Spain and North Africa, this time penetrating as far as the Balearic islands of Mallorca and Minorca. Southern French towns, such as Nîmes, were also targeted, and Viking ships reached as far east as the Ligurian coast of Italy. The clashes between the Vikings and Muslim forces at this time bring into sharp focus the role of the Mediterranean as a point of meeting and conflict for very different cultures from very disparate areas.

abundance of theories, some of which were to underpin modern western thinking for many years. Though many of these theories were, alas, wrong, they at least gave later scientists a point of reference against which to measure their own work.

In mathematics, however, the Greeks produced experts who were not just brilliant but whose works have stood the test of time and remain just as important today as they were in the ancient world.

Pythagoras

Perhaps the most intriguing of these geniuses was Pythagoras (*c.* 580–500 BC). Pythagoras did not invent mathematics any more than Homer invented writing, and we know that both the ancient Egyptians and the Babylonians wrestled with mathematical problems. The Babylonians in particular were very skilled practical mathematicians. Pythagoras did leave an enduring legacy, however.

First, he is forever associated with the famous theorem about right-angled triangles, which states that the square on the hypotenuse (the longest side) equals the sum of the squares on the other two sides. Second, he is important for his profound understanding of the importance of numbers in the universe. He was perhaps the first pure mathematician, concerned with the abstract as much as the practical application of mathematics.

Pythagoras was born on the Ionian island of Samos, a short distance from the coast of Asia Minor, though his father came from the Levant trading city of Tyre. As a young man he met and was influenced by the great Milesian philosopher Thales, and lived for a while in Egypt. When the Persians captured Egypt, Pythagoras was taken as a prisoner to Babylon, where he studied their mathematical techniques and problems, and according to some traditions spent time studying with the 'wise men' of the east – the Magi.

The time he spent immersed in eastern thought was to have a major influence on both Pythagoras' work and his lifestyle. Later, as a free man, he returned to Samos before setting up a school in Croton in southern Italy. This school was more than just a place of teaching and learning; it established a whole way of life. Pythagoras was as much a philosopher, astronomer, musician and mystic as a mathematician – one of his core beliefs was that ultimate reality was essentially mathematical in nature and that numbers were at the heart of the universe – and his followers followed strict rituals, owned no possessions and refused to eat meat. They regarded their teacher as a holy man, possibly even as divine.

Yet very little of the work of Pythagoras or his followers has survived, and in what we do have it is hard to disentangle his own work from the collective output of his disciples. It is also now clear that the Babylonians were aware of the famous theorem about right-angled triangles for perhaps 1,000 years before the time of Pythagoras. However, Pythagoras, fascinated with the abstract, may well have been the first to prove it.

Pythagoreans were also the first to realize that the earth was in the shape of a sphere – even if the empirical proof for this came a little later, in the time of Aristotle. As much as anything, it is Pythagoras' understanding of the purity of mathematics and its relationship with the universe that marks him out as such an important figure.

BELOW: When we think of Pythagoras we tend to think only of mathematics, but in fact this 6th-century Greek was more than just a mathematician: he was also a musician, a philosopher and, to his followers, a holy man.

Euclid

Arguably the most important mathematician of antiquity was Euclid (330–260 BC), a Greek who taught in the Egyptian city of Alexandria. By his time the city was a renowned centre of learning in the ancient world. We know very little about Euclid, though it appears he probably studied at the Academy Plato had established in Athens. His great achievement was his 13–volume mathematical work called *The Elements*. These volumes dealt with both geometry (plane and solid geometry) and number theory, and in effect codified and laid out all the major existing theories of Euclid's day. They were to endure for more than 2,000 years as the main source for geometric reasoning, theorems and method. *The Elements* has been described as the greatest maths textbook of all time. In fact, it is probably one of the most influential books in all human history.

Euclid's great contribution to mathematical thought was the clarity and precision he brought to his task, in the way he stated the problems and demonstrated the proofs. It is not thought that Euclid originated many of the proofs in his books, though he doubtless added his own improvements and refinements. Much of the books' content was based on the work of earlier mathematicians, such as the brilliant Eudoxus (c. 400–347 BC) from Cnidus in Asia Minor, a rival of Plato (and a much better mathematician than the Athenian). None of this detracts, however, from Euclid's remarkable and long–lasting achievement.

ABOVE: The famous mathematician Euclid (330–260 BC), who worked in Alexandria, wrote probably the most successful textbook of all time. The Elements *pulled together much of the mathematical knowledge of his day and its authority and clarity has stood the test of time. From the series of six corner reliefs in the Campanile of the Duomo in Florence, now replaced by copies. Florence, Museo dell'Opera del Duomo.*

Archimedes

There is no disputing the personal brilliance of another key figure in the story of mathematics, Archimedes (c. 287–212 BC). Archimedes is best known for the way in which he is supposed to have discovered his famous principle on the displacement of fluids. The story is that he was asked by Hieron II, the ruler of Syracuse in Sicily, where Archimedes was born and lived, to determine the purity of a golden wreath (a kind of crown) he had commissioned. The king suspected that the goldsmith had adulterated the wreath with a cheaper metal such as silver and pocketed the remaining gold.

Archimedes pondered how to test the purity of the gold without destroying the sacred wreath, which was due to be dedicated to the gods and had to be preserved intact. The answer came as he was bathing. The mathematician noticed that the further his body entered the water the higher the water level rose. This gave him a clue; in fact, he was supposedly so struck by the implications that he cried out 'Eureka! Eureka!' ('I have found it! I have found it!'), leaped out of the bath and dashed home, having forgotten to put on any clothes in his excitement. Archimedes had realized that the amount of water displaced was proportionate to the volume of the body being submerged in the water.

He also understood that as gold is heavier than silver, a given weight of gold will displace less water than the *same weight* of silver. This is because it occupies less volume than the silver.

Applying this principle to the golden wreath, the mathematician discovered that the crown displaced more water than it should have done had it been made of pure gold. The inevitable conclusion was that some other material had been added to it – as the king had suspected all along.

This charming story – though for the goldsmith the consequences may have been less charming – illustrates Archimedes' great inventiveness. The scope of his work is astonishing. Aside from the theory on buoyancy reputedly discovered in the bath, he produced theories on topics ranging from the principles of levers to the properties of cylinders and spheres. He is credited with coming up with a rough approximation for the value of pi, the ratio of the circumference of a circle to its diameter. His work also anticipated the later development of differential calculus.

Archimedes, who had studied in Alexandria, prized pure mathematics as the most important of the many areas in which he excelled, but his outstanding ability was also applied to more prosaic, even brutal purposes, such as creating weapons of war. Archimedes lived at a time when Rome's forces were fighting in Sicily as part of its ongoing war with Carthage, and Greek cities such as Syracuse were inevitably caught up in the conflict. When the Romans attacked Syracuse in 214 BC, machines designed by Archimedes were used to fight them. These included devices that fired missiles, a crane that dropped stones, and claws that pulled ships out of the water.

Even Archimedes' ingenious mind could not hold back the Romans for long, however, and the city was eventually sacked in 212 BC. There are conflicting stories about the precise circumstances in which he died, though it is clear he was killed by a Roman soldier – and despite orders that the great mathematician was to be taken alive. One tradition has it that when a soldier ordered him to come with him to the Roman commander Marcellus, Archimedes absentmindedly asked him to wait while he resolved a mathematical problem in which he was absorbed. Enraged at being made to wait in this way, the soldier stabbed him to death.

ABOVE: The great mathematician and inventor Archimedes (c. 287–212 BC) discovered various scientific theories and worked out the theory behind how levers can be used to move heavy objects; he is said to have demonstrated this by using a pulley system to launch the ship Syrakosia in Syracuse. Coll. Archiv f.Kunst & Geschichte.

The physical world

In common with many other mathematicians of the ancient world, Archimedes was also an astronomer. Many great Greek thinkers sought to understand the physical world around them, even if some philosophers such as Plato chose mathematics and metaphysics over science.

They were not the first to do so. The Babylonians, Persians and Egyptians had been keen astronomers in an age where no distinction existed between astronomy and astrology. The Greeks were inheritors of older traditions and thoughts about the world around them, out of which they tried to make sense with an array of new theories.

Early Atomists

Two early and important figures are Leucippus (c. 480–420 BC) and Democritus (c. 460–370 BC). Leucippus came from Miletus, following in the footsteps of that city's great philosophers such as Thales. Democritus, from Abdera in northern Greece, was a pupil of Leucippus, and developed his master's ideas. The two men held that the basic elements of the world were not, as many argued, water, earth, fire or water, or a combination of these, but instead tiny particles called atoms.

These atoms, which were surrounded by space, moved randomly and were indestructible and eternal in nature. Interestingly, Democritus described the movement of these atoms as rather like those of dust particles that we can see when they are illuminated by a beam of sunshine. Such views were a major departure from most accepted thinking of the time, though to us they sound very familiar. When Ernest Rutherford revealed the nature of an atom's nucleus in 1910, he was described as the greatest atomic physicist since Democritus. Sadly, however, this description only demonstrates how, despite the remarkable intellectual achievement of both Leucippus and Democritus, their atomic theory was largely ignored for more than 2,000 years – even though it held the key to understanding the nature of matter.

ABOVE: *Though atomic theory is essential to our modern understanding of the physical world it is not new. The Greek philosopher Democritus (c. 460–370 BC) proposed such an idea some 2,400 years ago, but sadly it was dismissed for centuries. Copper engraving, drawing by Joachim von Sandrart (1606–1688), engraving by Philipp Kilian. Coll. Archiv f.Kunst & Geschichte.*

Aristotle and Science

From the 4th century BC onwards, ancient and medieval thinking on the nature of the world was instead to be dominated largely by the astonishing mind and output of one man.

Aristotle's place as a philosopher and the importance he attached to human reason were discussed in the previous chapter. He was to have just as great an influence, however, as a scientist. His surviving works alone cover physics, biology, astronomy, psychology and meteorology.

There is a fundamental paradox concerning Aristotle as a scientist. On the one hand, notably in areas such as biology, he believed wholeheartedly in the power of observation, and his observations on matters such as the distinction between mammals and fish were not only important in themselves but mark him out as one of the first empiricists.

Yet in the realms of what we would call physics and astronomy, Aristotle was largely wrong about fundamental issues, at least in part because he gave greater priority to reasoning than to observation. Obviously, Aristotle was not alone in the ancient world in having genuine but misguided notions about the physical world. But his ideas were taken up so enthusiastically during the Middle Ages among western and Christian thinking that they came to acquire a force of dogma second only to that of the Bible itself.

Thus, when from about the 15th century AD scientists gradually (and often at great risk) began to challenge accepted Christian/western thinking on astronomy, it was often Aristotle's ideas the scientists were attacking, while the great Greek scientist was defended by dogmatic churchmen. In the bitter struggle that ensued, Aristotle's name

RIGHT: Aristotle was a teacher as well as a philosopher and scientist and taught students the value of observation of the natural world; his most famous pupil by far was Alexander the Great. Woodcut, German, circa 1480.

OPPOSITE: The astronomer Ptolemy (AD 100–170) elaborated a complex model of how the universe's celestial bodies moved that became accepted wisdom until the late Middle Ages. Despite his undoubted brilliance and ingenuity, Ptolemy was fundamentally wrong, because he believed that the Earth was at the centre of the universe. Painting, c.1476, by Justus van Gent, from a series of portraits of famous men in the Palazzo Ducale, Urbino. Paris, Musée du Louvre.

and reputation were dragged through the intellectual mud, with the result that modern generations have tended to have a rather negative view of Aristotle.

This, however, is unfair. For few people tried to understand the world as diligently as Aristotle. Indeed, his desire to explain the world rationally sets him apart as one of the great proto-scientists of human history. So where and how did the great man get it so wrong?

For one thing, Aristotle came out decisively against the atomic theory proposed by Leucippus and Democritus. Indeed, one of the reasons why we know so much about their theory is that Aristotle took time and trouble to reject it. His view was that such particles could not and did not exist; instead, he argued that you could go on breaking down matter into smaller and smaller parts. This was a view that would not be contradicted by observation for many hundreds of years and thus lodged in the collective western consciousness.

Aristotle seems to have adopted the view of earlier thinkers, such as the fascinating character Empedocles (c. 493–433 BC), that matter was created out of earth, wind, fire and air. (Empedocles, who lived on Sicily, is an engaging figure who among many other traits claimed magical powers, despised meat-eating and is said to have died after throwing himself into the crater of Mount Etna – possibly, it was said, to prove his divinity.)

Cosmology

Perhaps even more important was the direction Aristotle took on astronomy. Many in the ancient world, including the great Babylonian astronomers, had recorded their observations about the stars and planets. Making sense of how the heavens worked and how they related to the world was a different matter.

Philosophers such as Eudoxus of Cnidus built on existing ideas that the planets rotated round the Earth. Eudoxus devised an ingenious system to explain what was happening: he proposed that the celestial bodies were carried round the Earth on a system of spheres. The final version of Eudoxus' system contained no fewer than 27 spheres (including one for all the stars), and, as befits such an able man, the geometry of his argument is brilliant.

Several questions, however, remained. Despite Eudoxus' brilliance, the spheres he described mathematically did not quite match the observed path of all the planets. Also, we cannot be quite sure whether Eudoxus considered the spheres to be a physical reality – for example, glass–like structures of some kind – or whether they were simply abstract ideas to him.

These points matter because Aristotle added to the spheres to try to correct the anomalies (not wholly successfully), and ended up with an Earth surrounded by 55 spheres, an extremely complex structure. Moreover, he *did* think of the spheres as physical entities.

For Aristotle, the moon was the boundary between the earthly and the celestial. Beyond the moon everything was constant and essentially unchanging, and here he introduced a fifth element that existed in that domain only: ether. Below the moon, down here on earth, matter was composed of the four elements and was in a constant state of change.

To his credit, however, Aristotle did not get everything wrong. He not only accepted that the world was spherical rather than flat, but also demonstrated through observation why this must be so. For example, during lunar eclipses the image of the earth appears on the moon as a curved shadow.

Aristotle should certainly not carry all the blame for the persistence of this erroneous view of the solar system. The astronomer Ptolemy (*c.* AD 100–170) of Alexandria – not to be confused with the many rulers of Egypt who went by that name – constructed an even more complex and detailed model of the universe than Aristotle's, building on the work of an earlier astronomer from Asia Minor, Hipparchus, who was noted for the accuracy of his observations. Ptolemy's famous work the *Algamest* became an accepted model of how the universe worked. The Earth was still at the centre and surrounded by circular paths along which the planets moved. The main difference from Aristotle was that in Ptolemy's view the planets did not just go round the Earth. He said they also moved in loops – called epicycles – round the line of their orbit round the Earth.

This so–called Ptolemaic system was very complex, but it did have the virtue of matching just about all known observations of planetary movement at the time – unlike Aristotle's theory.

Between the two of them, Aristotle and, especially, Ptolemy dominated how humans viewed themselves in the universe – at the centre – for centuries. This idea survived until the late Middle Ages and became in effect an article of faith for Christianity.

One ancient voice did argue that the Earth was not at the centre of the universe: a Greek mathematician from Samos, Aristarchus (c. 320–250 BC). He was convinced that the sun was far bigger than the Earth, and that it was therefore the Earth that revolved round the sun rather than the other way around. He was ridiculed for such a view, and it never seriously challenged the Aristotelian/Ptolemaic view of the world.

Biology and medicine

Aristotle

One area where Aristotle's work has better withstood the test of time is biology. Here, his powers of observation of the natural world were outstanding. For example, he observed that, although a dolphin lived in the sea and swam like a fish, it gave birth to live young with the help of a placenta, just as land mammals did. So, he correctly classified dolphins as mammals. Aristotle also dissected animals to see how they were formed, and studied animal embryos and the stomachs of cattle.

He classified living things into a hierarchy with, naturally enough, plants at the bottom and humans at the top. It is true that even in this area Aristotle made some glaring mistakes – for example, denying that plants had different sexes. But on the whole, the more he observed, the more accurate Aristotle was. His extensive writings on the natural world rightly survived for a long time as models of their kind.

Aristotle's view of the human body, however, was less accurate than his other observations on nature. He gave primacy to the human heart as the seat of thought and the soul, and considered the brain little more than a cooler of the blood; humans were more rational than animals because – as had been observed – they had proportionately larger brains to cool their hot-bloodedness.

Hippocrates and Galen

In contrast to Aristotle, an earlier Greek, Hippocrates (c. 460–377 BC) had argued that the brain was the repository of intelligence. Hippocrates is generally regarded as the father of modern-day medicine, the man who made a decisive break with irrational and superstitious bases for treating the human body and tried to understand it using reason. One of his most famous contributions was the Hippocratic Oath, which still, in modified form, governs the way in which doctors are expected to behave in relation to their patients – especially in matters of confidentiality. Though it is doubtful that the oath was directly written by him, it is felt that it reflects Hippocrates' approach.

Hippocrates' own father was a doctor, which perhaps accounts for his own very practical approach to medicine. He believed in good diet and hygiene, and in moderation in all things, and thought that a doctor should intervene more drastically only when really necessary.

Hippocrates had a huge influence on a young doctor called Galen (AD 131–201), who in turn helped determine western medical practice until the end of the Middle Ages. Galen was born in Pergamum in Asia Minor and spoke Greek, though he spent a great deal of time in the imperial capital of his day, Rome. Among his practical experience was a spell as a doctor patching up gladiators, which gave him a valuable insight into wounds and the human body. He was also physician to several emperors, including Marcus Aurelius.

BELOW: The name of the Greek physician Hippocrates (460–377 BC) survives to this day because of the medical oath that bears his name. He probably inherited his interest in medicine from his father, who was also a doctor. Copper engraving, French, 16th century.

Galen both followed and developed the works of Hippocrates and other ancient physicians. For example, he expanded upon the traditional Hippocratic view that health and well-being depended on the correct balance of the four humours (bodily fluids), which were blood, phlegm, yellow bile (or choler) and black bile. These corresponded to the four elements – respectively, air, water, fire and earth – and also to four different temperaments: sanguine, phlegmatic, choleric and melancholic.

Galen understood that arteries contained blood, not air, but surprisingly did not make the small but crucial further step to understanding the true nature of blood circulation in the body. He was also a champion of bloodletting. Though Galen was himself keen on experimentation – including on live animals – for centuries after him physicians more or less simply accepted what he had written and generally did not conduct their own experiments. His influence on the practice of medicine was just as powerful as that of Aristotle and Ptolemy on physics and astronomy, and lasted until the 17th century.

The transfer of knowledge

The Tragedy of Alexandria
Nowadays we take it for granted that information and knowledge, archives and books are passed seamlessly on from one generation to another, even if occasional bouts of book-burning and censorship in modern history show that the flow can sometimes be

BELOW: The famous Library of Alexandria held much of the great learning and knowledge of the ancient world. Its destruction and the loss of its contents by the 5th century AD are still a source of great mystery and controversy. Coll. Archiv f.Kunst & Geschichte.

ABOVE: *Ptolemy II Philadelphus Egyptian King of the Macedonian Dynasty, 284-246 BC. Ptolemy and his sister (from 227 also his wife) Arsinoe. Coin portrait on an octadrachmon, c.285-246 BC.*

interrupted. The survival of ancient literature on a vast range of subjects was altogether more haphazard, and many of the works of great figures such as Aristotle are frustratingly lost to us for ever.

One of the symbols of the ancient world was the great library of Alexandria, a treasure house of literature from across the ancient world and a place that from the 3rd century BC attracted some of the greatest scholars in the classical world. It was founded by the ruler of Egypt, Ptolemy II (308–246 BC), the son of Alexander the Great's general who had started the Ptolemaic dynasty, and for centuries much of the knowledge and writing of the ancient world was stored here. It was said that the works of Aristotle himself formed the core of the collection at the great library.

At some point in the first few centuries AD, however, the library and its priceless collection of literature were destroyed.

Just who was responsible for this destruction, and in what circumstances such an important repository of knowledge was lost, are still matters of controversy. The library at Alexandria was a symbol of learning and culture, and thus different cultures and traditions have tried to blame its destruction on 'barbarian' rivals. The first person to be blamed for the loss was Julius Caesar, who, in 48 BC, in the course of his campaign against his rival Pompey, set fire to the Egyptian fleet in harbour at Alexandria. The resulting blaze is said to have destroyed parts of the city itself, including the library with an alleged loss of 40,000 precious volumes. It may be that, as some claim, the main structure of the library was destroyed at this time. However, there is strong evidence that a library of some kind continued to exist for many years after Caesar's time. There is, for example, a report that Mark Antony donated 200,000 books from another ancient library at Pergamum in Asia Minor to Cleopatra as an addition to the Alexandria collection.

The charge of the library's destruction has also been levelled at the Christian authorities, who destroyed or assimilated many of the visible signs of the pagan world when Christianity became the official faith of the Roman Empire. It is known that there was a satellite library to the main building, and that this was linked to the beautiful Temple of Serapis (the Serapeum) in Alexandria. In 391, the Emperor Theodosius ordered the destruction of all pagan temples in the city, an instruction that the Patriarch of Alexandria, Theophilus, carried out with some enthusiasm. The temple was duly razed, though there is no contemporary account telling us that any manuscripts were destroyed, or that the main library of Alexandria was attacked at the same time. However, there are also no ancient sources indicating that the library or the neighbouring museum survived into the 5th century AD.

Much later, some Christians claimed that the library and its contents were destroyed by the Muslim caliph Omar during the 7th century AD when the Arabs took control of Egypt. However, such claims can be dismissed as medieval Christian propaganda.

The likely truth is that the library and its contents suffered damage and destruction over a long period in a city noted for its volatility and unrest. With the advent of Christianity there was in general far less emphasis on science, philosophy and learning compared with theology, and libraries such as those at Alexandria probably dwindled in importance as a result. The main building may have been destroyed accidentally by Caesar. But this does not explain what happened to the many manuscripts and scrolls that existed in the city after Caesar's time. It could be that the ultimate fate of these volumes was linked to anti-pagan activity at the end of the 4th century AD.

The loss of such unimaginably important material – some claim the library at Alexandria may have contained 500,000 scrolls at its peak – did not cause the intellectual dark ages that were beginning to fall on west European thought at this time; but it was a symbol of them. What need had early Christians of Aristotle or Homer when they had the Bible? As a result, many ancient volumes were neglected, languished untranslated or

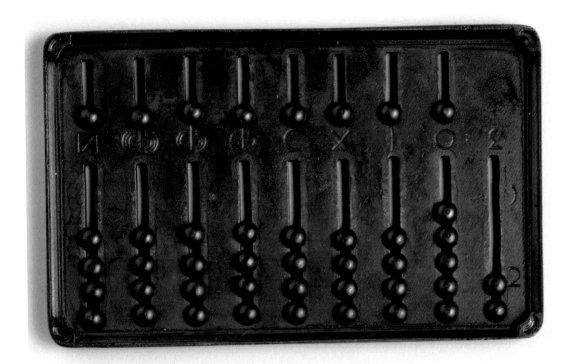

perhaps were even destroyed. For centuries to come the collective mind of western civilization was only dimly aware of many of the intellectual glories of the ancient world. Ironically, the salvation of western thought was eventually to come in the shape of a new power emerging from the east: that of the Arabs and Islam.

The Islamic Legacy

By the time Islam emerged from Arabia in the 7th century, much of classical learning was already a distant memory in the west. By the mid–13th century, when Islam was politically on the wane in the western Mediterranean, western civilization had rediscovered the lost teachings of the past, and itself stood on the eve of a cultural and intellectual renaissance.

What occurred in between was a remarkable transfer of information from east to west, from the Islamic to the Christian world, in some case via Christians in the Middle East and Asia Minor. Over the course of decades and centuries, the works of great classical writers were discovered, translated and often added to by Muslim scholars. Then western scholars, eager to find out more about this vast treasure trove of knowledge, travelled to great centres of learning in Spain and Italy to read and translate these ancient texts for themselves.

This flow of information was not, of course, the result of any deliberate policy. It was the norm for enlightened Islamic rulers to encourage the arts and education, and Moorish rule made Spain one of the cultural centres of the Mediterranean. The passing on of classical knowledge to Christian Europe was just an accidental by–product of Islamic practice.

What made the transfer of information possible was that in Spain, and also in Sicily and the Levant, Muslims and Christians lived side by side for centuries. In Spain, to be sure, this coexistence was often hindered by mutual mistrust, indeed, hatred, and punctuated by war and bloodshed. But in between crises there were relative periods of calm, during which lines of intellectual communication slowly developed. Once it was clear to scholars in the west that they had a hitherto unknown wealth of knowledge and learning on their own doorstep, the more intellectually curious of them made their way south and east. Some political leaders in the west actively encouraged this process.

AVICENNA

Ibn Sina (ad 980–1037), known to the west by his Latinized name of Avicenna, was regarded as the greatest mind of his day in the Islamic world. The Persian-born scholar was adept at both philosophy and medicine. In philosophy, he was regarded as an expert in the works of Aristotle, and his *Book of the Cure* (meaning the cure of ignorance) was a sort of encyclopaedia of philosophy, drawing not just on Aristotle but on Plato and the neoplatonists too. Just as important was Avicenna's *Canon of Medicine*, inspired by the works of Hippocrates, with which he was familiar via Galen's writings. This book was translated into Latin and became one of the standard textbooks on medicine in the west in the Middle Ages. Avicenna was said to have been something of a child prodigy, who by the age of ten knew by heart not just the entirety of the Qur'an but large amounts of poetry too, and who as a young man read Aristotle's work *Metaphysics* 40 times. Revered in Iran to this day, his significant influence on philosophy and medicine has been largely overlooked in the west.

The translation and development of classical texts began in earnest in the middle of the 8th century, when the 'Abbasid dynasty moved the centre of the Islamic world to Baghdad. The range of subjects in which the caliphate was interested was huge, and included philosophy, botany, agriculture, astronomy, medicine and surveying.

Many of the works of ancient scholars were translated directly into Arabic from Greek; some, though, were rendered into Arabic from translations of the originals made by Christian scholars in the east. For example, an eastern Christian known as George, Bishop of the Arabians (c. AD 640–724) had translated some of Aristotle's works into Syriac, and these Syriac renderings were later translated into Arabic. The 'Abbasid dynasty specifically commissioned an Arabic translation of Ptolemy's *Algamest*, while in the 9th century a Christian physician working for the caliph translated Hippocrates and Galen into Arabic.

The passing on of such texts to the west did not happen immediately. By the second half of the 10th century, though, the caliphate at Córdoba in Spain was acquiring a reputation for learning and culture; by the following century its library was claimed to contain some 400,000 volumes. Translated works on the subject of herbs by the Greek physician Dioscorides had already been circulating in Spain, while the great Arabic scholar and astronomer Maslama of Madrid was translating Ptolemy's *Planisphere* as well as contributing his own works on mathematics and astronomy.

An example of how the west gradually picked up knowledge via the Islamic world involves the abacus. Widely used by the Romans, this simple but effective aid to arithmetic had been lost to the west by the early Middle Ages. However, at the end of the 10th century, a Christian scholar called Gerbert of Aurillac (later Pope Sylvester II), who had spent some time studying in Spain, wrote a book on the subject. This text was almost certainly based on an earlier work written by a Christian or Jewish scholar, who had previously lived in Moorish Spain and who had picked up his knowledge of the abacus through scholars there.

The Islamic world was, of course, far more than just a passive conduit through which the great Greek writings passed en route to the west. Islamic scholarship, for example, had already absorbed and understood Aristotle. One of the greatest minds of the early medieval world was a brilliant 10th/11th–century philosopher called Ibn Sina or Avicenna. An equally talented later scholar was Ibn Rushd (1126–1198) – known in the west as Averroës – who wrote a series of brilliant commentaries on the Greek philosophers that helped shape both Islamic and Christian thought. Averroës was born in Córdoba and had trained as a physician, in which capacity he served the caliphate. He wrote extensively on a range of subjects, but was especially fascinated by Aristotle and sought to reconcile the Greek's philosophy with the Qur'an and Islam.

The history of algebra also owes much to the Islamic world – including its name. Algebra has its roots in Babylon, the ancient Greeks and Hindu mathematics, but Islamic scholars developed algebraic ideas of their own, and once again their knowledge was passed on to the west. The word 'algebra' comes from an Arabic title of a book on mathematics, published around AD 830, called  *al-Kitab al-mukhtasar fi hisab al-jabr wa'l-muqabala*. The author was a mathematician in Baghdad called Muhammad ibn Musa al–Khwarizmi, from the last part of whose name comes the word algorithm.

ABOVE: *The brilliant scholar Ibn Sina (980-1037), better known in the western world by the name Avicenna, was an important medieval figure who helped bring the knowledge of the ancient world into Christian culture. Born in Persia, he was an expert not just in philosophy, but medicine, too; and his work on medicine, inspired by Hippocrates and Galen, became a standard textbook on the subject in much of Europe. Engraving, unsigned, 16th century.*

The Classical Heritage in the West

During the 11th and 12th centuries, the translation of words and ideas gained pace. A scholar called Adelard of Bath (c. 1080–1150), who travelled in Sicily and also Syria, translated Euclid's *The Elements* into Latin – the language of scholars in the west. Adelard also wrote about the abacus, falconry and the astrolabe, in each case drawing on information gleaned from his travels in Islamic lands and his knowledge of Arabic.

The Arabic versions of famous texts even influenced their western names. For example, Ptolemy's great work on astronomy, the *Mathematike Syntaxis*, was known in the Arabic world as 'al–Majisti'; hence the name we know it by – the *Almagest*.

Around 1160, a translator known as Gerard of Cremona rendered the *Almagest* into Latin from Arabic, at the same time as another Italian scholar was translating a Greek version of the same work into Latin.

Gerard was a fascinating character, who translated no fewer than 88 works from Arabic into Latin. He carried out his work over nearly five decades in the Spanish city of Toledo, one of the most important centres of that period in the cross–fertilization of ideas and texts between the Muslim and Christian worlds. A number of such scholars were attracted to Toledo, including an Englishman called Daniel of Morley, one of Gerard's pupils and a fellow translator. It is through his accounts that we get a glimpse of how the process worked. Gerard first had a local scholar translate the Arabic text of a classical work into Spanish; he would then himself translate this version into Latin. This laborious approach was not only time-consuming but inevitably led to some quite imprecise translations.

Another British scholar involved in the transfer of knowledge was the Scottish astrologer Michael Scot. In the early 13th century, he was astrologer and alchemist to Frederick II, the Holy Roman Emperor. While in the emperor's employ, Scot translated a number of Aristotle's works on the natural sciences.

Another monarch of the period, Alfonso X of Castile, was so fascinated by what lay hidden in Arabic texts that he assembled a group of scholars whose task it was to render Arabic works into Spanish. The texts they translated ranged in subject-matter from astronomy and falconry to poetry.

This vast influx of material into the western canon of scholarship, so long starved of fresh material, soon found new markets. Up until this time, scholarship in the west had been largely confined within the Christian church and especially monasteries, where new ideas found it hard to penetrate. By the 12th and 13th centuries, however, separate centres of learning were starting to emerge in cities such as Paris and Bologna. This was the beginning of the universities, and an associated revolution in learning that was to sweep through Europe. The texts from the classical past rediscovered via Muslim Spain and Sicily were to have a huge impact on this new arena of intellectual endeavour.

The inventive mind and the development of technology

As well as laying the basis for our modern intellectual heritage, the minds of the ancient world applied themselves with equal enthusiasm and skill to solving more practical problems. Perhaps the most outstandingly practical people of all were the Romans, whose feats of engineering were to baffle and amaze people for centuries after their western empire had vanished into the chaos of the European dark ages.

The Roman Use of Concrete

One of the key Roman technological developments is also one of the most prosaic. The Egyptians had used a form of concrete in some of their building work, but it was the Romans who really perfected this very modern building material. The proof of their success still surrounds us: many Roman buildings made with concrete still stand, some 2,000 years after they were made.

By using concrete, the Romans could build larger buildings without compromising on their strength – as they did so effectively in the Pantheon in Rome (described in the previous chapter), which is one of the best examples of how this material was used. The secret ingredient that Roman engineers discovered to make concrete strong enough for large buildings was *pozzolana*, a sandy volcanic ash originally found and extracted at Pozzuoli near Mount Vesuvius. When this was added to the cement mix used to make concrete, the result was a material that set even under water and was far harder than the conventional concrete (which used lime or gypsum) they made. (We get our word cement from the Latin word *caementum*, which means 'rough stone'.)

It seems, however, that the Romans were not keen on the appearance of concrete, and it was standard practice to face the visible surface of a structure with a more attractive material, such as brick or marble – as, for example, in the Pantheon.

Bridges

The toughness of Roman concrete also made it an ideal material for use in the base of bridges, where strong water currents full of particles could quickly wear away a structure.

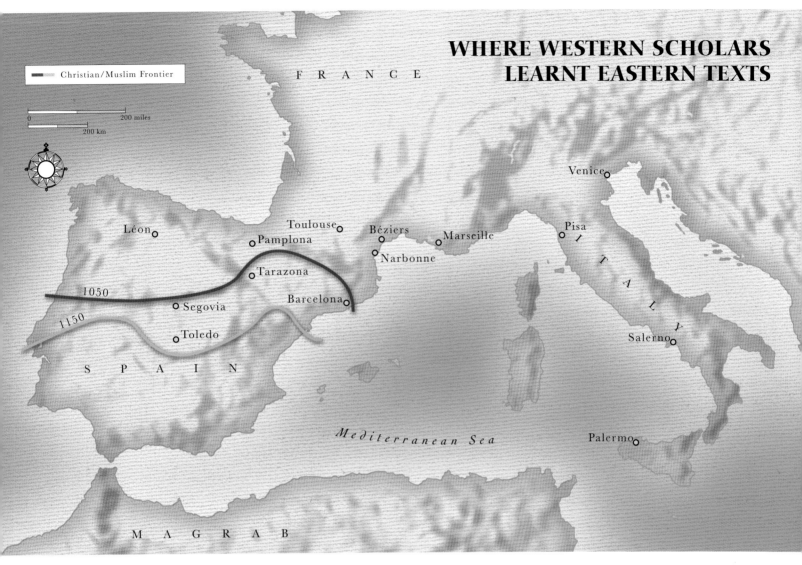

Christian/Muslim Frontier

0   200 miles
200 km

FRANCE

Venice

Léon

Toulouse   Béziers   Marseille   Pisa
Pamplona   Narbonne   ITALY

Tarazona

1050   Barcelona

1150   Segovia

Toledo   Salerno

SPAIN

Mediterranean Sea   Palermo

MAGRAB

Bridge–making was always a key requirement in the ancient world, when rivers, marshes and narrow stretches of sea provided natural barriers to the progress of horses, wagons and marching soldiers. Most of the early bridges were made of wood, but these, while relatively quick to build and strong enough to support most traffic, inevitably soon perished. In a few places stone bridges were used, but though these were more durable they were difficult and time–consuming to build.

One option for military or other short–term use was to build temporary floating bridges. In 480 BC, the Persian king Xerxes proposed taking a huge invasion army into Greece by land. This meant crossing the Hellespont (the Dardanelles) from Asia into Europe, and so he ordered his Phoenician and Egyptian engineers to construct two floating bridges. The first attempt was wrecked by a storm – for which the unfortunate engineers literally lost their heads – but fresh teams of engineers completed the feat, which, according to Herodotus, involved some elaborate engineering.

Herodotus says that 360 ships were used to support the bridge nearest the Black Sea, while 314 were needed for the bridge nearest the Aegean. Once the ships were in place, engineers stretched cables, some made of flax and others of papyrus, across and wound these taut with the aid of wooden winches. When the ropes were secured, wooden planks, brushwood and finally compacted earth were used to form the surface of the bridge. There was even a barrier put up on either side of the bridge, says Herodotus, so that horses and mules would not see the water below and take fright.

Once the bridges were finished, the Persians had to make the appropriate ceremonial

ABOVE: One of the accidental legacies of the Muslim influence across the Mediterranean was that it allowed Western scholars to rediscover much of the ancient learning of the classical world. This knowledge had been carefully preserved and elaborated on by Islamic academics.

ABOVE: At times, the Roman architects and engineers effortlessly combined great elegance with supreme practicality, as seen in the Pont du Gard at Nimes, France, which is the bridge section of an aqueduct.

preparations for such a major crossing. They burned spices on the bridge and placed boughs of myrtle at intervals along its length. At sunrise, Xerxes appeared with a golden goblet of wine, made a prayer for his invasion of Europe, and then threw the cup into the waters. Then the crossing began.

According to Herodotus, such was the size of the Persian army that seven days and seven nights passed before all the men, horses and provisions were safely on other side. This is almost certainly an exaggeration, but it must nonetheless have been an impressive sight as Xerxes and his men made this historic, if ill-fated, march into Europe.

Similar, but less elaborate, temporary bridges were used by Roman armies to cross rivers. In 55 BC, Julius Caesar had a wooden bridge built across the river Rhine in his campaign against the Germanic tribes. This mighty structure was built in ten days and was used to launch raiding parties against the enemy. But just 18 days after its completion the Romans dismantled it. Its real purpose was probably to demonstrate the might of Roman power and thus persuade the Germans that further resistance was pointless.

One of the greatest of Roman engineering feats was that of an architect called Apollodorus. In AD 104, at the demand of the Emperor Trajan, he built a bridge across the

river Danube at Drobetae in what is now Romania. Made of wood, it rested on solid pillars made from concrete and bricks and incorporated 21 arch spans: at more than 800 metres (2,600 feet) from end to end, it was the longest bridge ever built by the Romans. Little remains of this giant structure now, though some of the original pillars can still be seen on the banks of the Danube. Many Roman bridges have survived, however, including in Rome itself the Pons Fabricius, built in 62 BC, and the Pons Cestius, dating from three decades later.

Aqueducts, Baths, Sewers and Roads

The Romans also built some extraordinary aqueducts. Many of these were constructions of great beauty and splendour, such as that at Segovia in Spain, built around the end of the 1st century AD, or the magnificent Pont du Gard, the spectacular bridge section of the aqueduct of Nîmes.

Yet their main purpose was, of course, intensely practical – to bring water to large centres of population. By the end of the 1st century AD, nine aqueducts were bringing up to 386,000 cubic metres (85 million gallons) a day into Rome. Some of these brought water from more than 50 kilometres (30 miles) away. One of the great challenges of building such long channels was that they had to slope, very gently, in the right direction for their entire length as gravity was the only means of propelling the water. This called for extremely precise measuring and building. The 'fall' of the gradient was usually between 1 and 3 metres every kilometre (about 5–15 feet per mile).

Rome was not the only recipient of this marvel of technology: aqueducts supplied some 200 cities throughout the empire. The water was used by the imperial household and for public fountains, and was even supplied to some individual houses – provided the owners were wealthy enough; and, of course, among the main recipients were the public baths.

Bathing was an important feature of the Mediterranean world, and not just for the Romans. The Greeks had public areas where people sat in individual baths in a communal room. The superior engineering of the Romans enabled them to make bathing a rather more elaborate experience, and some of the baths were vast leisure complexes, complete with steam rooms, cold plunges, massage and exercise areas, and spaces to sit and chat.

A less glamorous, but equally important, Roman development was the sewer. The sewerage system under Rome was begun as early as the 5th century BC and was influenced by Etruscan practice. Ultimately, the huge sewers spread right under the city, to the point where Pliny the Elder, writing in the 1st century AD, described Rome as a 'city on stilts' in which the sewers were so vast that men had once sailed in them in 33 BC.

BELOW: Roman roads were a tribute to the ingenious and determined engineering of Roman experts. This road is found near Seville, Spain, homeland of Roman emperors Trajan and Hadrian.

Of all the remarkable engineering work of the Romans, one of the most noteworthy elements was their road-building. Once more, Roman engineers adapted Etruscan practices to lay roads on a scale never seen before – and not matched for centuries afterwards.

The first section of road was the famous Appian Way, which dates from AD 312 and ran south from Rome, first to Capua and later to Beneventum, Tarentum and Brundisium. At its fullest extent it was 563 kilometres (350 miles) long and was known among the Romans as the 'Queen of Highways'. This, however, was just the start: engineers would eventually build around 80,000 kilometres (50,000 miles) of road throughout the empire, much of it following very straight lines. The primary purpose of the roads was military: the legions could walk many miles a day on them, and messengers could carry their dispatches with maximum speed. Roads to and from ports were also used to carry goods.

The roads were built to a common standard, though precise techniques varied according to the importance and location of the route. Compacted earth and stone formed a base upon which a layer of stone was packed for drainage. A central layer contained concrete, gravel and sand, while the top was usually gravel, stones or sometimes slabs. Like so many of the Romans' physical achievements, many of the roads were left to deteriorate by local populations after the end of the empire in the west. Standards of transport, water supply and hygiene fell and remained below the levels set by the Romans for hundreds of years.

Industrial and Agricultural Engineering

The need to provide enough water to enable farmers to grow their crops was a major concern of the ancient world. The Egyptians had to learn how to channel the flow of the Nile, while throughout the usually dry Mediterranean region, water always had to be preserved and directed.

An early but limited invention for moving water over short distances was the *shaduf*, which dates from the 3rd millennium BC in Mesopotamia and around 1340 BC in Egypt, and later spread to the rest of the Mediterranean. The *shaduf* is a long pole fixed to a crossbeam. At one end is a weight; at the other a rope with a water container on the end. The idea was to dip the container into water, then swing the pole around to pour the water into a larger container, ditch or patch of ground. The use of the weight did reduce a lot of the backbreaking effort involved in carrying water by hand, but the device was slow and unable to carry large amounts of water any great distance.

More efficient was the *saqiya*, in which two interlocked wheels driven by cattle or other beasts pulled a chain of pots: this mechanism could move large quantities of water in a day. This technique was probably developed by the Persians from around 500 BC and was used in Egypt from the 3rd century BC.

More ambitious still was a device invented by the great mathematician Archimedes, whose technical brilliance has featured earlier in this chapter. This consisted of a cylinder, inside which was a helix or 'screw'; when this screw was turned, it drew water from one end to the other. Archimedes' screw may have originally been designed for pumping water out of a ship, and, according to the 1st-century BC historian Diodorus Siculus, it was also used by the Romans to drain water from mines in Spain.

Among the masters of irrigation in the Mediterranean were the Moors in Spain. Their sophisticated system of channels helped bring fertility to much of Andalucía and notably Valencia, where rice-growing remains a common form of agriculture. When, after the Christian reconquest of Spain in 1492, many thousands of Muslims were expelled, they took much of their knowledge and experience of irrigation techniques with them, and parts of southern Spain returned to drought conditions.

ABOVE: This very old and simple device known as a shaduf was first used to move water in Mesopotamia as far back as the 3rd millennium BC; here it is being used on the Nile as recently as the late 20th century.

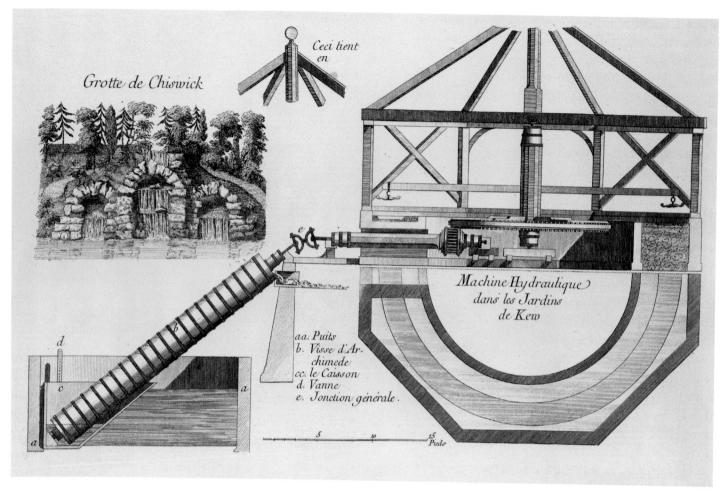

Grotte de Chiswick

Ceci tient en

Machine Hydraulique dans les Jardins de Kew

aa. Puits
b. Visse d'Archimede
cc. le Caisson
d. Vanne
e. Jonction générale.

5   10   15 Pieds

ABOVE: An ingenious device to move water, invented by Archimedes and known as an Archimedes Screw, was the basis of an engine used to pump water at Kew Gardens in London from the middle of the 18th century until the 1850s.

Writing Materials

The progress of writing, and ultimately the development of literature, philosophy, science and mathematics, all depended on another important area of technological advance – the development of writing materials.

The ancient Egyptians, apart from carving in stone, are well known for writing on papyrus, a flexible material made from the papyrus plants or reeds that flourished in the marshes that surround the Nile. Such material was widely used in the eastern Mediterranean.

Another common technique was to use wooden or sometimes ivory tablets held together with a hinge or a piece of cord. The Greeks and later the Romans used variations on such tablets, as well as rolls of papyrus. The Latin for a roll of papyrus was 'volumen', from which we get the English word 'volume' for a book.

An alternative material was parchment produced from animal skins – higher quality parchment is known as vellum. Rather than writing directly on the vellum in ink, sometimes people would cover the sheets of vellum in wax so they could be written on and then reused. Sheets of vellum were also bound together to form what are called 'codices' (singular 'codex'), which are the forerunner of modern books. However, the classics of the Greek and Roman world and, for example, the 'books' of the New Testament were written on papyrus. Many early Christian works were written on papyrus codices, that is sheets of papyrus bound together.

The English word 'paper' comes from 'papyrus', but in fact the two materials are different. Papyrus is made by overlapping layers of the papyrus plant, pressing them together and then allowing them to dry. Paper comes from wood that has been mixed with water, mashed into a pulp and then compressed and dried into sheets.

Paper was invented by the Chinese, probably around 200 BC, and it took a long time to come to the Mediterranean world. For centuries, the Chinese kept the process a closely guarded secret, but eventually the technique spread to the Islamic world. Exactly how it did so is unclear, though tradition has it that it followed a battle between Arabs and Chinese in central Asia in AD 751, after which the prisoners taken by the Islamic forces were found to include a group of Chinese paper-makers who were persuaded to reveal their secrets.

It was the Arabs who introduced paper into the Mediterranean world, and by the start of the 10th century it had reached Spain. This was a time when Moorish power under the Arabs and Berbers was close to its peak. By the 12th century, and possibly before, paper mills had been established in Moorish Spain. Meanwhile, the knowledge of paper and how to make it started to spread to Christian Europe, partly because of the gradual Christian reconquest in Spain, and partly because of the communication between Islamic and Christian scholars in Spain and Sicily.

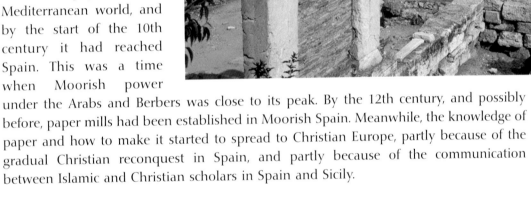

ABOVE: The fascinating Tower of the Winds in Athens dates from around 50 BC. It is thought to have housed sundials and an elaborate water clock, as well as a bronze weathervane in the form of the sea god Triton, which sadly has not survived.

Time and money

Calendars and Clocks

One invention that has become so integral a part of our lives that we can sometimes forget that it was devised by humans is the division of time into standard periods: years, months, days, hours and so on.

The ancient Egyptians came up with the 365-day year, an idea which came from the regular flooding of the Nile and which was in turn associated with the rising of the 'dog star' or Sirius at the same time. Their year comprised 12 months of 30 days each, with an awkward extra five days on the end.

An attempt to deal with the problem of extra days was made by the Romans during the time of Julius Caesar. The so-called 'Julian calendar' of 46 BC spread the 'spare' days around the months. To allow for the fact that a year is actually 365.2422 rather than 365 days they also introduced the idea of a 'leap year' of 366 days every four years.

This calendar remained in force until 1582 when, under Pope Gregory XIII, a new 'Gregorian calendar' was devised. This altered which years could be leap years. However, the Orthodox churches did not accept this new calendar until the 20th century, and even then not all of them adopted it. Indeed, all Orthodox churches – including those that otherwise use the Gregorian system – still calculate Easter by the old Roman Julian calendar.

ABOVE: Sundials, such as this Roman limestone example, have been used by humans to tell the time of day since ancient times; versions existed in Egypt, while the Greeks apparently learnt about their use from the mathematically minded Babylonians.

Our names for the months also come from the Romans. January derives from Janus, the god of doors and beginnings, who was depicted looking both backwards and forwards; March comes from the god of war, Mars; July from Julius Caesar; and August from the first emperor, Augustus Caesar.

The need to measure time on a smaller scale, in terms of times of day and hours, gradually became more pressing as society became more complex. No one is quite sure who invented the sundial – the mechanism was probably invented independently in different parts of the world – but we do know that a rudimentary sundial existed in Egypt around 1500 BC. Herodotus tells us that the Greeks learned about the sundial and the division of the day into 12 parts – hours – from the Babylonians. There is also a mention of what might be called an 'accidental sundial' in the Old Testament at 2 Kings 20, which refers to the shadow of the sun moving across the steps of a stairway built by King Ahaz: the word 'stairway' is sometimes translated as 'sundial'. This episode dates from some time in the 8th century BC.

The Greek–speaking Babylonian astronomer Berosus invented a more sophisticated form of sundial around the 4th century BC. His device was a hollow hemisphere, like a bowl, with a rod or a pin – known as a gnomon – inside it at the centre. As the sun 'moved' through the sky, the progress of the shadow cast by the gnomon was marked on the inside of the hemisphere.

Sundials remained popular throughout the Roman empire and into more modern times, though they did have severe limitations. They relied on the sun shining, obviously did not work at night, and required allowances to be made for the different lengths of day in winter and summer.

An alternative device was the water clock. Typically, this used a tank from which water was allowed to escape, slowly and at a regular speed. As the water level went down, a float in the tank fell with it, and marked the passing of the time on a scale on the side of the tank. The Tower of the Winds (otherwise known as the Horologion of Andronicos) in Athens, which dates from about 50 BC, is said to have contained an elaborate water clock.

Currency

Just as it became necessary to be able to measure time according to a generally acknowledged standard, so it also became necessary to have a universally accepted form of payment with which to conduct trade.

Money was used for thousands of years in the ancient world in the form of gold, silver, jewels and other materials regarded as precious. In Egypt and other societies, precious metals, such as gold and silver, were weighed accurately to test their value and thus assess how much they could buy.

A more standardized system of money was introduced first, as far as we can tell, by the people of Lydia in Asia Minor in the 7th century BC. The Lydians were known throughout the ancient world for their wealth – the fabulously rich Croesus, who died in about 546 BC, was the last king of Lydia before it was absorbed into the Persian Empire. Their coins bore the mark of the government that had issued them, which constituted a guarantee of their value and meant they did not have to be weighed each time they were used in exchange for goods. The citizens of classical Greece, who soon adopted the idea of issuing money, made coins with designs that referred to the individual cities where the coins were produced. The Romans had their own tradition of currency: by the start of the 2nd century BC their system was based on a silver *denarius* coin plus other coins made of bronze, and later a gold coin called the *aureus* was introduced.

Military invention

It was always essential for people in the ancient Mediterranean world to be able to defend themselves, as well as to attack others. Accordingly, much of the inventiveness of humans in the region was, as elsewhere, channelled into military technology. We have already seen how Archimedes helped design war machines; in fact, this was one of his main claims to fame in the ancient world, despite the fact that he much preferred pure mathematics.

Behind each dominant empire there was usually a military as well an economic or political reason why it prevailed over other peoples. For example, as noted in Chapter Two, the Macedonians and Greeks under Alexander the Great benefited not just from his inspirational leadership and personal courage but from rigorous training instigated by Alexander's father Philip, who introduced the new weapon of the sarissa (a long spear or pike) and the associated fighting formation: a tight phalanx of troops with the appearance of a giant hedgehog that made it hard for the enemy to get close without being speared.

The Romans, who produced perhaps the greatest military might ever known, pioneered a number of new techniques. They adapted the old round shield of the Greeks to an oval one that gave them better protection against, for example, the long, slashing swords of the Gauls. They also developed a double-edged sword with a blade of about 50 centimetres (20 inches) that was ideal for close combat. Another key development was the use of the *pilum*, a powerful javelin with a narrow neck that was designed to bend on impact with the enemy's shield or body. Even if the opponent was not killed, he was usually incapacitated or at least lost the use of his shield.

Roman troops were extremely well trained and drilled, and knew what was expected of them in battle. Under reforms instigated first by the great general Scipio Africanus, and pursued later by consul and general Gaius Marius (c. 157–86 BC), the army was put on an even more professional footing.

Roman soldiers were also immensely skilled and courageous in hand-to-hand fighting. As the popularity of gladiatorial competition showed, the importance attached to individual combat in the Roman world was immense.

The rapid expansion of the Arab/Islamic empire in the 7th century AD was a result of many factors, among them the undoubted ability of their generals and the quality of their forces: their soldiers were fierce and determined, their armies highly mobile. Moreover, the Arabs were adept at fighting in the desert and at using this environment, so hostile to others, as a place of refuge, a conduit for communications, and a source of reinforcements

ABOVE: Long before the Euro, Europe had a common currency in the form of the Roman system of money, which was based on the silver denarius, shown here with the head of the Emperor Augustus on a coin made in 19 BC. Found at Kalkriese (Osnabrueck region, Lower Saxony), probably the scene of the Varus Battle. Kalkriese, Museum und Park Kalkriese.

ABOVE: The 13th-century philosopher Thomas Aquinas sought to reconcile the beliefs of the Christian Church with the much older and, in theory, 'pagan' philosophy of the Greek Aristotle. Painting, c.1476, by Justus van Gent, from the series of portraits of famous men in the Palazzo Ducale in Urbino. Paris, Musée du Louvre.

and supplies. Some observers have even likened the Arabs' use of the desert to the way that later maritime empires used the seas.

One devastating military invention that played a significant role in the history of the Mediterranean was a substance known as 'Greek fire'. For hundreds of years, attackers and defenders alike had used flammable substances, including resins, sulphur, naphtha and petroleum, to attack enemy troops, buildings and ships, just as they had hurled a variety of other materials – such as venomous snakes and even plague victims – in catapults and other siege machines.

Yet Greek fire seems to have been even more dangerous. The name, given to it much later by the crusaders (original names included 'marine fire', 'liquid fire' and 'wildfire'), is somewhat misleading, for its invention is traditionally ascribed to a Syrian called Calinicus, who fled to Constantinople from the Arab invasions of the late 7th century AD. The precise nature of its composition remains a mystery: it may have been a mixture of petroleum with resin and sulphur; some have suggested that quicklime was a vital extra ingredient. What all contemporaries agree on is that the power of this liquid, once ignited, was greater than any other similar substance used thus far. It was used to devastating effect twice by the Byzantine Empire when its capital Constantinople came under attack from Muslim fleets. The first occasion was a long siege that began in AD 673; the second occasion was in 717–718. On each occasion the defenders shot the deadly liquid from metal tubes or weapons fixed on the front of their ships.

The formula for Greek fire was a closely guarded secret among the Byzantine elite, who were desperate to make sure that no enemy or potential enemy got their hands on it. It seems, however, that the Arabs did manage to copy it or invent a similar liquid, even if the material was never to have quite the decisive impact in later conflict as the original had when first used.

When the scientific output of the ancient world was rediscovered by the west, thanks largely to the work of Islamic scholars, it helped lay the foundations for the Renaissance and later the Age of Reason and Science in Europe. This outcome was not immediate, nor was it inevitable. In the 13th century, first Albertus Magnus, then his more famous pupil Thomas (later St) Aquinas (see box opposite) sought to reconcile faith with reason, Aristotle with Christianity. Their success in doing so was not necessarily an advance for science: Aristotle's theories in effect became part of accepted wisdom and teaching, errors and all, which did not encourage new thinking. However, there was now at least a discussion and a basic framework for the study of the natural world, however wrong, against which new scientists could test their observations and theories.

Slowly, new theories emerged from men such as Copernicus, Brahe, Galileo and Newton that changed the way humans saw themselves and the world for ever. In many senses, these pioneers of their age were completing the unfinished work started by the great minds of the classical world. As Newton himself famously once wrote: 'If I have seen further than others, it is because I have stood on the shoulders of giants.'

THOMAS AQUINAS

Thomas Aquinas (1225–1274) was made a saint in 1323 and is one of the most important figures in the history of western learning. Born in Italy into a well–connected aristocratic family, Aquinas wanted to join the Dominican monastic order from an early age. Initially he was 'kidnapped' by his family in a bid to dissuade him, but by 1244 he had got his way and was sent by the order to study under the great philosopher and scholar Albertus Magnus in Cologne. Here he developed his interest in the work of Aristotle. Up to this point there had seemed to be an inherent and irreconcilable conflict between the 'blind' faith of the church, and the reliance on reason urged by Aristotle. The Angelic Doctor, as Aquinas became known, reconciled the two in his work *Summa contra Gentiles (Treatise against Unbelievers)*, which was specifically designed to be used in Spain against the arguments of Muslims and Jews. Just as St Augustine had sought to reconcile parts of Platonic and neoplatonic thought with Christianity, so Aquinas worked to accommodate the church and Aristotle. Aquinas' best–known work was the unfinished *Summa theologica*, in which he laid out Christian beliefs – a work that was to remain at the centre of Catholic thought for centuries.

ABOVE: In war, as in so many other aspects of life, the Romans were inventive and good at developing or adapting new technologies; these are giant catapults used for war in around 52 BC. Woodcut after a painting by Henri P. Motte, c.1870.

CHAPTER 5
RELIGION AND BELIEFS

The history, culture and philosophy of the Mediterranean world can be fully appreciated only with an understanding of the varied beliefs of its peoples. Religion has played a central role in the story of the region, not least because three great world religions – Judaism, Christianity and Islam, whose followers are together called the 'peoples of the book' – have converged and often come into conflict there. The story of gods, faith and religion, however, reaches back far in time, long before these three monotheisms came to dominate.

RIGHT: Religion has played a crucial role in the story of the Mediterranean, often inspiring great art and architecture but also leading to many clashes of cultures and beliefs – tensions that still exist in the region today. This Byzantine mosaic shows Mary and child between John II Comnenus and Empress Irene. Mosaic, c.1118–22. Istanbul, Hagia Sophia, South gallery.

As so often in the Mediterranean, our story starts with ancient Egypt. The Egyptians worshipped a pantheon of gods thousands of years before the birth of Jesus Christ, and were greatly preoccupied with the afterlife.

In the beginning: the Egyptians

Ancient Egyptians even had their own guide book to death. This is often called *The Book of the Dead*, though it was known to them as *The Book of Going Forth by Day*. This remarkable collection of texts, which dates from the end of the 2nd millennium BC, was placed alongside the deceased so they could use it during their journey to the underworld. It revealed routes, shortcuts, prayers and spells, and acted as a kind of passport for the dead person's spirit. Wealthier citizens had sections of the texts prepared especially for them. The less well-off used existing templates of the book on which a scribe would simply add their name, and the scroll would then be buried with the dead person.

The Egyptians also had a variety of gods. According to tradition the first was Atum, though the sun god Re (sometimes written Ra) was usually regarded as the most powerful. In time, these two deities became merged into one as Atum-Re. Another important deity, from Thebes in Upper Egypt, was Amun, who again became associated with Re as Amun-Re. The historian Herodotus said that the Greeks identified Amun (or Amen) with Zeus.

The best-known names among the hierarchy of Egyptian gods, however, are Osiris, Isis and Horus. After Re, Osiris was probably the most important and powerful of the deities, and the story of his death and resurrection is a key part of ancient Egyptian mythology.

Osiris was a great ruler who taught the Egyptians the values of civilization, how to farm and how to irrigate. His brother Seth, however, was jealous of Osiris' power and status, and plotted his downfall. He laid on a banquet at which he displayed a marvellous coffin and promised that whoever could fit into it the best could have it as a gift. Osiris got into the

BELOW: The Egyptian texts known to us as The Book of the Dead *are a mixture of prayers, advice and incantations. They were designed as a kind of guide to the afterlife and intended to help the dead person's spirit find its way to the underworld. Painting on papyrus. Turin, Museo Egizio.*

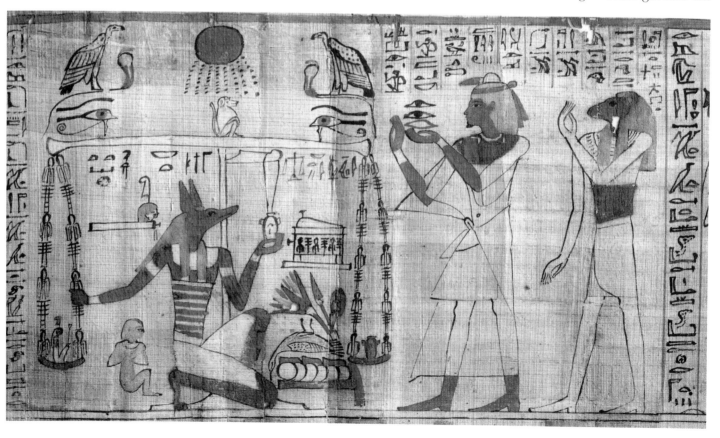

coffin and found it was a perfect fit – whereupon Seth sealed it tight and threw it into the river. A distraught Isis, Osiris' wife and sister, rescued the body, but Seth got hold of it once more. Seth then cut Osiris into 14 pieces, which he scattered over Egypt. Undeterred, Isis retrieved all the pieces, save for the penis, reassembled Osiris and brought him back to life; she even fashioned new genitalia for him. Though restored to life, Osiris chose to preside instead over the realm of the dead, but meanwhile he and Isis had miraculously conceived a child called Horus who ultimately avenged his father in battle with Seth.

For the Egyptians, Isis, who hid her son in the rushes of the Nile delta to protect him from harm, became the ultimate symbol of a devoted mother, while Horus' image was that of the devoted son. Horus was also closely linked with the worship of Re.

Images of Isis nursing her infant son Horus irresistibly remind us of the later Christian image of the Madonna and Child. Indeed, some scholars have suggested that there are a number of intriguing parallels between the stories of the birth, life and characteristics of Horus and those of Jesus.

Isis was an immensely popular goddess in the ancient world, not just with Egyptians but with the Greeks and Romans too – there is evidence there may even have been a temple to Isis as far away as Roman London. She was known by a number of titles, among them 'Queen of Heaven' and 'Star of the Sea' (in Latin, 'Stella Maris'); in some areas she became a patron saint of sailors. The Greeks also associated her with Demeter, the goddess of agriculture and the earth. It is possible that familiarity with the cult of Isis helped early Christian converts identify with the story of Mary, the mother of Jesus and thus, like Isis, the mother of a god.

Hittites and Phoenicians

The names and characteristics of different gods did not remain constant in the ancient world. The rise and fall of empires, the development of trade links and the constant movement of peoples meant that societies were often coming into contact not only with each other but with each other's deities. Sometimes these new gods were identified with a society's existing deities; sometimes they were simply added to the pantheon as new gods. Many of the gods that were worshipped by the Sumerians and Babylonians in Mesopotamia, for example, found their way into the religions of neighbouring peoples.

The Hittites in particular seem to have been very adept at collecting deities as their empire in Anatolia expanded. Indeed, ancient sources spoke of the 'thousand gods of Hatti', and many hundreds of their names have now been identified. The Hittites seem to have practised religious tolerance on a grand scale, simply adding a new god or goddess to their worship whenever they came across one. An important figure was Anu, who seems to be the Hittite version of An, an important Mesopotamian deity.

A popular goddess worshipped on the eastern edge of the ancient Mediterranean

ABOVE: *The goddess Astarte, depicted here in a sculpture dating from the 3rd century BC, was an important deity in Canaan and became an important goddess of the Phoenicians, who spread her worship throughout the Mediterranean. She represented nature, fertility and sexuality. Alabaster statuette with gold-plating. Paris, Musée du Louvre.*

ABOVE: This is the figure of Baal, who was one of the most important gods of the Canaanites. The Phoenicians spread his worship around the Mediterranean and Baal, who was thought to be able to protect sailors, was revered in Carthage. Gilded broze figurine. Minet-el Beida (Harbour of Ugarit, today Shamra, Syria). Departement des Antiquites Orientales, Paris, Musée du Louvre.

world was the Babylonian Ishtar, or Inanna as she was known to the Sumerians. Ishtar was a mother goddess and represented fertility and love, but she was also a goddess of war to the Assyrians, and before a battle she appeared dressed in body armour and armed with her bow and arrows.

A famous story concerning Ishtar relates her descent to the underworld, where she was imprisoned, causing the plants and animals of the earth above to become infertile. This story has strong parallels with the later Greek tale of Persephone, the beautiful daughter of Demeter and Zeus who was abducted by the god of the underworld, Hades. Demeter was so enraged at the fate of her daughter that she caused the earth to become cold and barren until she was released. Eventually, Hades agreed to let Persephone go, but tricked her into having to return to the underworld for part of each year. When she does so, the earth becomes barren once more, returning to fertility only when she reappears each spring. Thus her story and its yearly cycle symbolizes the endless flow of the seasons, a recurrent and important theme in ancient myths and religions, and often expressed in terms of death and resurrection – as in the story of Osiris.

The Canaanites, inhabitants of the Levant and known to us from the Old Testament, had similar stories. Their chief god was El, but another important deity was Baal – originally the name (which means 'Lord') given to a number of local gods before emerging as a god of weather and fertility in his own right.

In one Canaanite story, Baal fights and kills his bitter enemy, the sea god Yam, but then has to confront another god, Mot, who represents death. Eventually, Baal accepts that, like everyone else, he has to yield to death. However, the goddess Anat, who is both wife and sister of Baal, decides to fight on his behalf and, in the face of indifference from the other gods, attacks Mot with a knife. She cuts him to shreds, burns and grinds the parts, and then scatters them in the fields. Baal is duly restored to life. Anat was clearly a feisty character; as well as taking on death she also crushed Lotan, better known to us as the sea monster Leviathan (also mentioned in the Old Testament).

The Phoenicians, who are broadly synonymous with the Canaanites, also worshipped Baal. Being great traders, who depended on boats and sea travel for their living, the Phoenicians adopted Baal as the god who protected sailors on their long and perilous voyages. As a result of the Phoenicians' travels, Eastern gods such as Baal were known all over the region and worshipped in many different places.

Baal survives now in a rather different context, in the name of Ba'al Zebub or Beelzebub, mentioned in the Old Testament at 2 Kings 1, verses 1–6, 16. King Ahaziah of Israel has fallen and hurt himself. In pain he despatches messengers, telling them, 'Go and consult Baal–Zebub, the god of Ekron, to see if I will recover from this injury'. According to Kings, the Lord was so upset at the king consulting another god that Ahaziah was condemned to die in his bed.

The use of the name 'Baal–Zebub' in the Old Testament divides scholars. Its literal translation is 'Lord of the Flies'. Some believe that this was the real name of the god of Ekron, a Philistine town in Canaan, and that the name either reflects Baal's ability to destroy flies and keep them away from religious sacrifices or that as a sun god he is the bringer of flies. Another view is that 'Baal–Zebub' is a deliberate distortion by the author of Kings of the name 'Baal–Zebul' which means 'Lord of the Mansion'. Whatever the true explanation, the name came to be associated with a demon, and in many later Christian accounts 'Beelzebub' figures as one of the most important 'fallen angels' or devils – or even as a name for the Devil himself.

The most important Phoenician goddess was Astarte, a goddess of war, love and fertility known also as the 'Queen of Heaven'. The Phoenicians were not the only people to worship her. Indeed, the Old Testament tells us that King Solomon himself followed Astarte, the 'goddess of the Sidonians' (Sidon was a major Phoenician port in the Levant). Astarte had devotees as far west as Malta and Sicily, and at the North African Phoenician colony of Carthage. On Crete she became associated with the Greek goddess Aphrodite.

Another Phoenician god associated with death and resurrection was Adonis, better known to us as a god of the Greeks, who adopted the fertility cult linked to him. His name, which, like Baal, means simply 'Lord', from the Canaanite word *adon*, is now synonymous with male beauty. In Phoenician mythology Adonis was matched with Astarte, and each

BELOW: Adonis was a Phoenician god, whose name meant 'Lord' in Canaanite. Later he became better known as a Greek god synonymous with male beauty. In mythology, Adonis is killed, as shown in this image, but brought back to life each year with the Spring. Marble statue by Vincenzo de Rossi (1525–1587). Florence, Museo Nazionale del Bargello.

year followers held rites to mark the dying and rebirth of the god. His death occurred after Astarte and Adonis fell in love and a jealous rival assumed the form of a wild boar and killed Adonis. In her grief, Astarte promised to bring Adonis alive each spring, and the flowering of red anemones each year marks his rebirth.

The main deity of the important city of Tyre, and one of the most important Phoenician gods of all, was Melqart, whom the Greeks knew as Heracles and the Romans knew as Hercules.

BELOW: Zeus was the supreme Greek god, who came to power after usurping his father Kronos and the other so-called Titans; his wife and sister was the goddess Hera, the queen of the gods. Palermo, Museo Nazionale Archeologico.

Indeed, Herodotus tells us that he made a special trip to the temple to Melqart (he uses the name Heracles) at Tyre. He describes talking to the priests and also tells us about two pillars in honour of the deity, one decorated with pure gold and the other with emerald that 'gleamed in the dark with a strange radiance'. Once again, through their trading activity, the Phoenicians and Carthaginians spread the worship of Melqart throughout the Mediterranean, even as far west as Spain. It has been suggested that the famous Pillars of Hercules at Gibraltar were originally known as the 'Pillars of Melqart'.

At Carthage, Astarte was displaced as the dominant goddess in the 5th century BC by a moon goddess called Tanit, while the main male deity was called Baal Hammon, the protector of Carthage.

One of the most controversial issues concerning the religious rituals of the Carthaginians is that of child sacrifice. The Greek-speaking historian of the 1st century BC, Diodorus Siculus, tells us that this was their practice, and cites an example of their sacrificing 200 children publicly in the late 4th century BC. However, Diodorus is generally regarded as an unreliable source, whereas more trustworthy writers such as Polybius, who witnessed the destruction of Carthage in 146 BC, are silent on the matter. The discovery of thousands of terracotta urns at Carthage containing cremated remains of children appears, on the face of it, compelling evidence that such sacrifices took place. Some critics, however, point out that there could be other reasons for these remains, and that we do not know enough about how the Carthaginians dealt with the bodies of dead and stillborn children to be sure what the true explanation is.

Ancient Greece

The Greek Gods

We have already seen how Greek gods derived in part from the deities of other cultures in the Mediterranean. Herodotus was convinced that many of them came from ancient Egypt; his mistake was not in seeing other religious influences on Greek beliefs, just in singling out Egypt as the main source of them.

Ultimately, though, it is as Greek creations that the ancient gods are best known to us, and the many fascinating myths surrounding the gods and semi-divine heroes have formed an important part of western consciousness. Though no longer worshipped – except in a few modern revivals – gods such as Zeus, Aphrodite, Apollo (see box opposite) and Hermes are still familiar characters to us.

Homer and Hesiod set out the origin and character of the Greek gods; their tales were picked up and embellished by later writers. Before Zeus there had been Kronos, son of Gaia (the earth) and Ouranos (the sky), plus the other great early deities known as Titans. The wife and sister of Kronos was Rhea, who was also associated with the earth goddess Cybele from Phrygia in Anatolia. However, Kronos and the other Titans were usurped by his son Zeus – who had gained the awesome power of thunder and lightning. It was he who ushered in the pantheon of gods with whom we are more familiar.

Greek religion was polytheistic, but Zeus was the supreme deity, known as the father of gods and men. He lived on Mount Olympus with the other Olympian gods, of whom there were 12 in all. The cast occasionally varied, but it was usually Aphrodite, Apollo, Ares, Artemis, Athena, Demeter, Hephaestus, Hera, Hermes, Hestia, Poseidon and Zeus.

There is a theory that early worship in the Aegean, around the time of the Minoan and Mycenaean societies, was centred on mother or earth goddesses. When the Dorians and other migrants arrived in the area, they may have changed the emphasis to the worship of sky gods, making their religious culture more masculine. Certainly, the prime importance of Zeus in Greek mythology tends to support this view, even if

LEFT: In Greek mythology the gods mingled often with humans, even if their status was very different. The mortal Trojan prince Paris was asked by the goddesses Athena, Hera and Aphrodite to decide which of them was most beautiful (the Judgement of Paris, as it is known, depicted here by the 17th-century Flemish painter Rubens, 1577–1640). When Paris chose Aphrodite, she gave him as a reward the love of the beautiful Helen of Sparta. Vienna, Akademie der Bildenden Kuenste.

the memory of earth-mother worship survived in goddesses such as Zeus's wife Hera and in Demeter.

The Greeks were very close to their gods, in the sense that the deities inhabited the same earth and became intimately involved in the affairs of humans. Zeus, for example, slept not just with other gods but with nymphs and human women too. The gods took sides and fought over humans, whom they favoured or disfavoured for a variety of reasons, often to do with sexual attraction and beauty.

For example, the handsome Paris, son of the Trojan king, Priam, was asked by Zeus to choose who was the most beautiful goddess out of Hera, Athena and Aphrodite. Eventually, after cunningly insisting that they undress so he could examine their charms more intimately, Paris chose Aphrodite. This was probably because she bribed him with the promise that he could have Helen of Sparta as a reward. In the Trojan War, which was caused by Paris' elopement with Helen, the gods again took sides and intervened on behalf of their favourites.

Yet while the gods were close to humans, they were emphatically not the same. The Greek lyrical poet Pindar (c. 518–438 BC) may have written that humans and gods both drew breath from 'one mother', but he made it clear that in strength they were far apart. Indeed, the folly of humans in thinking that they could act like the gods or defy the gods' wishes was expressed in the Greek idea of *hubris*: extreme human pride or presumption which inevitably leads to the displeasure of the gods and ends in disaster.

Examples of *hubris* can be found throughout Greek stories and myths. Arachne, a girl from a modest family in Lydia, Asia Minor, had a remarkable talent as a weaver. It was said even to rival the ability of the goddess Athena (Minerva to the Romans). Unfortunately, Arachne refused to acknowledge the goddess as her teacher and went so far as to challenge the goddess to a contest. For her temerity in challenging the gods, Arachne was ultimately turned into a spider.

The apparently licentious behaviour of the gods – sleeping with whomever they liked, turning themselves into animals or condemning humans to endless torment – did not meet with the approval of all parts of Greek society at all times. As early as the 6th century BC, the philosopher Xenophanes argued that God was a single, undivided entity, and that humans sought to portray divinity in their own image. He famously asserted that if oxen had hands and could paint then they would depict gods in the form of oxen.

The Greek philosopher Heraclitus (c.544–483 BC) believed in a divinity but not in the personalized gods of the traditional Greek pantheon. He and other philosophers began the process of separating thought (*logos*) from myth

BELOW: The remains of the once elaborate gateway or propylaeum at Eleusis in Greece, the home to the famous rituals known as the Eleusinian Mysteries, which were held in honour of the goddess of fertility and wheat, Demeter. The Mysteries attracted followers from many different parts of the Mediterranean.

(*mythos*). Heraclitus was expressing a different approach to divinity and the world when he wrote: 'This world-order, the same of all, no god nor man did create, but it ever was and is and will be: ever-living fire, kindling in measures and being quenched in measures.'

The mystically inclined Plato was particularly scathing about the capricious nature and wicked acts of the gods as described by Homer and Hesiod. He and Socrates were far more concerned with the question of the human individual's personal ethics and with the idea of ultimate goodness than with the quixotic behaviour of Olympian deities. They could not accept that divinity could and did act in the way that the traditional Greek stories depicted. For Aristotle in the 4th century BC, too, the idea of god was something eternal and unchangeable: he or it was the Prime Mover, a far more abstract notion than that provided by a licentious Dionysus or sensual Aphrodite.

Thus, when in later centuries Christian and other scholars attacked what they saw as the immorality of the 'pagan' Greek gods, they were echoing views that had already existed during the classical era. It was not the Olympian gods, but philosophers such as Plato and Aristotle who put an ethical system of how to live into classical Greek thought – and thus into western consciousness.

ABOVE: *The god of wine Bacchus with one of his female followers, who were known as Maenads. Bacchus was the Roman equivalent of the rather wilder Greek deity Dionysus, though the Roman authorities initially took a dim view of the 'imported' rites and mysteries associated with Bacchus/ Dionysus. Roman wall painting. Naples, Museo Nazionale Archeologico.*

Greek Mystery Cults

Though the pantheon of gods was publicly worshipped in the Greek world in sacrificial ceremonies, believers also had a more personal, mystical relationship with divinity. In particular, various mystery cults promised different ways of experiencing the divine. Among the best-known were the Eleusinian Mysteries, based at the temple of Eleusis just outside Athens. The worship included a procession from Athens, during which initiates were bathed in the sea, and then secret rites held at the temple at Eleusis itself. The divine object of the rites was the corn goddess Demeter, whose daughter Persephone was taken to the underworld and whose re-emergence each year coincided with spring. These mysteries were held in great reverence and attracted followers from all over the Greek-speaking world; all were forbidden, however, to reveal the secrets of the cult's dramatic rites.

Another cult was connected to the powerful Dionysus, the god of wine, vegetation and ecstasy. Dionysus originated abroad – possibly in Phrygia – yet was regarded by the Greeks as immensely powerful. When Pentheus, the king of Thebes, tried to stop the worship of Dionysus (in Greek mythology Thebes was one of places the god was supposed to have been born), the result was horrific. The god's female followers, known as the Maenads, launched a bloody attack on Pentheus in which they literally tore him apart. The dreadful assault was led by the king's own mother Agave, who ripped off her son's head in the frenzy.

The rites associated with Dionysus were indeed wild: the 'orgies' of the Maenads supposedly involved frenzied dancing, loud shrieking, and the ripping open and eating of live animals, as well as the drinking of wine. The god was, like so many in the ancient world, associated with death and resurrection. In Roman times the rites continued, in slightly more moderate form, through the worship of the god of wine Bacchus.

Another tradition of mystery rites was Orphism, based on the legendary Greek poet and singer Orpheus, who so tragically failed to rescue his beloved wife Eurydice from the underworld. The Orphic priesthood shunned meat, which was quite a revolutionary concept in a society where animal sacrifices were customarily associated with civic and religious ceremonies.

The importance of religion and prophecy in the Greek world to even the most eminent and successful rulers is illustrated by an episode in the life of Alexander the Great.

By 331 BC, Alexander had reached Egypt, where he founded the great city of Alexandria and was poised to launch a decisive attack on the Persian Empire. But he interrupted his military adventure and crossed the desert to visit the ancient oracle of Amun (or Ammon or Hammon) at the oasis of Siwa, close to the current border between Libya and Egypt. One of the reasons why Alexander wanted to visit this oracle, despite the difficult and perilous trek required to reach it, was that Heracles, from whom he claimed descent, was supposed to have visited it. So, too, had Perseus, the legendary ancestor of the Persians whose empire Alexander was about to destroy. Doubtless Alexander wanted to make a point to the world about his destiny. But he also seems to have been on something of a personal religious mission as well.

Having been saved from thirst by unexpected heavy rain and then guided on their way by ravens, Alexander and his small band of followers finally reached the oracle. What happened next is unclear. A priest seems to have greeted Alexander as the son of god, of Amun, though some ancient reports say the priest spoke poor Greek and that this was merely a slip of the tongue. In any case, Alexander left the oracle more convinced than ever of his divine destiny and later worshipped Amun, the older Egyptian equivalent of Zeus. There was also a report that on his deathbed Alexander asked to be buried at Siwa.

The Roman Empire

The Roman Gods and Worship Practices

Though the Romans are well known for assimilating Greek gods into their religious framework, they had their own tradition, too.

Early Roman beliefs centred on what are called *numina*, nameless spirits who inhabited nature, plus household gods who were called *lares* and *penates*. The *lares* were the spirits of departed ancestors and were a sort of

BELOW: The Vestal Virgins were a rare example of women taking a formal part in Roman society and culture. Their task was to keep the flame burning in Rome's Temple of Vesta, the city's important goddess of the hearth. Roman marble bust c.120/130 AD. Florence, Galleria degli Uffizi.

guardian deity, while the *penates* were literally the 'pantry' gods, who stayed with a family and its home. Perhaps it was this plethora of existing gods that made the Romans so receptive to new gods and so ready to absorb them.

Public worship was common and very important. Gods were celebrated in feasts, sacrifices, boxing and wrestling matches, races and, ultimately, gladiatorial combats. These rituals were overseen by a priesthood, though in the Roman system there was little distinction between state and religious positions. The main priests were usually senators, while under the empire, the role of head priest or *pontifex maximus*, an elected position in the republic, was usually bestowed upon the emperor; it was later adopted by the bishops of Rome, i.e. the popes.

Other important players in what might be termed the state religion of Rome were the six Vestal Virgins. These women were, as their name suggests, virgins appointed to tend the temple of the hearth goddess Vesta in Rome. In particular, it was their job to keep the temple flame burning. This was a rare example of women having a formal role in Roman public life. They held their prestigious positions for 30 years: 10 to train, 10 to serve and 10 to teach. There were thus 18 women involved at any one time.

The major Greek deities all have their Roman counterparts. Thus the powerful Roman god Jupiter – after whom the planet was named, and from whom we get the oath 'by Jove', which is an English name for Jupiter derived from Latin roots – was associated with the Greek Zeus; Juno with Hera; Venus with Aphrodite; Diana with Artemis; Pluto with Hades; and Mercury with Hermes. To supplement this pantheon, the Romans, perhaps aware that they lacked some of the picturesque and powerful tales of the Greeks, came up with a mythology of their own. In this, Aeneas, who fought at Troy, became the legendary founder of what was to be Rome.

In addition to the worship of public and household gods, many mystery cults flourished in and around Rome, satisfying the private spiritual needs of worshippers. The authorities, who generally took a relaxed view of other gods and faiths, did not always approve of these groups and their practices. Perhaps it was the individualistic, secretive nature of the cults – in which people were initiated in private – that unnerved the civic mind; for, as we have seen, state and public religion in Rome were practically indivisible. In 186 BC, therefore, the Senate attempted to suppress the rites of Bacchus, and it is thought that many hundreds, possibly thousands, of followers were executed in the following clampdown.

Foreign gods, by contrast, were usually welcomed or benignly ignored so long as their worship posed no threat to civic order. For example, the Egyptian goddess Isis, to whom a temple was dedicated in Rome from the 2nd century BC, developed a strong cult following in Rome. We can be even more precise about when the worship of the Phrygian mother goddess Cybele began in the Roman capital, for in 204 BC a black stone associated with her worship was brought from Asia Minor to Rome, where she was revered as *Magna Mater* – 'Great Mother'.

Cybele's son and consort Attis was another god associated with death and resurrection. He bled to death underneath a pine tree – supposedly after castrating himself – but was miraculously brought back to life. Each spring, believers held a ceremony to mark

ABOVE: In the mystery religion of Mithraism, one of the central symbols was that of the god Mithras (or Mithra) slaying a bull to symbolize the renewal of life. It was once assumed that the religion, which was extremely popular among Roman soldiers and was a rival to Christianity, came directly from Zoroastrianism but is now thought to have developed separately in Asia Minor. Relief from Fiano Romano. Paris, Musée du Louvre.

the god's death, followed by a big celebration and procession in honour both of Cybele and of Attis' rebirth. As part of the sometimes bloody ritual, an effigy of the young god was tied to a pine tree and paraded through the streets. Acolytes cut themselves – or even castrated themselves – to symbolize the death of Attis. The day on which Attis was said to rise from the dead was the Roman festival of Hilaria – the Festival of Joy.

Cybele remained a very important goddess in Rome, and indeed in much of the Mediterranean, until Christianity became the dominant faith.

ABOVE: Abraham's wife, the beautiful Sarah, was thought unable to have children and instead the great Patriarch fathered a child with Sarah's maid Hagar. That son was called Ishmael and he became the father of the Arab people. Here, Sarah presents the Egyptian Hagar to Abraham.

Mithraism

From around the middle of the 1st century BC, another cult started to take a hold on many Romans – Mithraism. This mysterious cult spread throughout the empire, attracting many followers in Rome but also at the furthest outposts of Roman influence, in Britain, Germany and Palestine. Its followers included bureaucrats, merchants and above all soldiers, for whom it seems to have held a special appeal.

Mithraism was a mystery religion, to which entry was secured by initiation, and the rituals were kept secret: no Mithraic texts about the beliefs and practices of the faith exist, although tantalizing images in many temples have survived. Relatively small groups of male followers – women were excluded – met in private in their temples, which were usually built underground or adapted from caves. The central figure and motif of the faith, taking pride of place in the temples, was the god Mithra (or Mithras), who is depicted slaying a bull, a symbol of the renewal of life.

For many years it was assumed that this important and powerful Roman-based cult was a direct offshoot from Persia and was associated with the Persian religion Zoroastrianism, in which the figure of Mithra is an important heavenly being. More recently, however, doubts have been cast on this theory, largely because nowhere in Zoroastrian mythology does that religion's Mithra slay a bull – the central theme of Roman Mithraism. One view is that it may have emerged from Asia Minor, influenced by a variety of Roman and eastern sources, including eastern astrology, and have then developed a belief system of its own.

Part of the attraction of Mithraism, especially among soldiers, may have been the depiction of Mithra as a warrior deity. But the cult also developed the idea of personal salvation, and its rituals probably encouraged the development of a mystical relationship with god.

The cult was also linked to the worship of the deity of the sun, with Mithra sometimes portrayed as the 'invincible sun god' – Sol Invictus. It existed and flourished as a rival to the Christian faith, though the dominance of Christianity at the heart of the Roman Empire by the end of the 4th century BC helped ensure its demise. Even then, a few elements of Mithraism survived: for example, the selection of 25 December as Jesus Christ's birthday mirrored the traditional choice of date for Mithra's birth. This was the time of year in the northern hemisphere when the days of the year started to get longer, mark–ing the 'rebirth' of the sun.

Public and Private Belief

The fact that the Roman world had both state religion and mystery cults highlights a phenomenon common to most religious traditions – the presence of both public and private sides of belief. On the one hand, most faiths have an outward face which involves obedience to god or gods, the following of state rituals and the adherence to religious laws. On the other side lies the more mystical side of faith, which involves inner reflection and striving towards a personal relationship with divinity.

ABOVE: One of the most famous and important stories in the Old Testament is that of Moses leading his people out of captivity, and then receiving the Ten Commandments from God on Mount Sinai. The Commandments were the core laws by which the Israelites were expected to abide.

Judaism

Origins

Christianity may have borrowed some of its imagery from polytheistic ancient cults, but it sprang directly out of an existing monotheistic religion – Judaism. The most obvious demonstration of this is the fact that Christianity's central figure, Jesus Christ, was born and died as a Jew.

Judaism is crucial to the story of religion both in the Mediterranean and in global terms. Its heritage and traditional stories are shared by two other great world faiths, Christianity and Islam, the other 'peoples of the book'. Reverence for Abraham, the great patriarch, for example, is common to all three faiths.

The origins of Judaism are intimately connected with the issues of land and identity – subjects that still have massive significance for politics in the 21st century. But the concept of Jewishness is much more complex than can be subsumed under those two ideas, defying easy national, racial or religious definition.

The story starts with Abraham – who was probably born between 1900 and 1750 BC – at a place called Ur of the Chaldees in Mesopotamia, in what is today Iraq. All that we know about Abraham comes from the biblical Old Testament; there are no other accounts or archaeological evidence for his life.

According to Genesis, the first book of the Bible, God appears to Abraham and promises him that he will be the founder of a great people, a people who will inhabit a new land. That land is in Canaan and will be known as Israel. In obedience to God, Abraham journeys to the Promised Land, via Egypt; but his wife, Sarah, cannot conceive a child, so in order to found his nation he instead has a child with Hagar. She is Sarah's maid and the daughter of a pharaoh. This child is called Ishmael. Later, however, Abraham miraculously has a child with Sarah, and he is named Isaac.

The fates of the two sons are very different. Hagar and her son are banished, supposedly because of Sarah's jealousy, and Ishmael becomes the father of the Arab people, and thus of Muhammad and Islam. (In Islam, Abraham is revered and known as Ibrahim, and Ishmael is regarded as a prophet.) The Old Testament also tells us that Abraham had another, third wife called Keturah, who had six sons by him.

Meanwhile, Isaac's son Jacob has 12 sons, who give their names to the twelve tribes of Israel. Joseph, the favoured son, is sold into captivity in Egypt but rises to prominence and wins the confidence of the pharaoh, and eventually the whole family moves to Egypt to escape famine in Canaan. According to the Book of Genesis, the Egyptians even hold 70 days of mourning for Joseph's father Jacob (known also as Israel) upon his death.

Yet, soon after Joseph's own death, with a new pharaoh on the throne, the Israelites' status in Egypt changes, and they are enslaved. The second book of the Old Testament, Exodus, then relates one of the best-known stories in the Bible, indeed in all antiquity: the tale of how Moses leads the Israelites out of Egyptian captivity and back to the Promised Land of Israel. This is one of the key periods in the history of Judaism and of Jewish identity; the events the story describes probably occurred just after 1300 BC, though scholars are not sure of the exact date.

There are many very well-known stories concerning Moses. As a baby he is hidden in the rushes on the banks of the Nile, and is later discovered and raised by the pharaoh's daughter. Eventually, though, he finds that his destiny is to be the leader of his own people, and leads the Israelites away from enslavement and into the wilderness for 40 years. During this time God reveals to him the Ten Commandments, the basic laws that underpin traditional Judaism and are at the heart of the Old Testament. The many rules and rituals concerning daily life, including diet, which still feature so strongly in Judaism, were also developed at this time.

Many other tales come from the same period: the story of the burning bush; the parting of the Red Sea to allow the Israelites to escape their pursuers; and also the Passover, when the Angel of Death killed all firstborn sons in Egypt but spared or 'passed over' those of the Israelites – an event which is marked annually in the festival of the Passover or Pesach.

Though Moses leads his people out of Egypt, he dies before crossing the river Jordan into the Promised Land. That honour goes instead to the new leader, Joshua, the man who later brought down the walls of Jericho. Moses, however, remains the greatest of the prophets in Judaism.

The Jewish People After the Exile

Even at this early stage some of the fundamental elements of Jewish identity can be identified. One is the emphasis on geographical location and the primacy of the Promised Land, which go right back to the first divine revelation to Abraham. Another is the pact or covenant with God: the understanding that, in return for following God's will and explicit laws, the faithful will be protected. This leads to a very personal relationship with God. A third is strict monotheism, the worship of one god. This was a major shift in an ancient world where the worship of many gods (polytheism) was widespread, indeed the norm. Abraham himself questioned the worship of many gods even as a child – ironically, his own father was a maker of idols.

Yet the monotheism of Judaism did not go unthreatened, even after the conquest of Canaan and the establishment of an Israeli monarchy by the start of the 1st millennium BC.

The third king of Israel was the great Solomon (c. 974–937 BC), son of the equally famous David who established Jerusalem as his capital. Solomon is renowned for his wisdom as well as for his building of the first Temple in Jerusalem, one of the marvels of the ancient world and a focal point of the Israelites. It was Solomon who was asked to rule in the case of two women who both claimed to be the true mother of a child. By threatening to cut the child in half with a sword, Solomon discovered who was the real mother.

Solomon was also famed for his great love of women; for example, he entertained the legendary Queen of Sheba, and non-Jewish traditions even claim they had a son. According to the first book of Kings, however, it was Solomon's many foreign wives – Ammonites, Hittites, Sidonians and even a pharaoh's daughter – who turned him towards worshipping other gods as well as Yahweh, the one true God of Jewish tradition.

BELOW: In synagogues, the Torah, the Holy writings of Judaism, is always written on a scroll and the cupboard where the scrolls are stored is known as the Ark. When the doors of the Ark are opened everyone stands and the Torah is taken in procession to the reading desk.

Indeed, it was God's displeasure with Solomon over this that led to the splitting of the kingdom into two after Solomon's death. Ten of the 12 tribes of Israel formed the Northern Kingdom (Israel), while Solomon's son Rehoboam became king of the Southern Kingdom (Judea) with the two remaining tribes of Judah and Benjamin.

After this split, two more major traumas hit the Israelites. First, in the late 8th century BC, the Assyrians conquered the Northern Kingdom, and the fate of the Israelites subsequently exiled from there is unknown. They are known as the 'ten lost tribes of Israel' and their disappearance has spawned many myths and tales.

Then, in the 6th century, King Nebuchadnezzar of Babylon invaded Judah. The Temple was destroyed in 586 BC and the Israelite elite were taken into exile to Babylon.

This was an event of fundamental importance to the development of Judaism. The exiled Israelites were allowed to practise their faith in Babylon, but things were very different there. In the first place, they no longer had their great Temple, which had been a focal point of their religious world. They also had to adjust their views of a tribal god, one who was supposed always to protect them from exile or captivity. From now on the perception of God was less tribal, and Jews placed more emphasis on righteousness and on the development of a system of personal ethics based on God's teachings. To please God, one had to follow his laws.

SIMON BAR KOKHBAR

Under the Roman Emperor Hadrian, Jews were initially hopeful that their life in the Holy Land would improve. Many returned to Jerusalem and even hoped to be able to rebuild the Temple. However, their hopes were shattered and in AD 132 Jews began a new rebellion led by a charismatic leader called Simon. At first the revolt was successful and Simon founded a new independent state of Israel. It even minted its own coins with the words 'The Freedom of Israel' written in Hebrew on them. Simon was given the name bar Kokhbar, meaning 'son of a star' in Aramaic. Some even believed he was the Messiah, who it had been prophesied, would come to restore Israel's glory. Eventually, however, Roman military might won the day and in 135 bar Kokhbar and his followers were annihilated at the fortress of Bethar, southwest of Jerusalem. In the aftermath of the revolt, many Jews were deported and sold into slavery, while Hadrian completed the construction of a new capital in Jerusalem called Aelia Capitolina in honour of himself and the great Roman god Jupiter – plans for which had provoked the revolt in the first place.

There was also the impact of Zoroastrianism. This was the faith of the Persians who, led by Cyrus the Great, conquered Babylon and who later, in 538 BC, decreed that exiled peoples – including the Israelites – could return to their homes. Zoroastrianism was also monotheistic, though it did have lesser, semi-divine figures who were represented as emanations of the one true god. There is little doubt that both the shock of the exile and the subsequent exposure to the Persian faith had an important influence on post-exile Judaism. For example, it led to the formation of the idea of an afterlife – a concept that already existed in vague terms but had not played a central role in pre-exile Judaism – in which the good were rewarded while the bad were punished with hell. This was already a theme of the eastern religion and subsequently appeared in post-exile Judaic thought.

The idea of a saviour or 'Messiah' who would rescue the Jewish people may also have been influenced by Zoroastrian thought, as well as by their experience of exile and delivery. Part of the book of Isaiah – a part that scholars believe was written around the time of the end of the Babylonian exile – explicitly refers to King Cyrus. Relaying the words of God, Isaiah says:

'I will raise up Cyrus in my righteousness, I will make all his ways straight. He will rebuild my city and set my exiles free.'

It is not hard to see why the concept of a saviour became so important in Judaic thought, given the troubled history of the Israelites. We shall return to this key idea later in this chapter.

From Babylon to the Destruction of the Second Temple

After many Israelites returned from exile – not all chose to leave Babylon – the Temple of Jerusalem was rebuilt, and this Second Temple survived until AD 70. By then the region had been conquered by both the Greeks and later the Romans.

Following the invasion of Alexander the Great, the language, culture and philosophy of the Greeks had a significant impact on not just Judaism but the whole region. In Alexandria, for example, a team of Jewish scholars translated the Torah (the first five books of the Bible) from Hebrew into Greek. Many members of the Jewish elite became 'Hellenized' in this period.

The first Greek rulers of Judea were members of the Ptolemaic dynasty based in Egypt; they were followed by the Syrian–based Seleucid dynasty, another successor regime to Alexander. They took control in 198 BC and quickly provoked bitter resentment among the Jews, notably by attempting to rededicate the Temple of Jerusalem to Zeus. To the Jews this was blasphemous and intolerable; neither the Persians nor the Ptolemaic regime had gone that far. Members of a Jewish family called Maccabee led the ensuing revolt in 165 BC, recapturing and cleansing the Temple. (The Jewish festival of Hannukah each year celebrates this rededication of the Second Temple.) By 141 BC, Judea was once more an independent Jewish state.

This independence lasted until 63 BC, when Jerusalem was captured by the Romans. This occupation, too, led to conflict with the Jewish population. When a major Jewish revolt broke out, the Romans responded by crushing it and destroying the Second Temple in AD 70. After a second and unsuccessful rising in AD 132, led by a messianic figure called Simon bar Kokhbar (see box on page 207), the Roman army forcibly expelled the Jews from Jerusalem and Judea. They dispersed widely, many joining the communities of Jewish people already living outside Israel. There was a large community in Rome and Alexandria, for example, plus others in Arabia, Mesopotamia and even as far away as India.

Thus once again the Jewish people were removed from the land they saw as their own, and from the city they claimed as their capital. It was an exile that was to last until the 20th century.

ABOVE: The splendid 19th-century synagogue in Oranienburger Strasse in Berlin was restored in the 1980s and 1990s after being badly damaged in the Second World War. Following the destruction of the Second Temple in Jerusalem, the focus in Judaism switched more to worship and communities based around synagogues, which like this one have been built all over the world.

Jewish Scriptures and Doctrine

By the second century AD, the Torah was already a long-established base of the Jewish religion. (These five books, Genesis, Exodus, Leviticus, Numbers and Deuteronomy, are also collectively referred to as the Pentateuch.) Jews believe these texts were handed down by God to Moses on Mount Sinai as he led his people from exile, and scrolls containing the Torah are kept in every synagogue.

To complement these books of stories, laws and history of the people of Israel, there was an oral tradition of laws that also had to be observed by Jews. Although originally it was forbidden for these laws to be written down, by the end of the 2nd century AD Jewish leaders felt it was essential to do so if they were to be preserved. These laws and stories – the Mishnah – and commentaries on them – Gemara – together form what is called the Talmud. There were in fact two Talmuds, one from Babylon, the other from Jerusalem: the former is regarded as more authoritative. This era is part of what is sometimes referred to as the era of rabbinic Judaism, which runs roughly from the time of the destruction of the Second Temple to the current day. It was the time in which the teachings of the rabbis – the spiritual and scholarly leaders of the faith – helped shape and define the Jewish faith as we now know it.

As Jewish teaching developed, so different branches within the faith emerged, sometimes associated with particular tribal groups and often disagreeing upon doctrine and theology: these groups included the Pharisees, the Sadducees, the Essenes, Zealots and Samaritans.

An important trend associated with these developments was the movement away from Judaism's traditional focus on sacrifice and the Temple and towards an even greater emphasis on obedience to the laws, study of scripture, the synagogue and the rabbi – whose primary role was that of teacher. As the synagogue became the focal point of worship, so Judaism became a religion that could flourish away from the geographical land of Israel and the Temple, even if these were to retain a tremendous pull on Jews down the centuries.

The Figure of the Messiah and the Birth of Christianity

There were two important themes in Judaism during the period from the 2nd century BC to the 2nd century AD, a time of much uncertainty and unrest.

BELOW: One of the most powerful images of Christianity is that of the birth of Jesus, and of his adoration by the shepherds. The Old Testament book of Micah foretold that the Jewish Messiah would come from Bethlehem which is why the Gospel of Luke goes to great lengths to explain how Jesus came to be born in that town.

One was apocalypticism, the idea that the end of the world was coming, when God would come to judge the good and the wicked at the Last Judgement. Linked with this was a belief in a Messiah, the longed–for deliverer of the Jewish people. This developed after the Babylonian exile, as noted above, and grew ever stronger under first Greek and then Roman domination.

There were several requirements for a Messiah, according to Jewish teach–ing. He had to come from the House of David, that is, to be descended from the family of the great king; and it had also been prophesied that the Messiah would be born in Bethlehem. The Messiah would be a prophet, a priest or a king. Opinion was divided about whether he would be a political leader who would drive out the enemy, a wise scholar whose powerful teaching would restore Israel, or a great prophet like Moses.

ABOVE: For Christians, the image of the Crucifixion of Christ is immensely powerful because it shows that their god was prepared to die for them. The concept of a god dying and then coming back to life was a familiar one in both pre- and post-Christian religious cults.

One thing that Judaism was clear about at this time was the physical and spiritual nature of the Messiah. He would be human and emphatically not divine. The word 'messiah', coming from Aramaic and Hebrew, means 'anointed one'. In Greek – the dominant language in the eastern Mediterranean at this time – this was translated as Christos, while in Latin it was Christus.

The belief in a Messiah is absolutely central to the origins of Christianity and reminds us again that this new faith sprang directly from Judaism.

It is indeed in the context of Judaism, in the suffering and exile of the past, the simmering discontent under the rule of the Romans, and the hope and expectation that someone would come to deliver the Jews from this burden, that we come to the remark–able story of Jesus Christ and the eventual birth of a new religion called Christianity.

Christianity

Jesus and the Gospels

Exactly when Jesus was born is not clear, though it seems likely to have been between 7 and 4 BC rather than in the year identified by the traditional Christian calendar. His death occurred probably in AD 29 or 30. About his life in between these dates we know very little. Even the main biblical sources for our information about Jesus, the 'syn–

optic gospels' of Matthew, Mark and Luke (so called because, taken together, they provide a 'synoptic' life of Jesus) plus the gospel of John, are largely silent on the matter, focusing on his birth, the events leading to his execution, and the dramatic story of his resurrection.

This brings us to one of the central problems when discussing Christianity in terms of history: the lack of hard information. The gospels may be powerful and descriptive – and, of course, to many Christians, literally true – but, viewed purely as historical documents, they are not wholly convincing. The authors were not, after all, trying to write history in the modern sense of the word but instead trying to tell a story that had meaning and significance for their audience.

The result is an evocative but tangled mass of text, with many contradictions, and details inserted

ABOVE: In many senses, St Paul, depicted here preaching in Athens, was one of the true creators of Christianity as we know it. It was Paul, originally called Saul, who took the central message of the new belief beyond Judaism and spread it over much of the eastern Mediterranean to a non-Jewish audience.

to fit certain expectations. For example, the claim that Jesus was born in Bethlehem features in two of the gospels, Matthew and Luke. The author of Luke even outlines an elaborate and historically implausible reason why Joseph and the heavily pregnant Mary had to travel all the way to Bethlehem in Judea from their home in Nazareth in Galilee. The reason why this detail was included is that both authors knew there was a prophecy in the Old Testament book of Micah that foretold that the Messiah would come from Bethlehem. The inclusion of this detail about the birth of Jesus would have reassured much of their potential audience about the *bona fides* of his status as the Messiah. The author of the fourth gospel, John, also knew about this prophecy. But in John 7, verses 41–43, it is stated that people were divided about the credibility of Jesus as the Messiah precisely because they knew he had come from Galilee – and not from Bethlehem.

This is not to suggest that the authors of the four gospels – written some time after the middle of the 1st century AD – did not believe what they were writing, or that much of it was not based on personal accounts of what had happened. The gospels are simply a complex blend of history, Old Testament imagery and prophecies, symbolism and spiritual insight, all rolled together in a powerful narrative designed to convey the massive importance of this story of death and resurrection – and this has been called 'The Greatest Story Ever Told'.

The Historical Jesus

Outside the gospels, mentions of Jesus Christ are few, and even these are controversial. The Jewish historian Flavius Josephus, writing in AD 93, famously writes in his *Antiquities of the Jews* about a man called Jesus who was a 'wise man' and a 'doer of wonderful works'. Many, though certainly not all, scholars believe that this passage was inserted later by Christians to add to the weight of evidence for an historical Jesus. In AD 116 the Roman historian Tacitus referred to the founder of the 'Christians' as a man called 'Christus' or Christ, though not to his name Jesus.

Even the writings of St Paul, the earliest of which date from around AD 50, before any of the gospels were completed, are almost completely quiet on the life of Jesus.

Thus, the reliable historical record on Jesus remains very thin, even though there are many colourful myths and stories about him that have come down through the centuries.

In a sense, this lack of historical detail does not matter to the story of Christianity. For believers, faith in the story of Jesus and his resurrection is paramount. In any case, within a relatively short period of time this man from Palestine, supposedly born of a virgin, and crucified by the Romans, was the central figure in a new and vibrant faith that swept rapidly around the eastern Mediterranean and beyond.

Jesus' Jewish followers, men and women who followed Jewish custom and ritual to the day they died, may have found this odd. To them, Jesus was not the originator of a new faith called 'Christianity'; he was, however, a person of the utmost importance, namely the Messiah who had long been prophesied within their Jewish religion. To Jews who did not accept Jesus as the Messiah – the majority – the notion of Jesus founding a whole new religion seemed even more peculiar. The idea that someone could die and then be resurrected, and moreover that such a person could be the 'son of God', played no part in the Jewish creed.

BELOW: The Temple of Artemis at Ephesus, whose remains can be found in what is now Turkey, was once one of the Seven Wonders of the Ancient World and, according to reports, was twice the size of the Parthenon. The city's attachment to the female god Artemis later led to their development of a cult to Mary, mother of Christ. Coll. Archiv f.Kunst & Geschichte.

St Paul

The reason why and the means by which this new faith spread so rapidly are to be found in the figure of another individual man – Paul. In many senses St Paul, who began life as Saul, a Jewish persecutor of Christians, can be described as the true inventor of Christianity.

It is Paul, a man from the cosmopolitan town of Tarsus in Asia Minor, who in the course of his own preaching and writings separated the cult surrounding Jesus from the rituals and laws of Judaism. Judaism, of course, was passed on through birth, and was therefore essentially limited to people who were born Jewish. Paul honed the new cult's beliefs down to a very simple, basic truth applicable and open to all humanity – Jews and Gentiles alike. This was the message that Jesus died on the cross to pay for all the sins of humankind, and that, by placing trust in Jesus Christ and his resurrection, an individual would achieve personal salvation. Above all, faith in Jesus Christ was the key.

For Gentiles, including the Greek-speaking communities among whom Paul largely preached, his message carried an attractive combination of elements. It welded a faith based on an idea of universal and absolute goodness, familiar to those who knew Greek ethics and philosophy, with a very personal mystical relationship with God through the real person of Christ. In a world used to many gods, it was not hard for people to relate to the divinity of Christ. Nor, given similar myths attached to so many ancient gods – Osiris, Dionysus and Attis, for example – was it hard to relate to the idea of a god who died and came back to life. The claim that Christ died and came back to life specifically to save individual souls and out of his love for humankind simply made the message infinitely more powerful and seductive.

BELOW: The first recorded Christian martyr was Stephen, whose feast day is on 26 December, the day after the birth of Jesus Christ is celebrated. St Stephen is said to have been stoned to death by Jews who were angry that his message was blasphemous to their faith.

Christians and Martyrs

Paul's message soon spread around the largely Greek-speaking eastern region of the Mediterranean, both within the large Jewish diaspora and the Gentile world. Its adherents met a great deal of often brutal opposition. What might be called the 'Jewish' Christian group suffered, like other Jews, at the hands of the Romans. The followers of Paul's Gentile tradition of Christianity were also persecuted, and it is assumed that Paul himself was killed for his beliefs when he was executed in Rome, under the reign of Nero, around AD 68.

(There was another form of early Christianity known as Gnosticism, from the Greek word for knowledge. This more esoteric and philosophical tradition, which may have pre-dated Christianity, saw Jesus as a messenger or revealer of secret knowledge about the ultimate nature of the world and how to find inner salvation through the

ABOVE: The condemnation of Jesus. Pontius Pilate presided over the trial of Jesus, found no fault with the defendant and washed his hands of the affair by referring it back to the Jewish mob, he also signed the final death warrant. Later, a minor uprising by the Samaritans was put down with excessive cruelty, and Pilate was recalled to Rome to answer charges, he then disappeared from history. From a painting by Antonio Ciseri.

divine spark or soul that lies in all of us. Followers believed that other Christians had completely misunderstood and dogmatized Christ's teachings, and that Gnostics alone grasped their real meaning. (Most Christians later dismissed Gnosticism as a heresy.)

Though martyrdom – dying for the faith – was a depressingly familiar experience for early Christians, the new religion quickly gained adherents, as is clear from a glance at the titles of Paul's letters in the New Testament. His epistles went to fledgling Christian communities in Corinth, Thessalonica and Ephesus. Ephesus in particular was an important location in the development of early Christianity. This bustling commercial centre in Asia Minor was reputedly the place where Mary, mother of Jesus, went to spend her last years on earth. The development of the cult of Mary in Ephesus was probably linked to the fact that there had previously been a very strong attachment to the goddess Artemis in the city – in fact, the magnificent Temple of Artemis at Ephesus was one of the Seven Wonders of the Ancient World. Veneration of Mary would have been readily understood in the context of the Asiatic and Greek deity.

The initial Roman view of Christianity was that it was simply another sect of Judaism, a religion that had in Roman eyes already produced more than its share of troublemakers. Indeed, it is often suggested that the passage in Luke's gospel in which Jesus praises the faith of a centurion, and another in which a centurion praises the dead Christ on the cross, were written with the aim of reassuring the Roman authorities about Christians.

Yet Roman persecution of Christians, though occasionally barbaric and brutal, was by no means continuous or systematic. As we have seen, the Roman authorities were generally tolerant of faiths and beliefs different from their own, and certainly did not persecute Christians for what they believed. Their problem was with people who refused to toe the line on matters such as making sacrifices to the emperor and gods as expected under the laws and customs of Rome. Roman society was based on respect for the state and its ways of doing things, and the security that this provided. Anyone seen as threatening to undermine the authority of the state was therefore likely to be punished.

There are suggestions that some early Christians almost invited death and martyrdom, much to the bemusement of the authorities. In one encounter a small number of Christians were executed but the local governor then decided to release the rest of the group – to their annoyance. The official is said to have grumbled to them that if they really wanted to die there were plenty of cliffs for them to jump off. On the other hand, when they did occur, attacks on Christians could plumb the depths of cruelty. For example, under Emperor Nero (AD 37–68) Christians were said to have been crucified, or wrapped in animal skins and then attacked by dogs; women were allegedly tied to bulls and dragged to their deaths.

The first recorded martyr, however, Stephen – St Stephen, whose feast day is 26 December – was stoned to death not by Romans but by Jews. The early Jewish persecution of Christians was one of the causes of the Christian resentment of Jews and Judaism which grew over the centuries and which in turn led to widespread persecution by Christians of Jews. The main reason for this hostility, however, was the growing insistence inside the Christian movement that the real responsibility for the death of Jesus Christ lay not with the Romans, embodied in procurator Pontius Pilate, but rather with the Jewish elders who feared the Messiah's message. It was they who had demanded and got Christ's crucifixion, said the Christians. In Matthew's gospel, the author has the Jewish crowd explicitly taking on this responsibility when they shout the grim words: 'Let the blood be on us and on our children.' These words have haunted history ever since.

The Emerging Church

As the number of Christians grew, so did the organization of what was to become known as 'the church'. The key leaders initially were the apostles, the eleven remaining disciples of Jesus, who were sent out among the Jewish diaspora and the Gentiles to spread the word about Jesus, plus of course the crucial figure of Paul.

Soon, a hierarchy developed within the church, similar to those in other religions. The top position (after the apostles) was held by the overseers or 'bishops', followed by the elders or 'presbyters' (priests), with deacons occupying the third rung. Interestingly, women played an important part in the organization of the early Christian church – in contrast to, for example, Mithraism – and served as deaconesses.

What, then, did members of this new church believe? They believed in the potential salvation of the soul, though opinions differed on whether this was to be achieved through faith alone, that is, belief in the resurrection of Jesus Christ, or in good works in following Jesus' commandments, for example from the Sermon on the Mount. Many seem to have believed a combination of the two was required. They also practised baptism and celebrated the Eucharist in remembrance of Christ's Last Supper with his disciples.

There were numerous debates in the early years of the Church over exactly what a Christian should believe. Various figures, such as St Justin (c. AD 100–163; often referred to as Justin Martyr), Bishop Clement of Rome and a third-century scholar from Alexandria called Origen started to expound their views on Christian theology. One of the most troubling thinkers at the time, at least to many Christians, was Arius (c. 250–336), a Christian priest from Egypt, where Christianity was flourishing.

Arius was worried by the notion that God and Jesus Christ were both, as it were, equally divine, and he taught instead that God had created Christ out of nothing. This logically meant there had been a time when Christ had not existed. Arius was apparently concerned that the divine nature of Christ conflicted with the idea of

ABOVE: Christ's Last Supper with his disciples, shortly before he was crucified to death, remains one of the most potent symbols of Christianity and became part of Church ritual. This is Leonardo da Vinci's (1451–1519) wonderful and huge imagining of the scene, painted on the wall at the Convent of Santa Maria delle Grazie in Milan.

monotheism, which was as central to Christianity as it was to Judaism.

However, Arius' view of the nature of Christ conflicted strongly with what was by now the 'orthodox' view. This was that Christ was divine, and that he and God were one; Christ was simply God made flesh, and had been there from the start of creation. Such a divergence of view on the nature of Christ had to be resolved, and an attempt to do just that was made at a council of church leaders and scholars in the early 4th century.

But before that a development occurred that was to transform the history of Christianity and the history of the world for ever.

From Roman Persecution to State Religion

The fortunes of the Christians at the hands of the Roman Empire had waxed and waned over the years. The size of the empire and the relative peace it commanded allowed new ideas and faiths to spread through better and faster communications. But the authorities' periods of tolerance of this new faith were still punctuated by bouts of persecution. The first years of the 4th century saw such an episode under the Emperor Diocletian (AD 245–316), a powerful figure who divided the empire into east and west and who regarded himself as having divine-like status – he styled himself 'the son of Jupiter'. His restora-

ABOVE: Diocletian (AD 245–316) was a powerful emperor of the Roman empire who disliked the growth of Christianity and who encouraged the worship of the old Roman gods until, unusually, he retired from his position in 305. Late 3rd-century Roman bust found at Nicomedia. Istanbul, Museum of Oriental Antiquities.

tion of the old Roman customs and gods indicated that he had little time for what he saw as alien, foreign faiths such as Christianity. In 303, he ordered that Christian churches and scripture be destroyed and went on to order the imprisonment of all Christian clergy, unless and until they made a sacrifice to the Roman gods. Ultimately, he ordered that any Christian who refused to worship the Roman gods be executed. Fortunately for Christians, this bloody assault on them was short-lived, as in 305, following an illness, Diocletian stepped down as emperor.

The new emperor brought to the fore by Diocletian's retirement was Constantine, later to be known as Constantine the Great (AD 285–337), one of the seminal figures in the story of Christianity. In 312, he was forced to fight a rival, Maxentius, for the undisputed leadership of the western empire. On the eve of battle, Constantine claimed to have had a vision in which he saw the symbol of 'chi-ro' shining above the sun, and took it as a divine sign. Accordingly, he had his troops paint the symbol on their shields. (Chi and ro are the first two letters of 'Christ' in the Greek alphabet; the symbol, made up of these two characters, resembles a cross in the shape of an X with a figure of a P through the centre of it. This new battle standard became known as the *labarum*.) Constantine's forces, though outnumbered, then went on to win a decisive victory at the battle of Milvian Bridge.

The triumph was a major turning point, not just for Constantine, who was now undisputed emperor of the west, but for Christianity, too. Within the year, the emperor had formally recognized Christianity in his part of the empire. By AD 324, he had managed to reunite the whole empire, and then set about outlawing pagan sacrifices and cementing the position of Christianity throughout the imperial lands. This charismatic soldier is accordingly known as the first Christian emperor of Rome.

Constantine and Christian Doctrine

As befitted a military man, Constantine disliked the messy doctrinal divisions within the Christian church. In 313, for example, there was a bitter dispute about the attitude the church should adopt towards bishops and priests who had renounced their faith or handed over scripture to be burned under the persecution, but now wanted to return to the flock. On the one side were those who adopted a hard–line attitude, saying that such priests should not be readmitted: these were known as Donatists after an African bishop. Others, meanwhile, said waverers should be shown tolerance and leniency.

To resolve this conflict, Constantine convened two meetings of bishops to decide upon the right course. The outcome was a defeat for the Donatists, though their influence and staunch belief in the value of suffering and martyrdom survived, especially in Africa.

The episode shows how widespread Christianity had become around the Mediterranean. The main body of Donatists came from North Africa, and their main complaint was against a bishop of Carthage, the refounded Roman city in Tunisia. Africa was a stronghold of Christianity for centuries, though the Donatist split badly weakened it. The first of the two meetings took place in Rome, the second at Arles in Gaul; and a later and more important meeting of church leaders was convened in Nicaea, Asia Minor (now the Turkish city of Iznik), to discuss the views of Arius, who was from Alexandria. Christianity had thus become a widely established Mediterranean religion even before it was officially recognized in the Roman empire.

This outcome of the meeting at Nicaea, held in 325 BC and known as the First Ecumenical Council of the church, was a clear–cut rejection of Arius. It affirmed what is called 'consubstantiality' – meaning that God and Christ, Father and Son, shared the same divinity. The formula of belief adopted by the church became known as the Nicene Creed, a text which, in amended form, is what Christians still recite today.

Yet, despite the decision of the council, Arianism continued to flourish in parts of the church, especially around the eastern Mediterranean and its intellectual centre, Alexandria. It was also the form of Christianity first adopted by the so–called 'barbarians', such as the Ostrogoths and the Vandals, who helped destroy the western half of the empire. Despite its prohibition, Arianism took a long time to die out.

Another important act of Constantine was to found a new capital city on the site of the old Greek settlement of Byzantium and thus effectively to shift the centre of gravity of the Roman empire eastwards. Though the move would be gradual, the division between east and west, Greek and Latin, would be mirrored by a deep and lasting split in the Christian church. The eastern, Greek–speaking church came to be known as Orthodox (from the Greek for 'right believer'), while the Latin, Rome–based tradition became known as Catholic (from the Greek for 'universal').

There are elements of Constantine's life that have made some observers suspicious about his true motives in relation to Christianity. He was not baptized until just before his death in 337, and even while professing Christianity had appeared to retain some attachment to the old gods too, notably to the cult of 'Sol Invictus' – Invincible Sun – which is linked to the god Apollo and also Mithraism. However, it was often the custom

ABOVE: Roman coin showing the emperor Constantine (AD 285–337), who famously encouraged the spread of Christianity under his rule and was himself a convert, though he may have simultaneously kept some respect for the old gods and beliefs.

for converted Christians to be baptized late in life or on their deathbed. There seems little reason to doubt Constantine's personal commitment to Christianity, even if he undoubtedly did at times use the religion as an instrument of political policy.

Constantine's appreciation of the subtleties of Christianity probably increased over a period of time, during which he continued to see parallels between the new faith and parts of the old religions. This was indeed a common enough process in the story of Christianity and Christians and their reactions to other faiths. One reaction was to destroy old pagan symbols, temples and literature, and to abandon old customs – for example, putting an end to gladiatorial entertainments. Another was to absorb elements of the so-called 'pagan' world into the Christian world – for example, adopting 25 December as Christmas Day, and incorporating ideas of Isis and Horus as mother and child into Christian imagery.

The word 'pagan', incidentally, derives from the Latin word for 'country dweller', and was used as an increasingly pejorative term for those who, away from the supposed sophistication of Christianized towns and cities, still worshipped the old polytheistic gods. Such people were characterized as, in effect, country bumpkins. The irony is that, in the very early development of Christianity, many Romans and Greeks derided its followers as naïve and credulous for believing in the literal story of a resurrected god.

The reign of Constantine did not quite bring the final victory of Christianity as the official religion of Rome – that had to wait until the accession of the Emperor Theodosius at the end of the 4th century. But Constantine's rule did lay down the foundations for the triumph of the faith and assisted its spread to all parts of its crumbling but still large empire. The triumph of Christianity, however, did not bring Christian unity.

The Great Schism

The name often given to the deep rupture in Christianity that took place from the 5th century and was formalized in the 11th is the Great Schism (not to be confused with the temporary schism inside the Catholic church in the 14th century that is often given the same name).

ABOVE: Gregory the Great (AD 540–604), who was later St Gregory, became Pope in 590 at a time when the papacy had already grown in strength and prestige after the collapse of the Roman Empire in the West; he increased the unity of the Church in western Europe. Painting, c.1610/20, ascribed to Carlo Saracini (1579–1620). Rome, Galleria Nazionale, Pal.Barberini.

Although the political western empire came to an end in 476 BC, the Bishop of Rome (the Pope) and his fellow bishops in the west remained at the head of the Church across the former imperial territories. There was thus a division between political and spiritual power. In the east, by contrast, the emperor still continued to exert both political and spiritual power; crowned by the Patriarch of Constantinople, the emperor was God's representative on Earth. Indeed, as far as the east was concerned he was still head of the Roman empire, even if the capital was now at Constantinople. Both the emperors and the empire's eastern neighbours saw it as following in an unbroken line from the days of Rome. It was only in the west that the eastern empire was referred to as Greek and ultimately Byzantine.

The gradual rise to prominence of the papacy in Rome was inevitably one reason for the eventual split. Leo the Great, who became Bishop of Rome in 440 (technically, all western bishops could be called 'Papa' or father, and the title was finally reserved for the Bishop of Rome only in the 11th century), was one of the first to use the old Roman title of *pontifex maximus*. By 590, when Gregory the Great had become Bishop of Rome, the power and prestige of the papacy, which alone preserved the old glories of the Roman empire in the west, had grown considerably.

The two halves of the old Roman empire drifted apart in terms of practice, imagery and even doctrine. Indeed, one of the great dividing issues was over who decided Christian doctrine – the eastern church or the west. The deepening split was emphasized by the fact that the Byzantine Emperor Constans II, who visited Rome in AD 663, was the last to do so until the 15th century. Meanwhile, the last pope to go to the Byzantine capital was the appropriately named Constantine at the start of the 8th century.

The formal schism came in 1054, when a representative of Pope Leo IX and the Patriarch of Constantinople Michael Cerularius exchanged excommunications. These remained in place until 1965.

Heresy and Secession

There were also other disputes leading to splits elsewhere in the Christian church. The idea of heresy is almost as old as Christianity itself. Originally meaning a 'choice' or a set of principles, it came to refer to ideas held by Christian believers that differed from the accepted orthodoxy. A heretic was therefore someone who was a Christian but whose views differed from the norm; in contrast, an apostate was someone who abandoned their faith altogether, perhaps by embracing another religion. One important heresy in the 5th century was Monophysitism. Its supporters regarded Christ's earthly status to have been wholly divine, not both human and divine as the majority of the church held. Ultimately, this issue was to lead to the secession of the Coptic Church, the so-called Jacobite Syrian church and the Armenian church.

The Monophysite heresy had been a reaction against another called Nestorianism, named after a Syrian cleric, Nestorius, who was briefly Patriarch of Constantinople. This heresy held that while Christ was both human and divine, Mary was simply the mother of Jesus the man, not the god, and thus could not be regarded as the Mother of God. Effectively banned from the mainstream Christian world, Nestorians moved east and eventually reached China, India and Afghanistan, where they won a number of converts. Small pockets of Nestorian Christians still exist today.

Such examples show how complicated and controversial Christian theology and practice became. Its diversity reflected the many different cultures and traditions of the Mediterranean itself, from North Africans and Egyptians through peoples from Palestine, Syria and Asia Minor to those of Greece, Italy and western Europe.

Islam

Unlike Christianity, Islam started life away from the shores of the Mediterranean, deep inside Arabia. But its arrival in the region in the 7th century was even more explosive.

Origins and Outline

The story of the origins of Islam is in many ways more straightforward than that of Christianity, for which the plethora of different writings, opinions and traditions from the start fuelled a continuing doctrinal debate down the centuries.

At the time of Muhammad's birth in Mecca in about AD 570, most Arabs were polytheists, though there were some Christians and Jews in the region as well as some people who had rejected polytheism but who had not opted for any of the monotheistic faiths. Mecca was already a place of pilgrimage to which people came to worship their various gods.

According to tradition, Muhammad's mission began in about 610, when he was called upon to reveal and recite the word of the one and only true god, Allah. For the next 22 years, Muhammad accordingly spoke the revealed word to his followers. He was the Prophet of God – and God's final prophet. Within just two decades of his death in 632 his words were written down and became the book that is central to the Islamic faith, the Qur'an. In contrast to Christianity, therefore, there can be little room for doctrinal doubt in Islam. It is true that there have been differences of interpretation over Islamic law, as there have been over the *hadith*, the body of stories about the life of the prophet, which are a source of moral inspiration for Muslims. In particular, the differences

BELOW: Pilgrims standing before the Kaaba in the Great Mosque of Mecca in Saudi Arabia. The Kaaba is a cubic, stone structure – covered in a black cloth – which in Islamic tradition was built or rebuilt by Abraham. It is the holiest place in Islam and Muslims face in the direction of the Kaaba when they pray. From The Cairo Punch. Coll. Archiv f.Kunst & Geschichte.

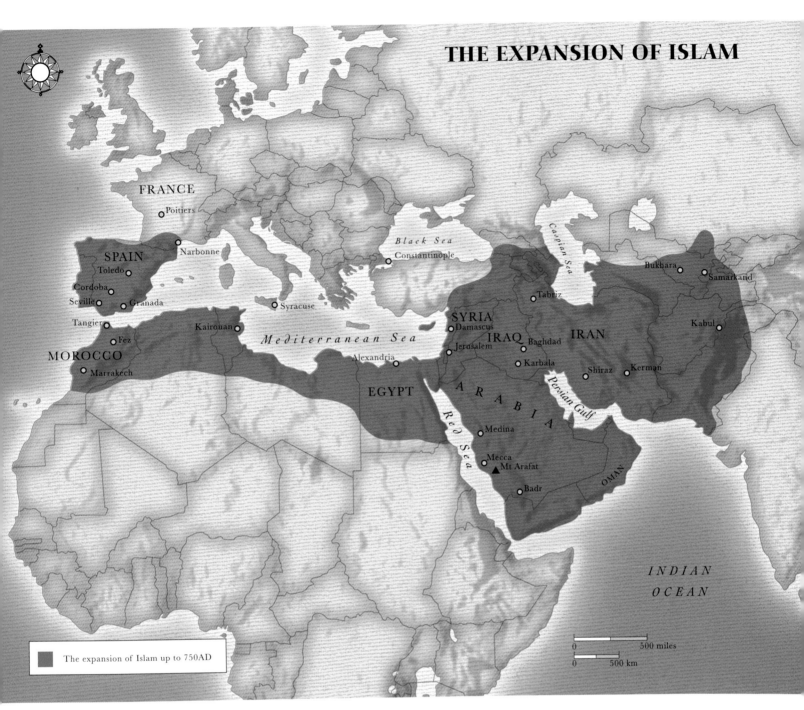

THE EXPANSION OF ISLAM

FRANCE
○ Poitiers

Black Sea
○ Constantinople

Caspian Sea

○ Bukhara
○ Samarkand

SPAIN
○ Narbonne
Toledo ○
Cordoba ○
Seville ○   ○ Granada
Tangier ○

○ Tabriz

SYRIA
○ Damascus
Jerusalem ○

IRAQ
○ Baghdad
Karbala ○

IRAN

Kabul ○

○ Syracuse

Mediterranean Sea

○ Kairouan

Fez ○

MOROCCO

○ Marrakech

Alexandria ○

EGYPT

A R A B I A

Red Sea

○ Medina

Mecca ○
▲ Mt Arafat

○ Badr

Shiraz ○   ○ Kerman

Persian Gulf

OMAN

INDIAN OCEAN

The expansion of Islam up to 750AD

0 ————— 500 miles
0 ————— 500 km

between the Sunni and Shi'a traditions, which were originally political, have led to the difference of interpretation over, for example, the method of prayer. However, these are small compared with the doctrinal fissures within Christianity. For all Muslims, the Qur'an is the revealed word of Allah and Muhammad is his Prophet, bringing God's final revelation to humanity.

Soon after Muhammad migrated from Mecca to Yathrib (later renamed Medina) in 622, he assumed military power and eventually defeated the Meccans in battle and brought Islam to his own city. The migration to Medina is called *hijra*, and it is from that year that the Muslim calendar is dated.

The word Islam itself means 'submission', as in submitting to the will of Allah. The five key aspects of the faith, often called the Five Pillars of Islam, take the form of obligations which all Muslims are expected to fulfil. These are: acceptance of the one true God and of Muhammad as his Prophet; saying prayers five times a day; the giving of alms or charity; fasting from dawn to dusk during the month of Ramadan; and making a

ABOVE: The expansion of the Arab Islamic world after its birth in the 7th century in the Arabian peninsula, was rapid and explosive; within a century its armies had conquered nearly all of Spain and had entered France.

pilgrimage (*hajj*) to Mecca once in their life if physically able.

Islam accepts that Christians and Jews worship the same God as Muslims, and that Moses and Jesus as well as Abraham were prophets, even if those faiths have since followed wrong paths. In particular, many Muslims regard the Christian assertion of the divinity of Christ as tantamount to polytheism.

Islam and Conquest

There is an important distinction between the natures of Islam and Christianity, associated with their respective founders. Jesus was executed having preached a powerful message but having neither achieved nor sought any temporal power. Christians were not to achieve political power for centuries, and in the meantime lived under the rule of an empire whose leaders practised other faiths. Partly as a result of this it was possible for Christians in later centuries – eventually – to accept a growing division between the Church and the State.

In contrast, Muhammad became a military and political leader as well as being the Prophet of Allah. So, from the start, Islam was always associated with state power – and this link has persisted to the present, even if there have been huge tensions between Islamic political rule and the demands of the faith.

ABOVE: A medieval map of the Indian Ocean showing the presumed location of Prester John. He was thought to be a Christian potentate who would help his fellow believers drive Islam out of the Holy Land. There is, however, no evidence that any such person existed. London, British Library.

After the Prophet's death in 632, there could be no more prophets – the divine revelation was complete – but there still had to be a successor to Muhammad as head of the new Islamic state. The term that came to be used for this position was khalifa (caliph), meaning successor and deputy; another title was 'Commander of the Faithful'. The issue of succession became the most divisive in Islam: if Christians squabbled mainly about what precisely they believed, Muslims argued primarily about who should be their leader.

In 656, the third caliph, 'Uthman, was murdered by mutineers and replaced as ruler by 'Ali ibn Abi Talib, Muhammad's cousin and husband of the Prophet's daughter Fatima. Ali's caliphate was short-lived: he was murdered by a lone assassin in 661, to be replaced in turn by Mu'awiya ibn Abi Sufyan, a member of the powerful Umayya family from Mecca and a strong military leader. This ushered in nearly a century of Umayyad caliphates at the head of Islam.

However, the followers of Ali were unhappy at the way the caliphs were being chosen; they insisted that the family of the Prophet had a right to head Islam, and that while Ali had been the fourth caliph he had been the first true successor. This group was to be known as the party of Ali or *Shi'at Ali* – Shi'a for short.

In 680, an event occurred which was to have enormous consequences for the Shi'a and how they saw themselves within Islam. Ali's son Husayn (a grandson of the Prophet), his family and supporters fought with an army of Umayyad soldiers led by Mu'awiya's son Yazid at Karbala in Iraq. Husayn's small band of 70 was wiped out, the only survivor

PRESTER JOHN

In the 12th century, Christians felt in need of a new hero who would help to save the Holy Land from Islamic domination. The object of their hopes was a mysterious character known as Prester ('Priest') John. No one knew exactly who Prester John was or where he lived. At various times he was thought to live in Africa or some part of Asia. But it was commonly held that he was a great Christian leader who would come to the rescue of his co-religionists and attack the Muslim rulers from the east. Stories about the existence of Prester John started to circulate from 1145, and in 1165 there was massive excitement in Christian courts when a letter from John arrived in Europe. In it, Prester John described himself as the ruler of 'Three Indias' and promised he would destroy the Islamic threat to the Holy Land. In 1177, Pope Alexander III sent a small embassy to find Prester John, a mission led by the Pope's own personal physician. The group reached 'Outremer' – the Christian enclave in the Holy Land – in safety, but thereafter vanished from history. In fact, the mission was doomed from the start as the letter from Prester John was a hoax. No such person ever existed.

BELOW: The caliph Harun al-Rashid receiving envoys from the Frankish ruler Charlemagne at the end of the 8th century. The reign of the caliph, who famously sent a gift of an elephant to Charlemagne, is regarded as one of the high points of the Abbasid dynasty and he and his court were immortalized in the famous collection of stories known as The Thousand and One Nights. *Painting, 1864, by Julius Koeckert (1827–1918). Munich, Maximilianeum Collection.*

RIGHT The familiar dance of the Whirling Dervishes, shown here, is a meditative technique used in the Sufi tradition of Islam. Other forms of meditation include the use of music and song.

being his young son, another Ali. The Shi'as regarded Husayn's demise as a martyr's death and the event still holds massive significance for the Shi'ite tradition. Followers trace much of their sense of persecution within the faith from this time. Around ten per cent of the world's Muslims are Shi'ite. The majority Sunnis take their name from the Arabic word *sunna*, meaning tradition.

Yet, even while there was internal strife over the issue of succession, the forces of Islam had already embarked on an astoundingly successful series of military campaigns. To the east, the desert-hardened Arab warriors destroyed the ailing Persian Empire and reached as far as China and India. Within the Mediterranean, the Arab soldiers drove the Byzantine Empire (seen by the Arabs as Romans) out of Syria and besieged the capital Constantinople.

Meanwhile, Islamic troops conquered Egypt and then, after a fierce struggle with the indigenous Berbers, took North Africa too. By the second half of the 8th century, much of the Iberian peninsula was under Islamic control. While it had taken around 300 years for the first Christian army to go into battle – under the Emperor Constantine – the soldiers of Islam dated back to the days of the Prophet himself and his conquest of Mecca.

It is probably accurate to describe this rapid expansion as an Arab rather than an Islamic conquest. Indeed, it was not a religious campaign to gain new converts to Islam; the Qur'an is quite explicit that there is to be 'no compulsion in religion'. Many scholars believe that the main motivation for the invasions was over-population in the dry Arabian peninsula leading to a quest for new and more fertile lands. Initially, most, if not

SUFISM

Since the 8th century Sufism has been an important, if controversial, tradition within Islam. Sufism is a mystical and ascetic tradition – the word comes from the Arabic *suf*, meaning coarse wool, and indicates the kind of garments worn by adherents. The aim of Sufis was the purification of consciousness, achieved by various forms of meditation – in this there is some similarity to Christian and other traditions of mysticism – including music, song and dance. The well-known dance of the Whirling Dervishes is the meditative technique of one branch of Sufism. The emphasis in the tradition of seeking union with God sometimes put Sufism on a collision course with the orthodox Sunni tradition, which has always insisted upon the strict separation or duality of God and humans. Orthodox Islam also sometimes accused Sufis of downplaying the importance of following the laws of God, and even of practising idolatry. However, in the late 11th and early 12th centuries, the respected philosopher al-Ghazali helped reconcile the spirituality of Sufism with the orthodoxy of Sunnism, and Sufism remains an important part of modern Islam.

ABOVE: The Dome of the Rock on the Temple Mount in Jerusalem (built 688-91 under qalif Abd al-Malik). Partial view of the octagon (built 1561 under Suleiman the Magnificent, replaced 1963) and gilded cupola. This was the place from where Muslims believe that the prophet Muhammad was taken into heaven to receive instructions for him and his followers from Allah.

all, Muslims were Arabs, and the Arab tribes, clans and families who came out of the desert remained a close-knit group. Under the Umayyad dynasty, in fact, only pure Arabs with Arabian family on both sides could gain the positions of highest power and prestige. One of the most important historical legacies of this expansion was the spread of Arabic, both as an oral and as a written language, through the eastern Mediterranean and along the North African coastline.

Yet, as more people converted to Islam, the Arab monopoly of power began to lead to some resentment. The Arabs had conquered some of the most sophisticated peoples in the Mediterranean world and beyond, for example in the Levant and the Persian Empire. They inherited a body of developed thought and philosophy, of scientific knowledge, along with traditions of bureaucracy and the apparatus of civil society. It was inevitable that this new world of ideas and culture would begin to impact upon the Arabs and Islamic society, just as Arab rule influenced the lives of the conquered. It was also perhaps inevitable that, as more of these subjects converted to Islam and the numbers of 'half-Arabs' – people born of Arab fathers and non-Arab mothers – grew, then so too did discontent with the Arab monopoly of power.

These disgruntled elements were among the strongest supporters of a revolution that occurred at the heart of Islam in 750. A new dynasty seized power, and the Umayyad ruling family were almost, though not completely, wiped out. The new caliph was Abu 'l-'Abbas, a member of the 'Abbasids, who were descendants of the Prophet's uncle al-'Abbas. The new leader also took the title al-Saffah – the Shedder of Blood – in recognition of his uncompromising treatment of members of the previous dynasty. The 'Abbasids were to remain in power until the middle of the 13th century, and from the start their regime was marked by a greater inclusion of non-Arabs. In particular, Iranians from the east, where Islam had replaced the Persian Empire, gained prominence. The physical centre of the empire also moved east when the small town of Baghdad in Iraq was transformed into a new purpose-built capital from 762.

BELOW: Saladin is one of the great figures of Islamic history. As well as recapturing Jerusalem in 1187 from the Crusaders, this Kurdish general is also credited with bringing unity to the Islamic world. Illumination, 15th century, from The Six Ages of the World. *London, British Library.*

Muslims, Christians and Jews

At first, indigenous peoples in the occupied lands were relatively slow to adopt Islam. Though the Arabs were conquerors, they did not embark on any campaign of forced conversion. Indeed, the Qur'an explicitly taught that the other 'peoples of the book' – Jews and Christians – believed in the same God as Muslims and that they should be respected. Thus, though there were restrictions – they were not able to build new churches or synagogues – for the most part Jews and Christians were allowed to practise their faiths and live their lives much as they had done before. In fact, many in the newly conquered lands in the Near East preferred the relatively relaxed Arab rule to that of Constantinople.

The need for administrators to keep all the conquered lands running also meant that many non-Muslims were co-opted into the bureaucracy. There is, for example, an intriguing story from the early 8th century about a Christian from recently invaded Spain who had apparently become a senior official to the caliph in Syria. Christians and Jews may not have been eligible for the

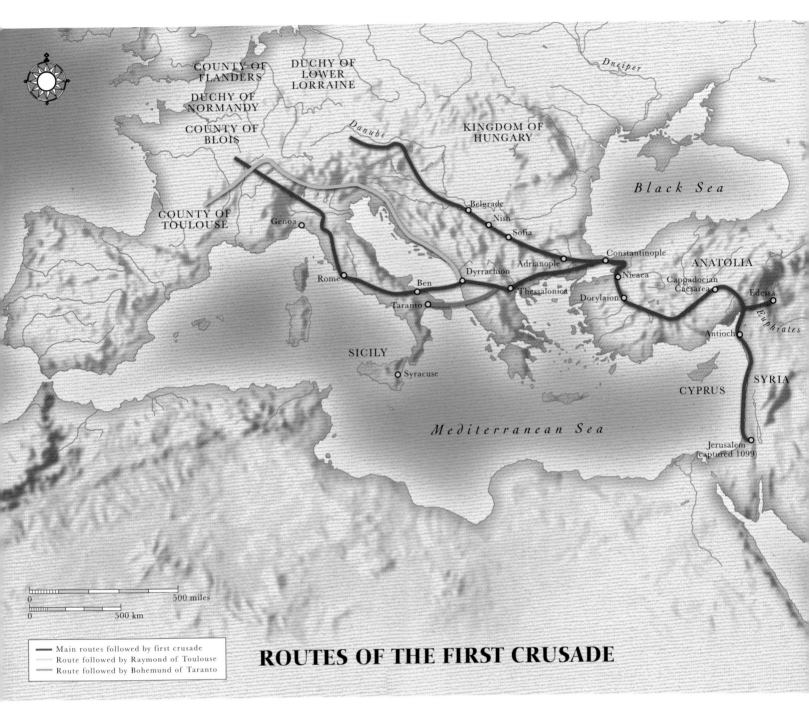

COUNTY OF
FLANDERS

DUCHY OF
LOWER
LORRAINE

DUCHY OF
NORMANDY

COUNTY OF
BLOIS

KINGDOM OF
HUNGARY

Danube

Dneiper

Black Sea

COUNTY OF
TOULOUSE

Genoa

Belgrade

Nish

Sofia

Constantinople

Rome

Ben

Dyrrachion

Adrianople

Nieaca

ANATOLIA

Cappadocian
Caesarea

Edessa

Taranto

Thessalonica

Dorylaion

Antioch

Euphrates

SICILY

Syracuse

CYPRUS

SYRIA

Mediterranean Sea

Jerusalem
(captured 1099)

0 ——————————— 500 miles
0 ——————————— 500 km

—— Main routes followed by first crusade
—— Route followed by Raymond of Toulouse
—— Route followed by Bohemund of Taranto

ROUTES OF THE FIRST CRUSADE

most senior positions, but the Arabs made the most of what talent they found in their new empire.

Nonetheless, the new rulers were keen to demonstrate the superiority of their faith. An example of this was the building of the magnificent Dome of the Rock in Jerusalem. This was constructed between 687 and 691 on the Temple Mount, the place where Abraham had been prepared to sacrifice his son Isaac to God, and thus a sacred place in Judaism. For Muslims, the place is revered as the spot from which Muhammad ascended into heaven in the company of the Archangel Gabriel to receive instructions from Allah. The Dome – a shrine rather than a mosque – is a beautiful building whose splendour was also designed to eclipse the nearby Christian Church of the Holy Sepulchre. The structure contains a key verse from the Qur'an in which the Christian idea that Christ is the son of God and divine is clearly rejected. It reads: 'Say that Allah is One, the Eternal God. He begot none, nor was He begotten. None is equal to him.'

The greatest period of conversion to Islam took place between the second half of the

ABOVE: The bloody First Crusade succeeded in its aim of capturing Jerusalem. However, in less than a century the city had been recaptured by Islamic troops under the leadership of the famous Saladin.

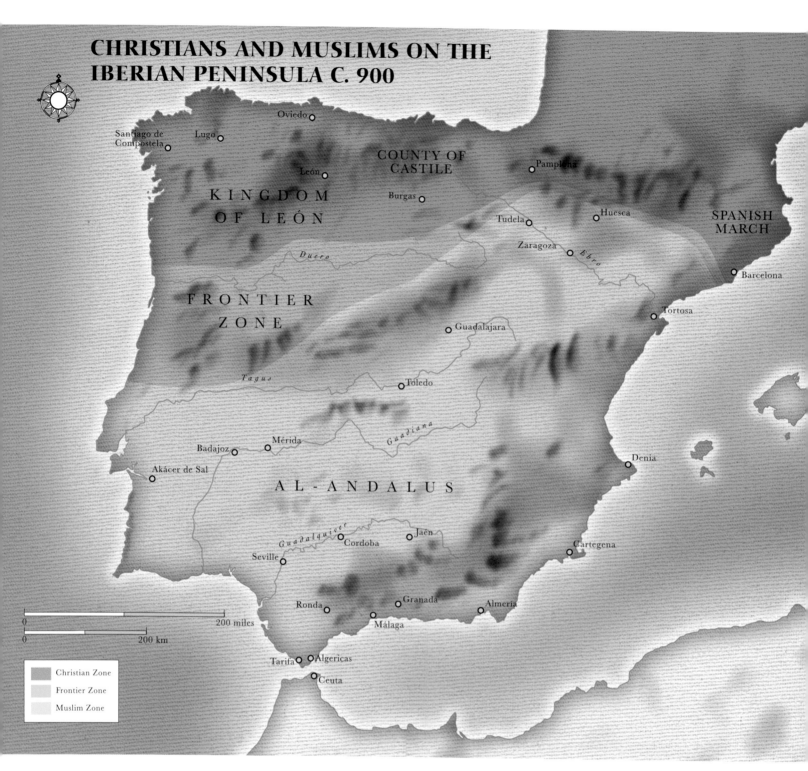

CHRISTIANS AND MUSLIMS ON THE IBERIAN PENINSULA C. 900

Oviedo

Santiago de Compostela · Lugo

León

COUNTY OF CASTILE

Pamplona

Burgas

KINGDOM OF LEÓN

Tudela

Huesca

SPANISH MARCH

Zaragoza · *Ebro*

Duero

Barcelona

FRONTIER ZONE

Guadalajara

Tortosa

Tagus

Toledo

Guadiana

Badajoz · Mérida

Denia

Akácer de Sal

AL-ANDALUS

Guadalquiver

Jaén

Cordoba

Cartegena

Seville

Ronda

Granada

Almería

Málaga

Tarifa · Algericas

Ceuta

0 ————— 200 miles
0 ————— 200 km

- Christian Zone
- Frontier Zone
- Muslim Zone

ABOVE: The arrival of Arab and Berber Islamic troops in the Iberian peninsula at the start of the 8th century changed the face of Spain forever; over the next seven centuries Christians and Muslims fought for supremacy there, though at times the two cultures managed to live side by side in relative peace.

8th century and the rise of the 'Abbasid dynasty to the end of the 10th century; it has been suggested that more than three-quarters of local populations under Islamic rule at the time, and possibly even 90 per cent, eventually embraced Islam. While the Christian world was not unaware of this, or of the Islamic presence in Palestine, the vast majority of western Christendom had little idea of what Muslims believed. Many, indeed, deliberately distorted or invented Islamic beliefs, while others thought that Islam was simply another Christian heresy, such as monophysitism.

It was in this context that the crusades to the Holy Land were launched by the Christian west, as described in Chapter Two. These were clearly major events in the history of Christian–Islamic relations. Even now the word 'crusade' still resonates in world politics. For the Christians who started them towards the end of the 11th century,

and who captured Jerusalem in 1099, these expeditions were of fundamental importance. Noblemen such as Raymond of Toulouse, Baldwin of Boulogne, Bohemond of Taranto and his nephew Tancred, who were all key figures in the First Crusade, were captivated by the idea. Curiously, however, contemporary Islamic writers made comparatively little of these supposedly cataclysmic events.

True, the great Kurdish leader Salah al–Din Yusuf, better known in the west as Saladin, became a great figure of his and later times, and was widely praised for his recapture of the holy city of Jerusalem in 1187, as well as for his generosity of spirit and dislike of unnecessary bloodshed. But even Saladin was famed as much for achieving a measure of unity in the Islamic world as for retaking the holy city. Overall, the crusades attracted a great deal less attention from Arab writers than one might suppose. Nor were these foreign Christian invaders referred to in any way that might identify them as religious warriors. Instead they were invariably referred to as *Franji*, i.e. Franks, irrespective of whether they were actually Frankish or not.

The main concern of Arabic writers before and during this period was internal dissension and the looming instability threatened by the Turkic peoples of central Asia. The most important of these in this context were the Seljuk Turks. They were displaced from their homelands by another Turkic people, the Kipchak, and moved westwards into Bukhara (Uzbekistan). By the 10th century they had become ardent followers of Islam after coming into contact with the Islamic world and continued a westward move into the Levant and ultimately Anatolia, seizing Baghdad in 1055. In the late 11th century, the Seljuks captured Syria and Palestine. In fact, it was the disunity of the Muslim world created by these invasions that enabled the crusaders to seize parts of the Holy Land in the first place. The Seljuks were members of the Oghuz group, a confederation of Turks. Another member was the Osmanli, who were ultimately to form the Ottoman Empire, marking a new high point for Islamic dominance around the Mediterranean.

For the most part, Muslims undoubtedly saw the Christians from the west as uncouth barbarians, as well as misguided in their religion. Yet this was also a common view in the sophisticated Byzantine Empire, whose members viewed the arrival in the region of large numbers of their western co-religionists with dread. Indeed, the Greek-oriented Byzantine authorities probably looked upon the Latin Christians rather as the Romans regarded the Gothic barbarians in the 4th and 5th centuries – a perception only increased by the sacking of Constantinople by members of the Fourth Crusade in 1204.

Cohabitation

The Mediterranean has been a key meeting place for the two faiths of Christianity and Islam. Often this meeting took the form of confrontation, leading to war, as we have seen. At other times it was possible for Muslims and Christians to live side by side in relative peace, notably in Spain and Sicily.

In Spain, for example, many Christians had to live under Muslim rule during the dominance of the Moors there in the 9th, 10th and 11th centuries. Telling fragments of documentation from this period record bans placed by the Islamic authorities on certain kinds of fraternization between Muslims and Christians, a fairly clear sign that the two sides did sometimes mingle. In one case, Muslims were ordered not to empty the cesspits of Christians; in another, Muslim women were told to keep away from churches to avoid the risk that they might drink, eat or 'fornicate' with the clergy.

Conversely, when the Christians began to re-exert control in Spain during the 12th and 13th centuries, Muslims had to live under Christian rule. The relative harmony that prevailed in this period is sometimes referred to as *convivencia*, which means 'living together'. However, it is easy to overstate the nature of this 'cohabitation'. Even when they were living in the same communities, Muslims and Christians generally led separate, parallel lives. There is plenty of evidence of discrimination against the governed. Also, not long after the last surviving Moorish kingdom of Granada was defeated in 1492, many of the Moors and Jews in Christian Spain were expelled, even though this had a damaging effect on the economy. It was moreover the case that when Christians and Muslims confronted each other in the Mediterranean, the losing party often ended up as slaves.

Nonetheless, the examples of Spain and Sicily show that it was, at times, possible for the religions of Islam and Christianity to co-exist in the same area in relative tranquillity.

After the eclipse of the Ottoman Empire in the 15th century, the formal boundaries separating the Islamic Mediterranean and the Christian Mediterranean became more settled. In the west, the Straits of Gibraltar mark the divide between Muslim North Africa and Christian Spain. In the east, a part of Turkey, including Istanbul, is on the European side of the Bosphorus, but otherwise the picture is broadly one of Christian Europe and Islamic Asia. Yet, a closer look reveals a more complex picture. In Europe, places such as parts of former Yugoslavia and Albania have significant Islamic traditions, while the south of France, Italy and Spain are now home to substantial numbers of Muslim immigrants from North Africa. There are, meanwhile, long-standing, if small, Christian minorities in Mediterranean Islamic countries such as Turkey, Egypt and the Lebanon.

The main area where the issue of faith still dominates in political terms is in the continuing Israeli–Palestinian dispute, inextricably linked with issues of nationalism and land. The modern state of Israel was created in 1948, and since then the Palestinians have been seeking a recognized and viable homeland of their own. Most of the Palestinians are Muslims – though a significant minority are Christians of various denominations – and this has led to the dispute being portrayed in terms of a battle between Jews and Muslims.

A lasting settlement of this conflict would write a new and more positive chapter in what has often been a turbulent story of religion and faith in the Mediterranean.

ABOVE: Mula Castle, Murcia, Spain. This 15th-century castle was built on the site of a former Moorish castle, and is an enduring legacy of the re-conquest of Spain. Isabel and Ferdinand succeeded in uniting the whole country under their crown, and their effort to 're-christianize' Spain eventually resulted in the Spanish Inquisition, when thousands of Jews and Moors who didn't want to convert to Christianity were expelled or killed.

OPPOSITE: The stunning mosque of Córdoba in southern Spain is a very visual reminder of how, despite the many tensions and obstacles of the past, the different cultures and traditions in the region have ultimately enriched the Mediterranean.

BIBLIOGRAPHY

General

ABULAFIA, D, editor, 2003. *The Mediterranean in History* (London: Thames & Hudson)
ASCHERSON, N. 1996. *Black Sea: The birthplace of civilisation and barbarism* (London: Vintage)
BRAUDEL, F. 2002. *The Mediterranean in the Ancient World*, translated by Siân Reynolds (London: Penguin)
HOMER 1987. *The Iliad*, translated by Martin Hammond. (London: Penguin)
HORDEN, P. and PURCELL, N. 2000. *The Corrupting Sea: A study of Mediterranean history* (Oxford: Blackwell)
HUTCHINSON ENCYCLOPAEDIA 1998. (Oxford: Helicon)
LENMAN, B.P. 2000. *Chambers Dictionary of World History* (Edinburgh: Chambers Harrap)
LEWIS, B. 1995. *The Middle East: 200 Years of History from the Rise of Christianity to the Present Day* (London: Phoenix Press)
ROBERTS, J.M. 1997. *The Penguin History of Europe* (London: Penguin)

Section one: Nature of the Mediterranean

AYTO, J. 1994. *A Gourmet's Guide: Food and Drink from A to Z* (Oxford: Oxford University Press)
DE BOER J.Z. and SANDERS D.T. 2005. *Volcanoes in Human History* (Princeton: Princeton University Press)
GROVE, A.T. and RACKHAM, O. 2001. *The Nature of Mediterranean Europe: An Ecological History* (New Haven: Yale University Press)
PHILLIPS, R. and RIX, M. 2002. *The Botanical Garden*, two volumes (London: Macmillan)
STERRY, P. 2000. *Complete Mediterranean Wildlife* (London: HarperCollins)

Section two: History and Politics

BARTLETT, R. 1993. *The Making of Europe: Conquest, Colonisation and Cultural Change 950 – 1350* (London: Penguin)
BOARDMAN, J., GRIFFIN, J. and MURRAY, O., editors 1991. *The Oxford History of the Roman World* (Oxford: Oxford University Press)

JORDAN, W.C. 2002. *Europe in the High Middle Ages* (London: Penguin)
MACKAY, A. 1977. *Spain in the Middle Ages: From Frontier to Empire 1000 – 1500* (London: Macmillan)
MACKAY, A and DITCHBURN, D. 1997. *Atlas of Medieval Europe* (London: Routledge)
MORRIS, J. 1990. *The Venetian Empire: A Sea Voyage* (London: Penguin)
GIBBON, E. 2003. *The Decline and Fall of the Roman Empire*, Modern Library paperback edition, edited by Hans–Friedrich Mueller (New York: Random House)
SABRI, S.M.K. 2000 *History of Muslim Spain* (Delhi: Adam)
TREADGOLD, W. 2001. *A Concise History of Byzantium* (London: Palgrave)
WOOD, M. 2001. *In Search of the Trojan War* (London: BBC)
ZIEGLER, P. 1997. *The Black Death* (London: Folio Society)

Section three: Art and Society

DOBSON, A. 2001. *The Hieroglyphics of Ancient Egypt* (London: New Holland)
HERODOTUS 1972. *The Histories*, translated by Aubrey de Sélincourt, introduction and notes by A.R. Burns (London: Penguin)
HOMER 1937. *The Odyssey*, translated by W.H.D. Rouse (New York: Mentor)
JOHNSON, P. 2003. *Art: A New History* (London: Weidenfeld & Nicolson)
JOINT ASSOCIATION OF CLASSICAL TEACHERS 1984. *The World of Athens: An introduction to classical Athenian culture* (Cambridge: Cambridge University Press)
JONES, P. and SIDWELL, K. editors 1997. The World of Rome: An Introduction to Roman Culture (Cambridge: Cambridge University Press)
SHARROCK, A and ASH, R. 2002. *Fifty Key Classical Authors* (London: Routledge)
VIRGIL 1991. *The Aeneid*, translated by David West (London: Penguin)
WAQUET, F. 2001. *Latin, or the Empire of a Sign*, translated by John Howe (London: Verso)

Section four: Adventure and Invention

ARTZ, F.B. 1980. *The Mind of the Middle Ages A.D. 200 – 1500*, 3rd edition (Chicago: University of Chicago Press)
CRUMP, T. 2002. *A Brief History of Science* (London: Robinson)
FAGAN, B. M. editor 2004. *The Seventy Great Inventions of the Ancient World* (London: Thames & Hudson)
FLETCHER, R. 1994. *Moorish Spain* (London: Phoenix)
PLINY THE ELDER 2004. *Natural History: A Selection* , translated by John F. Healy (London: Penguin)

Section five: Religion and Beliefs

COTTERELL, A. 1979. *A Dictionary of World Mythology* (London: Book Club Associates)
FLETCHER, R. 2004. *The Cross and the Crescent: The dramatic story of the earliest encounters between Christians and Muslims* (London: Penguin)
GRAVES, R. 1996. *The Greek Myths* (London: The Folio Society)
HOLY BIBLE, New International Version, 1978 (London: Hodder and Stoughton)
LEWIS, B. 2002. *What Went Wrong? Western impact and Middle Eastern Response* (London: Phoenix)
MAALOUF, A. 1984. *The Crusades through Arab Eyes*, translated by Jon Rothschild (London: Al Saqi Books)
RUSSELL, J.B. 2000. *A History of witchcraft: Sorcerers, Heretics and Pagans* (London: Thames & Hudson)
SAVILL, S., LOCKE, E., BARKER, M. and COOK, C. 1976. *Pears Encyclopaedia of Myths and Legends* (London: Pelham Books)
SMART, N. 1998. *The World's Religions*, second edition (Cambridge: Cambridge University Press)
WILSON, A.N. 1992. *Jesus* (London: Sinclair-Stevenson)
WILSON, A.N. 1997. *Paul* (London: Sinclair-Stevenson)

Useful websites

www.iep.utm.edu
www.fordham.edu/halsall/ancient/asbook.html
www.hti.umich.edu/k/koran
http://classics.mit.edu/
www.religioustolerance.org
www.worldwildlife.org/wildworld/profiles/terrestrial/pa/pa0904_full.html
www.worldwildlife.org/wildworld/profiles/terrestrial/pa/pa1214_full.html
www.bbc.co.uk/history/ancient
www.foodtimeline.org
www.helike.org
http://phoenicia.org
www.e-classics.com
www.nationmaster.com/encyclopedia
http://en.wikipedia.org/wiki/Main_Page
www.ehistory.com
www.bartleby.com
www.centuries.co.uk
Rohling, E.J. (2001), *The dark secret of the Mediterranean - a case history in past environmental reconstruction*. This can be found at: www.soes.soton.ac.uk/staff/ejr/DarkMed/dark-title.html
http://magma.nationalgeographic.com/ngm/0410/feature2/online_extra.html
www.teacheroz.com/generalancient.htm

Television

Who Wrote the Bible?, presented by Dr Robert Beckford, Channel 4, broadcast 25 December 2004.

INDEX

...dgements

...y agent Chelsey Fox for her ... writing of this book, and ...and for all her help from the ...y brother Jeff for his valuable ...rature of the ancient world and to my ...oos for her encouragement and general

improvements to the text.
The Royal Society for the Protection of Birds helped me clarify some details about the annual migration of birds in the region, for which I am grateful, and thanks also to the press team at Channel 4 for providing me with a cassette of one of their programmes.

Picture Acknowledgements

All pictures supplied by AKG Images except for the following:

Front cover (top): Alessandro Saffo/4Corners Images; (bottom middle and bottom left) akg-images/Erich Lessing
Back cover: akg-images/Nimatallah
Pages 1, 6 (left), 7 (right), 24, 31, 35, 36, 45, 52–3, 56, 59, 60, 62, 63, 64, 65, 73, 74–5, 80, 92, 104, 108–109, 118, 127, 128, 138 140, 141, 143, 156, 157, 171, 188, 190–91, 193, 194, 199, 201: akg-images/Erich Lessing
Pages 2–3, 116–117, 142, 150–151, 152, 192, 196, 197, 198: akg-images/Nimatallah
Pages 4–5: Bridgeman Art Library
Page 6 (right): akg-images/CGA Guillemot
Pages 7 (left), 124, 225: akg-images/Robert O'Dea
Page 10: Sotheby's/akg-images
Pages 12–13 & 28: NHPA/Alberto Nardi
Pages 15 & 54–5: Courtesy of Malta Tourist Office
Pages 20–21: akg-images/Hedda Eid
Page 22: Lloyd Cluff/Corbis
Page 23: Hilary Sharp
Page 26: Kontos Yannis/Corbis Sygma
Page 27: Courtesy of Slovenia Tourism Photo Library/D. Mladenovic
Page 29 Wellcome Trust
Pages 32, 209: akg-images/Gilles Mermet
Page 33: NHPA/Roger Tidman
Pages 38–39, 50, 96, 111 & 115: Courtesy of Egyptian State Tourist Office

Page 41: Reuters/Corbis
Pages 46, 133: akg-images/Electa
Pages 48 & 165: Mary Evans Picture Library
Page 51: NHPA/Daniel Heuclin
Pages 57, 76–77: Hervé Champollion/akg-images
Pages 58, 68: akg-images/John Hios
Page 95: akg-images/Joseph Martin
Pages 98, 99, 105: akg-images/cameraphoto
Page 121, 202–205, 210, 211, 213, 229, 230: Courtesy of Alan Marshall
Pages 124–5: akg-images/Gerard Degeorge
Pages 130–131, 180–181, 185: akg-images/Schuetze/Rodemann
Pages 134 & 137: NHP archive
Page 147: Werner Forman/Corbis
Pages 167: akg-images/Orsi Battaglini
Page 174: akg-images/CDA/Guillemot
Page 175: Science and Society Picture Library/Science Museum
Page 182: akg-images/Elizabeth Disney
Page 186: akg-images/Museum Kalkriese
Pages 195, 200: akg-images/Rabatti-Domingie
Page 224: akg-images/Rainer Hackenberg
Pages 222, 226: akg-images/British Library
Page 230: akg-images/Jean-Louis Nou